A
TIME
OF
RAPE

INGA L. CHESNEY

PRENTICE-HALL, INC.
Englewood Cliffs, N. J.

The author's German name has been concealed to protect relatives living behind the Iron Curtain.

PREFACE

To live in the past is the sad prerogative of those who have no future: the very old, or the very disillusioned. Yet we cannot afford to ignore the past, for it is from the past that we learn what mistakes we have made. The future offers no solutions since it does not yet exist, and the present keeps us busy with everyday living.

Looking back, we must also search for the truth, the only solid foundation on which to build our future. Truth does not have many faces; it has only one—its own. There is only one way to arrive at concrete and correct answers: to seek, tell, listen to, analyze, and evaluate the truth.

The Russian conquest of the city of Berlin in Germany 1945 was a nightmare. If I ask you to share this nightmare with me, it is not for the sake of sensationalism, but for the sake of asking questions and finding answers. Those that I found were paid for with the lives of millions.

All events in this book are true. I have described what happened to my family and me in our Berlin home during the short life of Hitler's Third Reich and for one year thereafter, as seen with the eyes of a seventeen-year-old girl—a girl who was suddenly confronted with the possibility that there might not be a future. Officially the events described are nothing but statistics. Statistics are numbers, but each number represents the life of one human being; and it is one human life multiplied thousands of times that formulates the impressive impact of statistics. Who, then, would want to say that what happened to one family should not be of concern to millions of others, when that family could have been yours? Who would want to say that what happened all those years ago is outdated, when we are daily confronted with the fact that we live in the "age of conscience"?

Some survived, some did not.

But if survival is to be regarded as a blessing, then it is only so and of value if it also involves the survival of spirit and soul.

Although my book is an autobiography, I prefer to call it "a document of survival."

CONTENTS

CONTENTS

For I hear the sound of the trumpet, the
alarm of war.
Disaster follows hard on disaster, the whole
land is laid to waste.
Suddenly my tents are destroyed, my curtains
in a moment.
How long must I see the standard, and hear the
sound of the trumpet?

Jeremiah 4:20-21

1

THE DAY OF THE GRAY SUN

To hide in this basement is not exactly the nicest experience.

I am lying on my folding bed trying not to think about the future. The prospect of this future is not what a seventeen-year-old girl is usually dreaming about—no parties, no dancing, no dating, maybe not even living. . . .

As a matter of fact, there is hardly any food left. We have barely enough to survive for the next six days—then what? I shut that thought out very quickly—in these days one does not think even as far as tomorrow. Today we live, and that is something to be thankful for.

The place is Berlin. It is either March or April (one does not notice dates in times of terror), the year is 1945, and the world outside should be beautiful. It is springtime; there should be blossoms, and flowers, and green trees, and birds singing. . . . But the blossoms have been replaced by shell splinters; most of the flowers have not dared to come through the protection of

1

the earth; the trees lie like fallen monuments of peace on the ground; and the birds have fled in terror. Had they stayed, their song could not be heard; the voice of the guns and cannons is too loud. . . .

I wonder if the sun is shining outside. Inside the basement one cannot tell. Not a glimmer of daylight peeks through the solid walls or blocked up windows. The stubby candle is slowly burning down to a small insignificant blob. In its dim light everybody looks spooky and weird, like people from "Tales of Hoffman."

It is not the conventional clubroom-type basement, and has never before been used for any purpose other than storage. There is only one exit, a door and stairway leading up to the ground floor apartment.

The house is about one hundred years old, and although it is built sturdy and solid, it is not blessed with many of the modern luxuries that make life easy. There are three windows in the cellar, each one level with the ground outside. Now they are completely blocked up with sandbags for protection from bombs, shells, or any other dangerous moving objects. . . .

The cellar consists of two sections, each about 20 x 18 feet long, with a smoke chamber in the middle from which the chimney leads up through the roof. Through the years one section has always been used for storage of our winter potatoes, the smoke chamber for storage of perishable food not immediately being used. Once in a while it would hold (lucky for us) a beautiful smoked ham. Since the temperature is almost always the same, summer or winter, it is ideal for storage purposes, but at the moment it is empty. Six years of war have depleted supplies. . . .

Now the only thing lingering in the air is the musty earthy smell left over from the last few potatoes.

Uninviting, uncomfortable as it may be, at the moment it most certainly is the safest place to live—if anyone can speak about safety at all.

We have been in the basement for approximately four days,

but since we are closed up in our shelter it is hard to tell how many days have gone by—day and night seem the same. Anyway—does it matter?

Since yesterday, so it seems, the antiaircraft guns have stopped. The only noise we hear now are the "Stalin Organs," a nickname for the very heavy Russian cannons, and now and then some machine gun fire. None of us talks much. What is there to talk about when you know that your world is just about to end?

To pass the time I count how many of us there are—my mother; my two sisters, Chris, nine, and Monika, only six months old; my eighty-year-old grandmother, whom we call "Omi"; granddad, whom we call "Opa"; Uncle Carl, middle-aged; our two lodgers, Mr. and Mrs. Schulmann; the lady who owns the restaurant next door, Mrs. Stromberg; and last, our little dog "Lux"—ten people and one dog.

Mama's sister, Evi, and her family had decided to stay in the earth-bunker some distance away, together with the other occupants of our small apartment house. Approximately sixteen people are over there. I must say I miss them. Uncle Fritz is always cheerful, always ready with a joke. His sense of humor would be comforting now, it would help to pass the time. . . . They have four children, ranging in age from six months to twelve years. The youngest, Rita, was born at about the same time as Monika.

When we all had realized, a few days ago, that we had better find shelter for the duration of the war, which was obviously coming to an end, we had also realized that only half of us could live in the basement. Some would have to take shelter in the little earth-bunker fifty yards outside the house, which we had built ourselves and reinforced with thick, solid tree trunks. It is not a bad little place, and frankly I would have preferred to be there rather than in the basement—the thought of being buried alive under a heap of bricks seems less attractive than the thought of one quick blast and bang! you're gone. Death is something we have become very familiar with. Nobody can live

3

through two air raids with heavy bombing each night and not realize that one could be the next victim.

The baby starts crying and interrupts my thoughts. "Please get me the bottle from over there," Mother says, pointing in my direction, and while she busies herself with the feeding procedure, I look at her closely.

Her face is still beautiful, but it looks thin and worried now with sharp lines around her mouth, which has forgotten how to smile, dark shadows under her eyes from endless nights without sleep. Nights filled with fear. The baby lies in her arms, sucking at the bottle, content and happy, making little cooing and smacking sounds. Mother's eyes are not fixed upon the baby, they are looking somewhere, nowhere, into space, not seeing anything at all. . . .

Maybe she is thinking about Papa. We have not heard from him for several months and do not know whether he is still alive. I wish that my father were home. Here we are—five women, three men, and two children. Uncle Carl does not really count too much, he had been in the First World War and became shell-shocked. For several years he could not talk, until one day another shock brought back his speech. He certainly has had his share of war—I am sure as far as defense is concerned he cannot be counted on too much. There is just so much a man can take; young as I am, I realize that.

So now, suppose the Russian troops come here soon. (We know that they are already about two miles away across the canal.) What will happen to us? From refugees we have heard terrifying stories—are they true? Being seventeen, I have some optimism left and decide that people sometimes exaggerate, and possibly it will not be so bad after all.

As if little Chris reads my gloomy thoughts, she has started crying. Her pretty blonde hair has not been washed in many days. Some leftover candy, the last of our ration, hoarded and cherished until now, is smeared all over her face and mingles with her tears—all in all she looks a pretty sorry sight. She also

4

has the funniest voice, deep and coarse. We are used to calling her our little "coal carrier" because her voice always sounds as if she has just swallowed a pound of charcoal.

"What's the matter?" Mother asks.

"I am scaaaared," Chris sobs.

I poke her. "Don't be such a crybaby."

"Leave her alone," Mother says. "I am just wondering how long all this is going to last. . . . Anyway, all of you better behave, and save all your strength for what is coming next. . . ." She stops short. Apparently the continuation of the thought is too unpleasant.

"Papa said in his letters not to worry, that it is all a bunch of propaganda!" I throw in, defiantly.

"And what would you know about propaganda?" Mother asks sharply, then checks herself. "Never mind, we'll just take it as it comes."

Monika has finished her bottle. Mama starts to change her diaper, when suddenly there is a terrific crash—the house shakes in its foundations, glass splinters, and then there is quiet, except for Monika and Chris. Monika has been pricked with the diaper pin by my mother and lets loose with a wail; Chris is just plain scared and is crying, holding on to my mother; my grandmother is saying over and over, "Oh my God, we're hit"; Mrs. Stromberg is mumbling something I cannot understand, and my uncle just sits in shock.

While we have been talking we have not realized that the noise outside has increased, the shelling has become louder and more frequent. It sounds like an inferno out there. What concerns us in the basement is the possibility that the house may have been hit by a firebomb or shell. If there is a fire, then we shall either burn to death inside or be faced with the necessity of leaving, and either prospect does not seem too nice. It's like someone asking you "Which way do you prefer to die, by fire or by a shell?" The thought seems funny in a sordid way, and I start giggling. I guess Mother realizes that I do it with a slight

5

hysteria and she does not say anything. She is busy trying to calm down the baby, so I grab Chris and pull her over, pressing her against me.

I remember an incident about a year ago, when Mama had gone on a short trip to visit my father who was stationed in Kiel. Chris and I were alone, Monika had not been born yet. I had taken care of my homework for school, tucked Chris into bed after supper, taken care of the dishes, dusted a little, and gone to bed with the comforting thought that all was well.

Of course, it was not a surprise when I was awakened by the sirens. Air raids were the rule, not the exception. Our suitcase with the few valuables, papers, photos, certificates, and other such items, was always packed and ready to go wherever and whenever we were going. The shades had been dutifully pulled to comply with the blackout regulations. The suitcase stood in the hallway ready to be grabbed for our nightly trip into the shelter.

I tried to wake Chris, but what a sleeper she was! It took me several minutes to just get her out of bed. "Get dressed in the kitchen," I told her, "it's warmer in there."

I still had things to do, which kept me busy for about five minutes; then I came back to the kitchen to see if Chris was ready. Danger and all, I burst out laughing—little Chris was standing there, eyes closed, and in a very rhythmical way, one–two–one–two–one–two, was trying to put her leg through a kitchen towel! At first I did not quite know what to make of it, then I realized that instead of her panties she had grabbed a kitchen towel and tried to step into it. Of course there was no leg hole, but faithfully she tried again and again after the motto, "If at first you don't succeed. . . ."

Outside, the antiaircraft guns were loudly proclaiming their existence. But that was not the only noise—a very familiar hum indicated that the attacking airplanes were already above, or at least getting close, and a more frightening sound, that of falling bombs, made me grab Chris in a hurry and drag her and the

6

suitcase into the shelter. It was always the same—you just ran for your life, hoping you would make it.

We have been lucky—we are all still alive. But here it is 1945, and all that is over. What is over? The air raids? The shortage of food? The sleepless nights when you lie awake worrying over people you love? If all this seemed rather uncomfortable at the time, it certainly had not been the most unpleasant part of the war. In all its nervousness, its cruelties, its uncertainties, there still had been a certain normalcy, a kind of routine. You learned to live with it, like with an ulcer. Right now, it seems like a million years, yet it was only a few days ago that I got up in the morning to go to work, have my lunch at noon, wait for five o'clock to come, to go home to avoid the first air raid, read a little, listen to the radio, go to bed.

According to the news, Germany was not in bad shape then at all. The Government admitted a few losses here and there, but all in all it was not too bad—after all, they said, the relief troops were only a few miles away from wherever they were needed!

I was a typist in the Personnel Department of a Military Supply Office. One of my uncles was the Personnel Director there, and so I had a relative as my boss. That was not bad at all—he was a friendly, easygoing man with a good sense of humor and made me laugh many times. His name was Wilhelm, but he had been nicknamed "Mutzi." I was the only one in the office who knew that! In front of others I would call him "Mr. F" since he was my boss; only on rare occasions, when we were alone discussing personal matters, did I call him "Uncle Mutzi." All in all, work there was pleasant. It was my first job and people were kind to me because they knew I was shy and self-conscious about not being more experienced in office work. My typing was terrible!

But those days did not last long. The time came when from day to day work became less and less important. Only one thing was in our minds—what was going to happen? None of us was fooled by the apparent optimism of our government officials, especially since I had in my office a gorgeous radio with which one could hear all sorts of foreign stations. The best to listen to was the BBC in London. Of course, had anybody seen me I would have been in serious trouble, since it was strictly forbidden to listen to any other than a German station. But the very young have an insatiable curiosity! I could speak and understand English fairly well even then, and so I was rather well informed about Germany's situation. The omens were all bad.

As was to be expected, the day came when we were all asked into the Department Head's office. "Okay, sit down fellows," Uncle Mutzi said in his usual casual way. His eyes had always been full of humor; today they looked worried. He called everybody "fellows"— that was his way.

"There are not too many supplies, but down in the basement are cartons and cartons of cigarettes. Take what you want and go home."

It was two o'clock in the afternoon. "Go home?" one of us asked.

"Yes," he replied, "go home. This is good-bye. Any questions?"

We did not have to ask any questions, and he knew that.

I took that information with mixed feelings. It was nice to think of a vacation, and since I was still living at home, I did not have to worry much about finances—but that kind of a vacation meant only one thing—the war was coming to an end, and that end was not the way Mr. Adolf Hitler had taken great pains to glorify. But then there were the relief troops—or were there?

By that time I had begun to wonder about a great many things.

Just as I was ready to leave the office, the sirens were sounding the alarm—another air raid! These daytime air raids were always much worse than those at night—why, I don't know. At night, possibly, it was always a kind of gory celebration; the "Christmas trees" lighting up the sky always added a touch of glamour to the destruction. If this sounds satirical, then it explains the mood of the Berliners at that time; they called it

8

"Galgen Humor" (gallows humor)—and it was this that kept them going. The day when that was gone too—that was the day a magnificent, courageous city was dead . . . but that day had not yet come.

I suppose I should explain what those "Christmas trees" were. They were flares dropped from the bombers at night, in the shape and form of lighted Christmas trees, so that the bombers could see the targets better. Unfortunately, this did not help much as far as hitting the targets was concerned. I would like to see the bomb that can be dropped from several thousand feet up in the sky and still hit the target!

The Berliners took it all in good stride. It was Germany that declared war, and they knew it. Besides, the Berliners are also a very good-natured people, with a fair sense of justice and an almost unbeatable humor—they could not change the situation, so the only thing to do was to take what was coming and try to survive with as much dignity and pride as was possible. And that they did!

Anyway, this was to be my last air raid away from home. Along with all the others, I entered the office air raid shelter. There we sat for about two hours, just waiting for it to be over, one way or the other. It was a really bad one this time—the walls shook several times as if we had been hit. Of course, the real impact never struck home until after the air raid, when you would set your foot outside and for a few moments wonder whether you had been condemned to hell.

One of my colleagues asked, "Do you live far from here?" He was in his late thirties, slim and handsome.

"If I have to walk it," I said, "it is far—about three or four hours' walk."

"Well, I wish you luck," he said. "It looks to me like after this one there will be no more air raids necessary—there won't be anything left to bomb."

He offered me a cigarette (I had just started smoking) and together we smoked and talked as if we were sitting in somebody's cocktail lounge. Well, what else was there to do?

"What are you going to do?" I asked him.

9

He looked around to see if anyone could hear us. Then he came close to my ear. "I am going to try and get through to the American lines," he said. "One thing is for sure—I am not going to stay here to experience the Russian conquest."

"What makes you so sure that the Americans and the English are not going to be here sooner?" I asked.

"Kid, wake up!" he exclaimed—then lowered his voice again. "Don't you know that the Americans are stopped at the Elbe for some reason, and the Russians are already close to Berlin? Believe me, it's only going to be a few days before they'll be here."

"Oh, come on now," I said indignantly. "You are just telling horror stories." I knew he was right, but I did not want to face that possibility yet. Once more it was my privilege, being so young, to play the game of make-believe. "After all, there may be some relief troops after all, Hitler is not going to give up the capital without a pretty big struggle. Maybe he can hold it until the Americans get here."

"Boy, are you naive!" he said. "Do you really think that the Americans are eager to conquer Berlin? I have a hunch that they have orders to stop right where they are. Something is fishy— why have they been at the Elbe for so long now without getting any further? After all, the German Army is finished—finished, I say!"

I changed the subject. "How will you get through?" I asked him.

"Frankly, I don't know yet," he replied, and his face looked worried. "But I'm sure going to try. As far as I'm concerned, I would rather be dead than conquered by the Russians."

Just then the "all clear" sounded. I wished him good luck. I never knew whether or not he made it.

When I went upstairs into what had been fresh air, I was met with a shock.

It had been a bright sunshiny day. Now the sun had disappeared behind an ugly, dirty, smoke-filled inferno. Flames were leaping up into the sky, greedily eating up everything they

10

could touch. I had seen this sight before, but never so fierce, so hopeless, so deadly. And one more thing was different from the times before—the silence. It was as if the city had finally succumbed, laying down its weary head to find a peaceful sleep, a peace and sleep it had been denied for six years. . . .

I started to make my way towards home, if there still was a home. It would be a miracle if the inferno had missed my own house. I took my time—what was the hurry? What would I hurry to?

As I slowly walked through the rubble, the fires, the crying people, the children with soot-smeared faces, I thought of what Berlin once had been. My Berlin, my beautiful city, all the work that had gone into its making, years and years, even centuries, of building magnificent pieces of architecture, parks with flowers, ancient monuments, the cathedrals, churches, castles, the Opera House, waterfalls—all that gone. . . . I knew that it could never be the same again; some things just cannot be rebuilt in weeks or months or even years. And as I realized that, it seemed rather insignificant whether I would find my home or not, I just wanted to find my mother and sisters alive.

I walked and looked around me, and my heart slowly but very persistently filled with a sadness I had never known before, with only one question—why?

All that seems like a million years ago as we sit here in hiding. The city has not been destroyed entirely. There are still basements in which one can live like mice in a trap. There are still some stores that have some food supplies. It's just a question of getting to them—alive! There are still some waterlines underground, not destroyed, but, most important, there are still millions of Berliners with one hope—that it will all be over soon. Now the question is: what is to come next?

The chances that all of us can live through this are small. Our house is located right in the line of fire from both sides. On one side, our own people are desperately and hopelessly trying to

11

defend what is left of Berlin. On the other side are the Russian troops trying to conquer a heap of rubble, ruins, torn-up ground, and sunken bridges.

In the middle are we, a bundle of frightened people. And the shelling and shooting hits us from both sides.

"One of us will have to go and see how badly we are hit," says Mother, looking at Uncle Carl. He stares blankly into space.

"I'll go, Mama," I say.

"No, you will not! If anyone goes it will be me, since we don't have any volunteers."

"Mama, be reasonable," I argue. "You are needed for the two little ones, Omi and Opa are too old, and Uncle Carl. . . ."

She knows what I mean. Besides, it is our house; we can hardly expect the lodgers to feel responsible for it, and Mrs. Stromberg is just a neighbor.

I feel very grown-up at that moment, and am proud of my logic and my decision. I do not give Mama much of a chance to protest. I leave in a hurry and proceed to go upstairs.

It is not a very large house; it has only the basement, the ground level, and one floor upstairs. A building has been added adjoining; that is where Mother, my sisters, and I lived after we had lost our first home in one nasty night of bombing. The lodgers live on the ground level, my grandparents on the top floor.

I look around.

The damage is not too bad. Fortunately it was not a fire-bomb that hit the house but a fairly powerful shell (or shells). It is all rather badly torn-up, but the house is not falling down on us, and I consider that quite a lucky break. But how much longer will our luck hold out?

It is impossible in the inferno of shelling and bombarding outside to go next door and see what damage is done there, but from an upstairs window I can look down on the roof of the adjoining area and see that there also the damage is not too bad. I catch a glimpse of the sun shining, and with a sigh of relief I go back downstairs.

12

"Everything is okay," I say. What else is there to say?

"I'm hungry, Mama." Chris' bright blue eyes look bored. Poor little darling—nine years old, and nothing to play with, no one her age to talk to, locked in a cage like a little bird. . . .

"Well, I guess we all ought to eat something," Mama says.

We have a few loaves of bread left, some sugar, a few pounds of potatoes, and a few packages of cigarettes. I am the only one who smokes, and only once in a while. The most precious belonging we have, however, is a small suitcase full of "Nestlés" baby food for Monika.

Mama cuts two slices of bread for each one of us. Although I am hungry, it just does not taste good at all; I guess I am too tense. Somehow I manage to get the bread down; then I decide that it would be best to sleep a little.

I say good-night, but I cannot sleep.

The thought of what may lie ahead of us is too much to cope with, so I decide to think of nice things in the past.

I am wondering what Annie, my girl friend, is doing right at this moment. Is she as frightened as I am? Maybe the Russians are already at her home, and for her it is all over . . . over? In which way? Death? . . . I get angry at myself. Why do I have to keep thinking about death? I want to think about nice things. . . .

Oh, the fun we used to have on Sunday afternoons! In summer, we would go swimming in the Wannsee, let ourselves be roasted in the sun and ogle the boys (or better, let them ogle us!). Still, there were not too many boys our age around; they were either in the "Arbeitsdienst" or drafted. The only eligible bachelors were foreign workers, and our mothers did not like dating of that kind. In most cases, we did not like that either. The only other kind were soldiers on leave or wounded, and if you dated these, you always knew it could never last more than a few days.

But going swimming was fun. At least we could loaf in the

sun and play the game of make-believe. No one could deprive us of dreams, and for hours on end, we would tell each other what we would do, if. . . .

Then there were always movie stars we could idolize, and we would dream up situations where fate would throw us right into the path of some famous hero. It went something like this. . . .

We would be in an air raid shelter; across from us would be Mr. X, the famous film star, aloof and very reserved. And then suddenly there would be a terrible crash, the house would shake and we would be thrown right into his arms, trembling. He would suddenly realize he held a pretty girl in his arms; of course by then we were quite sophisticated and very, very beautiful, and he would look at us and say, "Why did I not notice you before?" Then after the air raid was over he would take us to a "Weinstube" and we would talk and be envied, and then he would take us home and kiss us good-night. Oh, boy!

Of course, the same idea could be applied to our heroes. There were quite a few war heroes—good-looking, courageous, dashing, smart. But there again, one would never know if and when they would ever return. . . .

Then there would be a more realistic version of daydreams. There would be a surprise air raid. We would walk past a burning house and see some people trapped there. We would courageously risk our own lives and help to get everyone out and bring them to safety. Then we would be decorated with a medal and be famous and meet lots of nice boys. Where they would come from all of a sudden is still a mystery to me, but if you dream, you may as well dream big!

After we had had enough of the sun, we would treat ourselves to coffee and cake. Usually it was not too hard to scrounge some bread coupons from Mother with which we could purchase some delicious bakery goodies—our allowances were ample. War mothers were generous—the motto was "Live today, for who knows what's going to happen tomorrow." In a way, when I think back now, they had to live in such terrible extremes. They did not have to fabricate a boogie man, they all had a built-in one called "war". Yet, like every mother, they

14

had to provide hope, encouragement, security, and love. And some fun, too. All of that they had to do alone, with the husbands away in the war, not knowing when they would come back, if ever; not knowing if any of their children would be alive the next day. They could not tie the children to their apron strings all the time. . . . They had to stand in line for hours to provide for the food, carry on normal life with a minimum of sleep with numerous air raids every night and day, wash their clothes by hand, chop and saw wood, take little wagons and carry hundredweights of coal to their homes, send packages to their husbands and sons and provide them with hope for the future, tell them everything was well at home when it wasn't, and emerge from heaps of rubble and ashes as ladies. . . .

I salute all the mothers of 1939 to 1945 in Germany. If the word "heroism" can be applied to any people's actions, then it is they who deserve it.

My thoughts wander back once more to Annie.

If she were here with me it would help. We could sit and occupy our thoughts with pleasant things to come and play the game of make-believe. But it's pretty hard to daydream when you are alone and outside is death and destruction and uncertainty. . . .

I wonder if she feels at this moment, the way I do. Then I fall asleep.

2

A DAY OF APPREHENSIONS

Lux, the dog, wakes me by nudging his head against me. I pat him and play with him for a few minutes.

The others are still asleep except Grandfather.

"Good morning, Opa. What time is it?"

He pulls his watch from his pocket, dollar-sized, on a gold chain.

"Six o'clock," he says.

Then I have not slept too long. Hours and hours of suspense and waiting ahead of us yet. When will it end?

The thought of just sitting there in the basement, waiting for something to happen, with nothing to do, nowhere to go, seems almost unbearable.

"If I could only sleep until it is all over," I find myself thinking.

I look at Opa, hoping I will come up with a subject to talk about to pass time. Instead I look at him closely. What are his thoughts? Is he thinking back into his life, maybe of happy times when he was younger?

The expression on his face indicates none of his thoughts. Strangely enough he looks as kind and cheerful as ever—is it because he proudly wears a "Kaiser Wilhelm mustache" that, ends brushed up, seems to hint at a smile?

As a matter of fact, he looks a lot like the old Kaiser; they were even born on the same day. I remember Opa saying on all his birthdays that the flag would come out in honor of his day of birth. I believed him, of course. I knew Granddad, but I did not know the Kaiser!

When he was younger, he must have been a rather impressive man, tall, broad, carrying himself straight and proud. I had seen him as a young man in photographs. Now he is an old man; I am sure the first World War must have left scars.... He was in France during the battle of Verdun and in the Argonne, which were quite horrible I had been told.

He never talks about that experience, although I have asked him many times. The only subject he ever discusses is the song the soldiers used to sing when it had been quiet on the Western Front for a while:

Die Voeglein im Walde, die sangen so wunder-wunderschoen,
In der Heimat, in der Heimat, da gibts ein Wiedersehn...

I used to sing it when he went to feed the chickens, taking me with him. I always tried to be with him. I loved him very much. There was never, not ever, an unkind word from him to me, and somehow, somewhere he always managed to have a piece of candy hidden for me. He permitted me to search his pockets and would apparently help me find the treasure. But at the beginning he always managed to point out the wrong pocket so that I, disappointment after disappointment, would have to search several times until finally—oh bliss!—I came to the right pocket. It was always an instant treasure hunt.

Now here he is, going through another war. It seems to me at this point that life is one continuous war—what on earth makes people want to fight?

"Opa, are you going to play a game of "Cheating" with me later on?"

"All right, get the cards," he says good-naturedly.

The game is not too much fun anymore, he always lets me win, and to a child that is nice; now that I am older it provides no challenge. But today it does not matter—anything is better than sitting, doing nothing but waiting.

17

For a while we forget what is going on outside, until our laughter wakes the others, one by one.

We have something to eat which can be called "breakfast"; one courageous person has gone upstairs to brew some "Ersatz" coffee. After we have had our meager nourishment, we all feel a little better. It is then that we realize that the shelling has decreased slightly—there are times in between when it is fairly quiet. The pause never lasts long, but it is still a relief.

"You know," my grandmother says, "I should go and milk the goat. The poor thing has not been milked in several days. I am sure she is very uncomfortable."

"Omi, you can't go out there," Mama protests.

"Goodness, you know it is not that quiet out there yet!"

"Well, just listen to her."

And indeed, we have not noticed it before—vaguely, but still very disturbingly, we hear her pitiful cries: "Maeeee, maaaeeee, maaaeee. . . ."

"The milk has accumulated and hurts her," Omi says. "Sooner or later I shall have to go."

I want to volunteer again but decide against it. I have never milked a goat, and surely this is neither the time to learn nor to gamble with my life. I feel very sorry for the goat, but I also do not feel like dying.

"Omi," I try to comfort her, "wait just a little bit longer. Maybe the shelling will decrease some more. Then it will not be quite so dangerous."

"I guess you are right," Omi sighs.

I know it bothers her. She is a conscientious woman, and she also loves her animals. But for the time being, there is just no other solution.

I decide to freshen up a little. Considering the circumstances all of us still look fairly neat and tidy—somehow surprising in a dark and dreary basement with no water and not the usual aids to hygiene available. The waterlines have long since been destroyed by the shelling. What water we have left has to be saved for drinking and cooking.

I have brought some of my beauty aids down into the cellar

18

with me, although my thoughts are everywhere else but on personal appearance. I guess it is habit—but how marvelous some habits are!

Now I look at what is me: skinny, scrawny, rather undeveloped, dark circles under my eyes from tension and lack of sleep for years. I do not consider myself very pretty at all. Contrary to the belief of most people outside Germany that all Germans are blond and heavyset and rather clumsy, I am not, nor is my mother. She has a tendency to be a little on the chubby side. I take after my father, who is very slim, but both my mother and I have dark hair and green eyes. I always considered Mama to be very beautiful, and she is. She has a fine-featured face, a very lovely nose—almost, in profile, with typical Greek features. Mine is not half as beautiful—slim, but pug-nosed. And my legs are nothing to rave about—just as skinny as the rest of me! Not that it makes much difference to me; at this point in my life I am just beginning to outgrow the tomboy I have been. All my playmates have been boys. More than once we would get into a wholesome fight over who would be captain when we played police and robbers. Sometimes I even won!

Now a problem has come into my life which so far has never been one.

From the refugees whom we had talked with we have heard some gruesome stories about the Russian soldiers raping women, sometimes even killing them afterwards or when they met with resistance.

I know, of course, enough about sex to know that rape is not the way I want to have my first encounter with sex, and the thought just terrifies me. It is a comfort to know that I am not too pretty, but then I have heard that the Russians are not particular. Either way I look at the situation, no part of it is in any way close to what I had hoped peace would bring us.

If only Papa were here! Papa had wanted a boy when I was born. He was very disappointed when the firstborn was a girl, but later on we became great pals. He took me hunting and on motorbike rides, and almost always talked to me like an adult. That was not because I was mature (I was not) but because he

19

did not know what to do with children, especially girls, and so our relationship was sometimes nice, sometimes awful. He was also a great critic, and I had a pretty hot temper! But now I desperately want him to be here, and I find that I am slowly beginning to get angry at the whole adult world which has put me into this situation. It is an unpleasant thought, and so I let my mind wander back into the past.

Thinking of Papa and wondering where he is at that moment, and if he is still alive, has brought my thoughts back to his home town. He came from a farm family, and during summer vacation from school, I would visit his brother on the farm, eat homemade bread, delicious ham, drink pints and pints of milk, eat the country-fresh butter—oh, thinking about it makes my mouth water, and makes me very hungry. Those were glorious days, carefree and happy.

The last time, however, my visit there was not under the same happy circumstances. When the air raids became heavier and heavier, my mother decided that it would be best to take some of our more valuable belongings to my father's relatives. We figured that in the country, where there were no air raids, they would be safer.

It was already close to the end of the war. Travelling was not a pleasure any more, it had become a trial. Sometimes it would take days for a trip which would normally have taken a few hours. In between travelling one would always have to figure on air raids, destroyed railroad lines, or other obstacles.

Mama hesitated to let me go, yet I was the only one who could. Chris was still too little to be left alone, and for Mama to go and take Chris with her was out of the question. She could not hold Chris with one hand and also carry luggage.

So I proceeded on my journey. At that time the desire of the very young for adventure was still strong with me, and I said good-bye with no misgivings.

Getting there was no problem. I arrived safe and sound,

20

stayed overnight and—heavenly bliss!—could sleep a whole night through without a single air raid!

When I said good-bye to my relatives, I did not have the vaguest feeling that it would be the last time I would see them.

The return trip met with obstacles almost immediately. My train had just arrived at Wittenberge (about an hour's journey from where my relatives lived) when it was stopped and everybody was told to leave the train and go for cover. It seemed rather silly to me, for there was not the slightest indication of an air raid. After all, I was an expert on that!

I stood around for a few minutes and looked up to the sky. The familiar sound of bombers was not there, and I thought that it might be just a blind alarm. I was standing next to a refreshment booth, looking at what was displayed in the window. Suddenly I heard the sound of airplanes. I expected that these were probably German fighter planes going after the enemy. Little did I know that at that time there were hardly any German fighter planes left to defend the civilian lives—those that were left had a bigger job to do at the Russian front!

The planes flew in beautiful formation, I could not help but admire them. They were up rather high, and I could not see the insignia. I counted them: one, two, three, four, five, six. . . .

Suddenly, to my surprise, they dived upon us with a frightening sound. In a second I realized what was going on—these were not German planes! They were enemy planes who were coming for us! At that moment I heard a sound I had never heard before, the fast and deadly fire of machine guns. Instinctively I looked for the best available cover and decided that there was no time to escape except underneath the train.

Next to me stood a little girl of about three or four years of age. Where her parents were, I did not know, there was just too much confusion, people running and screaming, trying to find cover from the guns—panic! I grabbed the little girl, who did not utter a sound. I pulled her down with me underneath the train, and there we lay, shaking and terrified. I realized that we were pretty safe where we were from machine guns—but what if

21

the fighter planes were followed by bombers? I prayed that this would be all, that there would be no bombers coming too. Luckily, at that time my prayers were still heard. . . .

After it was all over and I crawled away from the train I saw that the glass window of the refreshment booth suddenly had been beautified by an intriguing design— a lovely, neat half-circle of bullet holes embroidered the area where my head would have been had I not sought cover under the train. Some people are just lucky!

I took the little girl to a station attendant, explaining the situation, and went back into the train. It took me two days to get back home. Normally it was a journey of five hours.

"I just can't stand it any longer to hear the goat cry," Omi interrupts my thoughts. "I have to go and milk her."

This time nobody tries to talk her out of it. The shelling has decreased considerably.

Silently I admire her courage. She is only a frail, tiny woman, but she makes up for her small physical features with a great amount of fortitude. Her hair is not white as would have been expected at her age, but gray—a rather dark gray. She is extremely neat in her appearance and would fight us tooth and nail if we tried to do something for her that she thought she could do herself. Pride in everything she does, and especially in doing things herself that most people her age would not be able to do, is one of her main characteristics. She has the kind of sense of humor that is only known to a Berliner—rough and biting, yet full of wisdom and good-naturedness. This is also her second war. The First World War had been quite rough on her. She had adopted two children, my mother and another little girl, Aunt Evi, who now, with her family, is one of the occupants awaiting the end of the war in the nearby earth-bunker we had built earlier for an air raid shelter. My mother told me that she remembered Omi sitting up till midnight almost every night during the First World War sewing buttonholes into uniforms.

22

She was able to provide extra food from the Black Market that way.

Thinking about all that now, my heart goes out to her—dear, dear Omi, now she has to face it all again, and this time so much worse. . . .

"Omi has certainly been gone a long time," Mama says. "I am beginning to get worried. We should not have let her go."

I realize then that I have not paid much attention and not even noticed that Omi has left the cellar.

"How long has she been gone?"

"Well," Mama says, "it has been about twenty-five minutes, and it does not take that long to milk the goat. Besides, can't you hear the shelling? It's started again."

"Don't worry just yet, Mama, maybe she is feeding her too, and that could take a little more time," I try to comfort Mama. "Twenty-five minutes is not really that long."

But if I am very honest with myself, I have to admit that I am beginning to get worried too. A feeling of danger arises inside me, making me shiver a little. Another five minutes pass—where in heaven's name is Omi? Surely she cannot turn this into a leisure and routine excursion with all that shooting and shelling going on outside!

I cannot stand it any longer. "I am going to see where Omi is," I say.

"Inga, you are not going to do any such thing!" Mother says, more than firmly. But I am already halfway up the cellar stairs and am gone before she can protest any more and possibly hold me back.

As I reach the outside door, I pause for a moment. My heart is pounding, and I am frightened. The shelling sounds a lot louder and much more threatening than when we hear it down in the basement. Do I really dare go out into that inferno? But out in that hell is Omi, and any normal human being in their full possession of wit would hurry to get back into safety, unless . . . it is then that I know something must have happened to Omi—she would not be out there any more, unless she could not come back! Suddenly I do not hear the shelling anymore; all I have in my mind is to get to Omi and maybe, possibly, save her. I throw open the door—and there she is!

With one hand she is holding the milk pail, with the other she is holding herself up on the door frame. Her face is pale white, and I see that she is ready to faint. Quickly I look her over to see if she is hurt. Down her right leg comes a stream of red. She is bleeding profusely. Where she stands, a pool of blood accumulates fast.

I take the milk pail out of her hand, with the other arm I get hold of her waist and half-carry her inside the house.

"Shell," Omi whispers.

"It's okay, Omi darling," I say. "Don't worry, you'll be all right, we will have you taken care of, you are safe now." But I am shaking all over and try hard not to cry.

I put the milk pail on the table and yell down into the basement. "I need help! Omi is hurt!"

Everybody wants to get there at the same time, and so we have a congestion on the cellar steps. Somehow we get her down into the basement without too much trouble and put her on the bed.

With all the blood, it is hard to see where the wound is located. I have to clean all the blood off first; then I see that it is quite a large but not dangerous wound on the very upper part on the inside of her right thigh. Omi tells us that she was already on her way back, when a shell came down a few yards away from her and a splinter hit her leg. It was a miracle that not more splinters had found their way to her, but probably she was so close to the explosion that most of it went right over her.

"All right," I say. "Someone give me some bandages!"

There is an embarrassed silence—in all the preparations for survival we have forgotten to provide bandages! What to do now? Omi is bleeding heavily and needs something to stop it.

Temporarily we collect all the handkerchiefs available and dress the wound with them. It is all right for the moment, but

24

she also needs to have the wound sterilized—and the first-aid kit is over in the earth-bunker!

After Omi's wound is primitively fixed up, I have to sit down for a moment. I am not shaking any more; something needs to be done and I need time to prepare myself to do it. Until now I have hardly ever smoked—now I want a cigarette. There are plenty, so it is no problem. It makes me just a little dizzy but not badly so; rather it elevates me a little—or so I think.

What has to be done would be under normal circumstances very simple: I have to go into the earth-bunker and get the first-aid kit, but that is about fifty yards away. Fifty yards of shelling and shooting! If I go, it will be senseless to crawl towards it—the chances of being hit are just too great. The only way I can succeed is to stop the shooting, and I know just how to do it. If the Russians see that I am a woman (or girl) they will probably figure I mean no harm, and if I somehow wave my hands, indicating that I am unarmed, they will probably stop for a moment.

This kind of thinking is proof of my youth. The optimism of the young is unbelievable, but among all this the word "probably" keeps coming up. I guess I'm not entirely convinced myself of the success of this mission. However, it helps to kill my fear.

I tell everybody of my intentions. By this time Mama does not protest anymore. First of all I have always been rather headstrong; secondly she is tired and weary from carrying too much responsibility for too long alone. Besides, I have done a pretty good job of convincing everybody that the way I plan to do it is quite without danger, and so I leave.

The shelling outside is temporarily not too bad, but I still think there will be less danger if I walk upright and proceed with my original plan. The only thing that separates the Russians from us is a big canal close to our house; they have dug themselves into the earth on the other side of the waterway. As I walk towards the canal, which is the way I must go in order to reach the earth-bunker, I vaguely see something move on the

25

other side. I have walked about fifty steps, when I hear a noise coming from the canal that sounds like a gunshot. Instinctively I throw myself to the ground. Nobody has taught me what to do in a case like this, but I guess something like it comes naturally! A bullet flies past right above me, there where my head would have been. I lie flat, thinking what to do next.

It would be sheer suicide to try and make it to the earth-bunker. We will just have to find another solution for Omi's wound. But now I have to get back. Now that the Russians know that there is someone across the canal, any movement they can detect means death for me. I start crawling back slowly and carefully. Where before optimism has prevailed, fear now has entered my heart, and it turns the journey back into a nightmare, but I make it.

"It is impossible to get to the bunker," I say. "But we all have petticoats, and Omi has some marvelous pine spirits—let me have some of these."

"Here," Mrs. Stromberg happily volunteers, "my petticoat is linen, that's just perfect for the occasion!"

She starts to tear up her petticoat. I have to smile a little—she is such a big woman, there certainly is enough petticoat to bandage two people!

"Thank you," I say, "but hold it for just a moment, will you?"

I look for the pine spirits. Omi, in her efficient ways, has collected pine needles over the years and has poured pure alcohol over them—this is supposed to be an excellent help against rheumatism. I have suddenly remembered this—and it is ideal for cleaning up Omi's wound.

"Omi, where are the pine spirits?"

"Right behind you," she answers.

They are standing on a shelf right behind my bed in a huge green bottle. Omi is marvelous when I clean her wound. It must sting a great deal, but she bites her lips and does not say a word. Bandaging it is not easy, the wound is up so high on her thigh that the bandage has a tendency to slip down. I don't dare make

26

it too tight either for fear that it may interfere with her blood circulation. But finally it is all done; Omi sits back and relaxes, and I, exhausted, sink on my bed and fall alseep.

I have only slept for about two hours, and when I awake, everybody else is sleeping. I do not like that at all, it means that I will have to sit and think—and thinking right now is not the best pastime. However, since there is nothing else I can do, I decide to play a game with myself, a game called "What are people?"

The game means looking at every individual present and trying to remember everything I know about them.

My mother and my two sisters, my grandparents and I myself are familiar—I decide to start with Mrs. Stromberg.

I was never sure whether I liked her or not during the past years. She owns the restaurant next to our house, and since her husband's death she has had to run the business herself. She looks the part all right: heavyset, gray hair with a bun at the neck, broad features, muscular, capable of handling any happy-under-the-influence lad who gets out of line with too much "Schnaps" in him! She speaks with a heavy gutteral accent which suggests either Slavic or Baltic ancestry.

Nobody quite knows where they came from. They never spoke about a home town or a family. One day they arrived, and that was it. Her husband, a slim, bald, quiet man, died a few years later.

There are times when I like her, and times when I do not. She has never been unkind to me; in fact I think she likes me, but our communication has never worked well enough to establish any kind of personal relationship. I am very sensitive, shy, and try to be polite—she is just the opposite. Her manner of speech sometimes irritates me; it is drastic, outspoken, and sometimes even crude. Why she has chosen us to be with during these days I will never know—I guess she likes us more than we think. I always suspect that she speaks either Russian or Polish or some

27

other Slavic language. Looking at her now, I wonder where my friend Paula is.

Paula is a girl from the Ukraine, one of the millions of foreign workers who came to Berlin during the war, and I like her tremendously. She is pretty in an unpolished way—not too slim, not too well shaped, not too sophisticated, everything about her is just average, but she has a very kind and warm heart, and although the language difficulty prevents us from complete understanding, I sense enough of her qualities to be very fond of her.

Once in a while I would invite her over to dinner, or offer her one of my dresses. Despite the shortage of food and clothing, we were still a lot better off than the foreign workers. Mostly I felt sorry for her because she was away from home and had no one to look after her. I knew myself what a dreadful experience it is to be all alone in foreign territory! Mrs. Stromberg had rented out a room to her, and although to my knowledge she was not unkind to Paula, she also was not exactly the motherly type. Paula and I in this way have developed a casual friendship. That friendship later will save my life more than once.

Paula could not pronounce my name properly. Instead of Inga she would say "Engel"—something like "Angel," although I am sure that is not what she meant—it was just the way she said it.

About a year before the war was over, I had noticed Paula getting heavier, mainly so around her middle.

"Me, baby," she said, beaming all over her face and pointing to her stomach. "German soldier—war." To my knowledge she was not married, but if it made her happy, I saw no reason not to be happy for her.

Two months later I found her crying. "Baby gone," she said, and her eyes had lost the sparkle. "Me sick."

Apparently she had had a miscarriage. I comforted her as best I could, but because of the language barrier I could not say too much. Still, I am sure she felt my sympathy and maybe it was a small comfort to her. Three months after that she came running

28

to me, sobbing bitterly, her eyes filled with tears. At first she could not talk, and I tried to comfort her. Then she said: "German soldier, dead. War." The only person who had ever really cared for her. This is the way I figured it, anyway, from bits and pieces of conversation between her and me. Now he was gone too.

About a month before we had to move into the basement, Paula had disappeared. I have never had the right moment to ask Mrs. Stromberg what has happened to her, and in all the turmoil, I have almost forgotten about Paula. Now that I remember again, I want to ask Mrs. Stromberg where Paula is, but I do not want to wake her and decide to save that for later.

Over there are Mr. and Mrs. Schulman. They are a couple who have been lodged in our home by the government. It has been a law that anybody who had a spare room would have to take as lodgers people who had lost their homes by bombs. Nobody really complains about it—after all, the next person in that situation could be yourself! So we have tried to make them as comfortable as possible. They are quiet, pleasant lodgers, minding their own business, exchanging a few polite words now and then with us. We never get too close, since we know that their political opinions are contrary to ours. They are very much for Hitler, while my parents and grandparents have never recognized anyone but the Kaiser, and do not care for any "Führer." The Schulmans have not tried to convert us and are not eager busybodies, so we avoid political arguments and on that basis get along very well.

I look at everybody sleeping peacefully: Mama and Chris together in one bed, Chris sleeping with the tranquillity of the child; Mama even during sleep with lines of worry in her face; Opa is snoring slightly, his Kaiser Wilhelm mustache lightly bobbing up and down; Omi is next to him, sometimes stirring and groaning in her sleep—the wound must have started really hurting; Mrs. Stromberg looking, as always, broad, unperturbed, also snoring lightly; Mr. and Mrs. Schulman sleeping holding each other, almost as if they knew. . . .

29

I suddenly realize that someone is looking at me. It is Uncle Carl, who must realize that my thoughts are anything but happy.

"What are you thinking about?" he asks.

"Everybody and everything," I say. "What do you think, Uncle Carl, are the Russians going to come here, or maybe the Americans?" From the tone of my voice he detects which is my preference and my hope.

"Don't worry, my little one. I am sure we have at least enough troops to hold Berlin until the British and the Americans can get here. I don't think that they will let the Russians have the capital. You must know," he adds, pointing a finger to emphasize his statement, "that whoever gets the capital will be the official victor." Despite his try to comfort me, he realizes that I am not too well convinced yet. He fumbles around in his pocket.

"Look here, little one," he says, and holds in his hand a small, pretty pistol. "If it comes to the worst, I have something to defend us." I absorb this with very mixed emotions. I cannot quite see how a small pistol could possibly defend us against a company of Russian soldiers. But somehow I sense that it gives him a certain amount of security to think he has a weapon with which to defend us, and so I say, with a halfhearted smile, "Oh, good!"

"What do you think Uncle Fritz and Aunt Evi are doing?" I change the subject.

"Oh, I'm sure they are all right," he says. "At least they can peek out once in a while and see if the sun is shining outside. We here," he adds with the slightest touch of fear, "we are in here like mice in a trap. . . ." It is then that I realize how hard it must be on him to be sitting in the dark basement. After all, during the First World War he was buried alive in a shell crater: that was when he lost his speech. He was dug out and saved, but for many years he could not talk. It was strange how he regained his ability to talk. He had, despite his defect, married a lovely young girl. They lived very happily together. One day, when she was sitting near the window in their home during a thunderstorm, lightening struck close by. It did not hurt her, but Uncle Carl, in shock, yelled out to her and dragged her away from the window. Suddenly they both realized that he had talked. What a blessing! But now he is alone; his wife passed away several years ago.

This time the roles are reversed; I try to comfort him. "We are not so badly off, Uncle Carl," I say. "At least we are pretty safe here for the time being, and who knows, maybe the English or the Americans are going to be here soon."

My thoughts wander back again to my aunt and uncle over there in the earth-bunker. Aunt Evi, Mama's sister, is a slender, pretty woman, seven years younger than my mother. Despite the fact that she has had three children, she has a beautiful figure, and always keeps herself neat and well-dressed. I always thought she was terrific. Our families were neighbors for many years. I always liked their apartment much better than ours. They had a beautiful view towards the surrounding woods and in the far distance more houses, but right in the immediate neighborhood were small lovely gardens and tiny wooden houses, lots of fruit trees, lilac bushes, and flowers. When I lived there I made friends with almost everybody in the neighborhood, and wherever I went, I was given toys, candy, or a bouquet of flowers, if I pointed out that I liked a particular kind of flower. One day I wandered off further than I was really permitted to go—it was not really very far, but I was only four or five years old. I remember this a little myself and Mama loves to tell the whole story about me. Mama began to worry a little, but she knew I was always playing at some neighbor's home, especially if they had pets. I was crazy about animals—all animals, and it seems that this love was always returned. My poor mother; if she had kept all the animals I brought home— "they just followed me home"—we would have had to open a zoo!

31

She was walking along the road looking for me when a neighbor came towards her and said, "Mrs. L, I was looking for you. I want you to come and see your daughter."

"She is all right?" Mama asked anxiously. "Is she all right?" The man grinned from one side of his mouth to the other, "I wish I had a camera to take a photo of how all right she is!"

When Mama had entered his yard, she almost fainted.

Mr. Schroeder raised pigs, but his yard was immaculately clean considering the circumstances! One of his sows had had little ones about four weeks before. These little pigs had taken my fancy, of course, and I had asked him if I could play with them. He agreed, and about an hour later he looked to see what I was doing. The little piglets had decided that I was more fun than their mother, and in play we had all gotten tired and fallen asleep. There I was, deep asleep surrounded by six sleeping piglets, cuddled up to me as if I was their mother! Mama hated to wake me, but she did anyway. At home she put me in the bathtub and I had the most thorough bath of my life.

Uncle Fritz, a broad, heavyset man, growing slightly bald, used to love to tease me about my name. My birth certificate states my name as "Ingeborg," but nobody ever called me that. It was always "Inga." "Borg" means "lend" in German, and Uncle Fritz would come up to me and say "Inga, borg mir mal zehn mark." ("Inga, lend me ten marks!") I still don't know why it infuriated me—maybe because he made fun of my name or because I knew that he knew I did not have ten marks—anyway, he always succeeded in making me mad as a hatter. I would run towards him and hit him with my fists, but he would just pick me up like a toy, laugh good-naturedly, and lift me up into the air.

"Ah," he would say, "Inga, you are a good little girl, but you ought to eat more. You ought to get some weight on you, skinny little thing." That was another thing that would irritate me. I did not want to be skinny. But I always heard my mother say, "The clever one gives in," and decided that was not a bad policy in life. So I would laugh halfheartedly. Besides, he was a lot stronger than I was!

As a matter of fact, his strength was quite outstanding; he was an extremely hard worker and had rough, thick fingers. Yet, the amazing thing was that he could play the mandolin or accordion like a real professional, and I used to love to sit with him and his family in the little garden and listen to his gay, happy, carefree playing and singing, watching him drink a few bottles of beer, although he was never drunk. He was not drafted during the war since he worked in a steel factory.

When I was ten years old a scholarship to high school was offered to me, and we immediately started to learn English. By the time I was twelve years old I had started to speak French, and when I was fifteen I could speak both foreign languages well enough to converse in them. It was not easy to keep up my grades with air raids night after night and many times during the day too. There was no father around to keep a firm hand, and not much fun as a reward for good grades! But I was in an elite class; it consisted only of girls who had won scholarships throughout the city. As a result, great things were expected of us. I remember our teachers saying "You are an 'A Class'—you are supposed to be bright—so prove it!" We had, of course, also elite teachers, but they were hard on us!

Uncle Fritz, who did not know any languages, would always coax me into talking to him in English or French, and I would willingly comply, mainly because I suspected that he did not really believe I could speak English and French! But this time I had the upper hand—if I wanted to, I could have called him all sorts of nasty things. He would not understand them! On my honor it may be said that I never did.

One day he came to me and said, "You are going to have a nice opportunity to practice your French. I have invited a Frenchman for dinner, and I cannot talk to him. But he is such a good worker and a very nice guy. And the foreign workers don't get much food, so I thought inviting him to dinner would show him I appreciate his good work."

Of course I accepted. I was very excited about the whole thing. This was the first time I could use my knowledge practically and for a good cause.

33

It turned out not to be as easy as I had thought. Maurice, that was his name, was from Brittany, and did not speak the clear French we learned at school. He spoke in dialect, and I had a very hard time understanding him. But we managed to get a conversation going, anyway, and I have the feeling he did enjoy his evening. One day I received a great big bar of French chocolate through Uncle Fritz from Maurice, the largest chocolate bar I ever saw. That was quite a treat—sweets were rationed in those days.

Now Uncle Fritz and Aunt Evi are sitting in the earth-bunker; we are only about fifty yards apart and yet we cannot communicate with them. I wonder if Uncle Fritz still has his sense of humor—right now his teasing me would be quite a treat. . . . Is Aunt Evi as frightened as I am? I wish that they were here with us now; it would help to pass the time. If only the others in the cellar would wake up! Are they going to sleep forever?

I decide to play with Lux. Cute little Lux—he is really fun; a brown-haired, fat, short-legged little mongrel of the canned-soup type—several different ingredients, and no one knows what they are! But I love him; he is never any trouble, he is loyal, faithful, and devoted. When the sirens went off early in the war, he would run towards the door, and scratch; we would open the door and he would run outside towards the earth-bunker, our air raid shelter. He was always the first one there, and he would greet whoever came after him with a big tail-wagging. Then he would lie down and sleep peacefully and unperturbed, paying no attention to anything going on outside. He was also the first one out when the "All-Clear" sounded.

He is lying there, panting a little. I figure he is probably thirsty and give him some water. He drinks it, then comes over and licks my hand in a thank-you gesture. I play with him for a while, rolling him over on his back and pushing my hand back and forth for him to catch. The noise wakes the others.

"What time is it?" Mama asks.

I look at the gold watch Papa has sent me from Denmark. It

is the most beautiful present I have ever received. It is delicate, with a mother-of-pearl dial, and very precious to me, especially since it has come from my father, who had never been able to lavish presents upon us.

"Quarter of six," I say.

"I have to feed Monika," Mama says. While she prepares Monika's food, she looks over to me and says, "Inga, I think we'd better hide your watch. It's best not to show it so obviously. You could put it inside your clothing somewhere."

"What for?" I ask, then hastily add, "Never mind, I'll hide it." It was a stupid question.

"Shall I give Chris something to eat?" I offer, trying to make up for my stupid behavior.

"Please," Mama says. "Oh, what would I give for a nice cup of coffee—real coffee, not that 'Ersatz' stuff made from chicory we've been getting."

"Would you settle for a mix of both?" Mrs. Schulman says. "I have some in my pocketbook; we wanted to save it for a special occasion. I did not exactly have in mind the occasion we are having now, but we might as well use it."

"Oh, that is wonderful," Mama replies, "but I wouldn't want you to go upstairs right now to make the coffee. It's just too dangerous."

"It is amazing," Mr. Schulman puts in a word, "how people forget what they are doing in times of stress. I just remembered that packed among some of our things here in the basement is a little kerosene stove, complete with fuel and in working condition. We could have ourselves a feast."

All of a sudden everybody seems to feel slightly revived.

"We could even cook a meal," Mrs. Stromberg throws in, enthusiastically. "I have two small cans of corned beef, Mrs. L has potatoes, we could cook us a nice meal."

Mr. Schulman has already started unpacking his belongings.

"There!" he says, triumphantly. "There we are!" and he holds the kerosene stove up for everyone to see.

I almost feel like applauding. The prospect of a proper meal seems to make our fate so much easier to take.

35

"I have nothing," Uncle Carl says sadly, but he searches his pockets. "Yes, I do! Yes, I do!" he cries out, and in his hands he holds a bar of chocolate.

"Oh, good, we will have that for dessert," Omi says. "By the way, I still have the pot of milk from the goat, also some cereal, and Liz has sugar. So tomorrow morning for breakfast we can have some sweet porridge."

"Well," Opa says cheerfully, "we are not so badly off after all."

Mama has already started putting the potatoes on the stove. After they are done, Mrs. Schulman makes the coffee, then we fry the corned beef. What a delicious meal!

"Now let the Russians come!" Mrs. Stromberg says. "I will hit them over the head with a noodle roller!" We all laugh—we can just see her doing it!

But the most amazing thing is that this incident of sharing our meager possessions all of a sudden has turned a basement of neighbors into a family.

———————————

After the first exhilarating effects of the meal have worn off we sit quietly, each person dozing a little.

I don't know what possesses me to say what I do, but a feeling of foreboding, of impending danger, of near panic, grips my heart, and into the silence I say, loudly and clearly, "Tomorrow night at six o'clock the Russians will be in this house!"

The city lies in ashes.
The sun has changed to sinister and threat'ning gray.
We look for God . . .
But even He, in all His mercy,
Has turned His back, and—blindly?—walked away.

3

DAYS OF TERROR

Since my last rather disturbing remark, hours have passed. I cannot remember what we did during that time other than just passing time. I do remember, however, that Mama was very angry at me for making such a statement, for which, she felt, I had no reason whatsoever. And up to a point I had to agree with her. What in heaven's name had made me say it? Berlin was not an easy city to conquer; even a strong force of troops would need time and an awful lot of soldiers, weapons, and supplies in order to conquer it. If the German troops could hold it a few days longer, chances were that either the relief troops would come or the Western Allied Forces: the English, Americans, or the French. Any one of these would be better than the Russians!

I try to think about my country logically, realistically, although at seventeen I have not had much practice in such deep matters. Why are we in this situation? How did we get here?

Something strikes me as strange. Here I am, a seventeen-year-old girl, and instead of looking forward into the future with hope, as is normal for a teenager, I cannot even look into the present without fear, let alone the future! Instead, all I have to occupy my mind with is the past—a situation that is normally reserved for very old people. . . .

Politics never held any attraction for me. My future, I thought, would be much more interesting. I wanted to go to college and study journalism, with a scholarship, of course. My teacher had already indicated that I would get one—she had great faith in my abilities. Now there is no future.

I vaguely remember when I was five years old that some excitement had taken place over a period of time, and it was all about voting. I asked Mama what "voting" was, and after she had explained it to me I asked her whom they had voted for.

"That is a secret I cannot tell," she had answered, which, of course, made me even more curious. It was also the first time that my mother had kept a secret from me, and for the longest time I could not understand why and was temporarily rather peeved at her. When I had grown a little older, I realized why. Had my parents voted for Adolf Hitler, she would have been pleased to tell me whom they had voted for—after all, he was the top man!

My grandparents were great believers in the "Kaiserhaus"; it was the only way of life they knew, and nothing could change that belief. My mother shared that viewpoint—a country should have a king or a kaiser, anything else was just not acceptable. My father was the only one who did not believe in a monarchy. He felt that social reforms were needed in Germany and would have been very happy if a government of Social Democrats came to power in Germany. He had a mind of his own. A national socialist system represented too much of a dictatorship to him.

I was pretty sure that neither of my parents had voted for Adolf Hitler, but I was smart enough to know that this was best not mentioned in public.

At that time a few hundred yards away from our small apartment building was the house my grandparents lived in. It was a very large property which kept them busy. But for a child there could not have been a nicer place to play. I could pick

38

fruits from the trees: apples, plums, cherries, pears, even a peach tree had managed to grow, and produced the most delicious fruits I ever ate. There were strawberries to pick and flowers; birds to watch and butterflies; and when I tired of doing this, I could play with the puppies, or lie in the grass and watch the passing clouds, making believe I saw figures in the shapes of the clouds, and some of these figures looked like God. . . . I saw emerge from nothing but an egg the most adorable living creatures: little chickens, ducklings, fluffy and cuddly and helpless. Paradise lost. . . .

Sitting in the basement now I wonder where it has all gone, and my heart aches with nostalgia.

The only thing I did not have plenty of were playmates my own age. To my utmost delight one day, when I was nine years old, a large group of girls close to my own age appeared on my grandparents' grounds. Under the supervision of an older girl, they played games and sang and seemed to have a terrific amount of fun. I stood a few yards back where they could not see me and watched them. They came again, week after week, and I desperately wanted to join them.

Just about a year before, Chris had been born, but she was such a tiny baby, I would have to wait an awful long time before I could really play with her! I asked Mama to go to the girls and ask them if I could join them, but she refused. I persisted and would not leave her alone until she agreed. She went out with me to see the girls.

"My little girl here," she said to the older girl, "wants very much to participate in your games. She has been after me for days now to ask you if she could join your group."

"How old is she?" the young lady asked.

"Nine years," Mama replied.

"Well, she is too young to officially join the Hitler Youth," the girl said regretfully. "But each ten-year-old is registered as an official member of the Hitler Youth anyway, so she won't have to wait too long."

I took all the courage I had into my hands and spoke up, close to tears, "But one year is so long!"

"Well," the girl smiled, "in that case why don't you just join us whenever you feel like it. We can always use an extra hand at our games."

From that day on my loneliness was gone. Once each week the girls would come to play their games, I would join them and have the time of my life. Once in a while the word "Führer" appeared in the discussion, but I did not pay much attention to it, and nobody expected me to, since I was neither an official member nor old enough.

By the time I reached the official age of registration—each ten-year-old child was automatically registered as a member of either the H.J. (Hitler Jugend) for the boys, or the B.D.M. (Bund Deutscher Mädchen) for the girls—it was the year 1938, and other important things had come about.

My father, who worked for the City of Berlin, had been approached again and again to join the Party. Favoring the social-democratic system, he was not at all willing to do so, but there had been instances when some of his colleagues had suddenly lost their jobs—for obvious reasons. He was in a quandary. He did not want to sell out his political beliefs, but he also loved his family and had just lived through a rough time of unemployment. He was an eager worker, almost always finding some way of making enough money to provide us with what we needed. When other men had been out of work for long periods on end, he always had worked at something.

Now for the first time in his life he had a secure job, with an old-age pension ahead of him. Should he risk his family's security for a political belief that did not have a chance?

Besides, looking at the overall picture in Germany then, was the present government really so bad? From depression and poverty, Germany had emerged with hardly any unemployment left; with enough food for each family; with the building industry flourishing; some people could even afford a car (that was the Volkswagen—Adolf Hitler called it "the working man's car"); with the young taken off the streets and away from

crime; with the "Winterhilfe" brought into action (a social
service for the very poor)—all in all, things in Germany had
certainly changed for the better since Adolf Hitler had come to
power. At least, that is what it was on the surface.

Underneath, there were rumors. Rumors that whispered of a
war planned (more "Lebensraum"), rumors that spoke of incidents where children informed on their parents if they happened to have a different political viewpoint from the government's. Everything pointed in one direction—dictatorship.

Papa had to make a decision.

Rumors were what they were, just rumors. How true were
they? At this point, it did not officially look as if Germany was
planning to go into a war. Would anyone planning destruction
go ahead and build as much as the Third Reich did? There was
the "Autobahn"—a magnificent piece of road, well-built, big,
easy to drive on. There were public buildings being erected:
stadiums, recreation centers, new housing, everything was made
neat and tidy. Who in his right mind would build so much and
then plan destruction?

Besides, everybody knows about rumors: a mountain made
out of a molehill. So the only question for Papa to answer was
the question of his own political convictions, and that was
hardly a question. A political viewpoint does not feed your
family—a job does. That left only one more problem to be
solved: which was the branch of the party to join that posed the
least involvement in politics?

He thought he had found the answer: the N.S.K.K. Music
Corps! Papa had a little musical talent and therefore found no
problem in joining. In other ways it worked very well, too. The
only thing he had to do was practice the flute, and that
presented no problem to him! Once in a while he would have to
march in a parade playing his flute, and that was not too bad
either. There was no political involvement other than that, just
as he had hoped. So, all in all, things seemed all right.

At about the same time, I was ten years old and registered as
a member of the B.D.M. The way this happened was very
simple: my parents received a card (or letter, I do not remember

which) simply stating that from such and such a date on, their daughter Ingeborg was registered as a member of the "Bund Deutscher Mädchen" (in actual translation it would be "Circle of German Girls") and was assigned to Group so-and-so and the first meeting would be at such and such a place.

Mama was rather irritated at that. She had not filled out an application form and resented what had been done. However, I was very much for the idea. I finally was accepted by my earlier playmates as one of them, and that made me feel a little more grown up. I was not a baby anymore!

For parents violently opposed to their children joining the organization, the situation presented quite a problem. The only way to keep their children out of it was to withdraw the membership they had never applied for—and they were forced to give an adequate reason for withdrawal.

Mama did not put up much of a fight (and I am sure a lot of other mothers did not either!) for there were more important problems creeping up. The rumors about an impending war grew stronger and stronger every day. If it happened, then Papa would have to go too. It was not a pleasant prospect.

———————

Something else happened which is important.

I overheard a conversation between my mother and Omi. Mama was extremely upset upon returning from a visit to our family doctor. He was an elderly, gray-haired man with extremely gentle manners, who had been our physician for many years. His name was Dr. Ehrhardt, and he was Jewish. He always had some candy ready for me when I had to be examined, and that endeared him even more to me. But it was mainly his kind and gentle ways which made me feel at home with him.

"Omi, Dr. Ehrhardt is leaving Germany," I heard Mama say to Omi.

"But why?" Omi was shocked.

"Why?" Mama got red with anger. "Why? Because these terrible people. . . Oh, I can't even find words to tell you how mad I am. Here is a wonderful man—dedicated to his profession, to his patients, a marvelous doctor, who's been in this country almost all his life, and now. . . ." She paused for a moment. "I have never seen him so sad. . . . 'Do you know, Mrs. L,' he told me, 'that I fought for Germany in the First World War? It was always my country, too, and I have always felt it my duty to support it. But now. . . .' Well," Mutti said furiously, "he did not have to tell me any more. All you have to do is read the "Stuermer," and you know which way the wind is blowing! The audacity of these people!"

"Shshsh!" Omi said, "don't talk so loud, Lisa!" She pointed to me.

"Inga," Mama said, "go outside and play." I would have given a lot to know who "these people" were, but never remembered to ask.

A week later, during which time Mama was very quiet, Dr. Ehrhardt left Germany. From some patients with whom he had been close friends we heard that he had arrived safe and sound at a foreign country—I cannot remember whether it was Palestine or America. His replacement was a doctor I learned thoroughly to dislike. What a contrast between the two men! After the gentle, understanding ways of Dr. Ehrhardt, this man was a monster (at least in my child's perspective). He was fairly young, abrupt, brusque, arrogant, self-assured, and a most dedicated believer in Hitler's philosophies. But he achieved one thing: he had an awful lot of suddenly-turned-healthy patients! I could sense that Mama hated him almost as much as I did.

Naturally, as a child, I understood not at all that one man was Jewish and the other a political fanatic; what made the difference was that one was a nice man and the other was not.

As I said, when I was ten years old I received a scholarship to high school. It is because of this and my change in schools that I remember the other incident well enough to know that it must have taken place sometime between the years 1938 and 1939.

To get to school, I had to take a bus, change once to another bus, and then walk for about one mile along a well-populated business street, with store after store. I could never afford to dally in the morning going to school, but I could afford to take my time after school to look into the store windows and admire all the pretty things.

One morning, hurrying as always, I saw that most of these stores had been completely devastated. The windows had been broken, clothes torn from their hangers, other things lay broken on the floor, but most of the contents were just gone. I could not possibly believe that that many thieves would have had the opportunity to break into that many stores all at once without getting caught, and I was puzzled. I did not have much time to look any further, school was close to starting and I had to be on time, but I had time to notice big yellow stars on every store.

In school nothing was mentioned about the yellow stars. If our teacher had any political ideas at all, they were hardly ever expressed. When she did speak, it was obvious that she did not agree with the doctrines of the Third Reich, but she was careful and never got into trouble. Besides, she was an excellent teacher and could hardly be spared. Today, I realize that she got away with a lot more than most people. . . .

That day she looked weary and sad. I decided to wait until I got home and then ask Mama about the yellow stars.

I had at that point not yet developed much interest in newspaper reading—adventure stories held a lot more fascination. I enjoyed geographical facts about the Mississippi in a country called America. Our geography teacher was a tiny, frail, funny man with a gray mustache and false teeth, which he used to clap about in the midst of a speech—a fact that made concentration difficult. It speaks for the Mississippi and its points of interest that I was so fascinated despite the obstacles! It was then that I developed a longing for far horizons, and it was then that I made up my mind to visit there when I was grown up.

Contrary to beliefs outside Germany, our churches were not closed during the government of the Third Reich. Two denominations were permitted: Lutheran and Catholic. I remember that during Lutheran class the Catholics left to go into another room to be taught facts about the Catholic religion, while we were learning the life of Christ the Lutheran way. Our Religion class teacher was excellent. When she talked about Christ, it was as if He Himself was somewhere near, so vividly did she bring out His personality. I cannot remember one boring or inattentive moment, and as a result I always brought home a grade of "good" or "very good." Later on it became more difficult because then it was not just the life of Christ, but facts and figures which had to be studied for confirmation—and that was never my cup of tea! The important seed had been planted, and even confirmation class was interesting up to a point. Whenever it became too much "fact and figure," I could always picture Christ on the water, or changing water into wine, or in the Garden of Gethsemane, or healing the sick. I did not think about Christ on the cross too often; it was just too sad to be remembered, but it was then that I got an inkling of the story of mankind. . . .

———————

When I got home the day the stores were smashed, Mama looked like my teacher—tired and unhappy. I told her what I had seen and asked her if she knew what it was all about. First of all, though, I wanted to know about the yellow stars, because I had also seen people walk past me with yellow stars on their coats or suits or dresses. I thought the stars looked somehow pretty but did not seem to match the expression on the faces of those who wore them.

"The stars are supposed to be a symbol of Judaism," Mama said.

"What is Judaism?"

"A religion different from ours."

"I know," I said. "We learned that in school in Religion class—but you know that too. Anyway, why are they wearing the star? Do they want to be different?"

"No," Mama said, "I don't think so. From what I have heard, they have to wear it."

"Who says so?"

"Our government."

I thought about that for a moment. I didn't see anything

45

wrong in people wearing a star—after all, if I wanted to wear a certain pin or brooch that looked pretty to me, I saw no reason to feel bad about it. On the other hand, if Mama were to force me to wear a pin I didn't like at all, I would be most resentful. I guess it is fortunate for all ten-year-olds that life is still fairly uncomplicated—and so to me, that problem was solved. As far as I could solve it, anyway.

I had been taught right from wrong, and somehow I sensed that something was wrong somewhere and it had something to do with our government. No ten-year-old will go and pursue a criminal, and by the same token I did not pursue the question of the yellow stars or the broken shop windows any further. . . .

Besides, life had become even more complex. When I went to the movies and saw newsreels, I saw falling bombs and dead people somewhere in another country; I believe it was Spain. There were a lot of battle scenes. People were talking a great deal about war. Many times war, threatening and evil, was in my dreams.

In September, 1939, the Second World War broke out. It would be useless for me now to go into political details of that era; the facts are known to the world. The German population was committed by Hitler to a war, whether they liked it or not.

About a year later, Papa was drafted into the Air Force. Mama, Chris, and I were alone.

The shelling has started again. Is it never going to end? I have reached the point where I feel anything is better than this waiting. There is the saying, "Better a horrible end than a horror without end." I decide to go upstairs and peek outside to see if anything new can be detected, anything at all that would indicate that maybe soon it would all be over. Or maybe just to catch a little bit of daylight. . . .

Upstairs everything looks the same, fortunately. At least our house has not yet been hit too badly; all four walls are still standing, though damaged. Despite the shelling, I decide to look outside, but never have a chance to do so.

46

Just as I go to open the door, it is opened from the outside. Standing before me, as much in shock as I, are two very rugged-looking people. At first glance I think they are Russians and I stand paralyzed with shock. Then one of them says, "Guten Tag—können wir für einige Minuten hier ausruhen?" (Hello, may we rest here for a few minutes?)

I thank God that they are Germans and look at them more closely. They are two men about sixty years of age, unshaven for days, eyes hollow, exhausted, dirty and dusty. They wear badly fitting German uniforms.

"Water, please," one of them asks.

I run down into the basement after I have told them to sit down and relax. I tell Mama what has happened and run back upstairs with some water.

They drink greedily, as if they have not had any water for quite a while.

Mama is standing behind me, in her hands a loaf of bread.

"You are Volkssturmmen, aren't you?" she asks. They nod.

It must be explained that in the last desperate struggle of Berlin, all available men were drafted, but by then there were only men over sixty, too old to fight in the war, or boys under sixteen, too young to be in the war. Now they are all in it. But then, so are we. . . .

"What is the situation?" Mama asks.

"Well," one of them answers, "we heard that Hitler is in the bunker of the Reichskanzlei saying to hold out, that the relief troops are just around the corner and so on and so on. Lies!" He looks disgusted.

"If they think we are going to stay around just waiting to be shot they have another think coming," the other one puts in. "I have a family who needs me, now more than ever."

They gratefully take the loaf of bread Mama has offered them and tell us that they are going to try and break through to their families.

"Which way do you think would be the safest and shortest way to get to Charlottenburg?" one asks Mama.

The question is not hard to answer. About a mile away,

where the breakthrough to the new canal has been made, a huge pipeline has been put across it, about thirty feet above the water. From where we live we can see that it is still intact, but it would be difficult to climb up onto it.

They have already mentioned that they cannot swim; to climb across on the pipeline will be their only way to cross the canal to get to their homes.

"I can give you our long wooden ladder," Mama says. "That should make it possible for you to climb onto the pipe during the night; or, if you don't want to wait that long, it could be used like a raft to get across the water."

They are very happy about that offer, and after wishing us good luck and our wishing them the same, they depart with our ladder.

Mama and I return to the basement and report to the others.

"I am glad they left," Mrs. Stromberg says. "We are civilians and the Russians may not hurt us, but if they found people in uniform here, they might take another viewpoint."

I do not quite agree with her—it seems kind of cruel to wish the two poor soldiers away from here where they might be safe. Who knows if they will ever make it? But in some odd way what she said does make sense, a kind of sense I do not particularly like. I suppose it is another lesson in maturity—or is it just a lesson in selfishness?

The rest of the day goes by—just like all the others before then.

We are all at the point where nothing really matters too much, only the wish: please let it be over with, and soon! Uncle Carl is dozing in his chair; Mr. and Mrs. Schulman, as always, are close to each other, now half-asleep; Opa and Mrs. Stromberg are lightly snoring; Omi is trying to sleep, turning and tossing; Chris and Monika are sleeping peacefully; Mama is lying on her bed, waiting like a tigress guarding her young; and I am trying to sleep as on so many nights before, and finally have succeeded in dozing a little, half-asleep, when suddenly we hear the door open upstairs and the sound of heavy footsteps.

In an instant every one of us is wide awake. No one dares to speak. I think we all know whom the footsteps belong to—and suddenly I remember my exclamation made last night: "Tomorrow night at six o'clock the Russians will be here!"

"Mama, what time is it?" I whisper.

"Five minutes before six," she says quietly.

These are the only words spoken, until finally we hear the cellar door open. I am lying facing the cellar steps. The first thing I see is a pair of heavy boots, then a hand holding a pistol, pointing in my direction. There is a shot and something behind me breaks. I close my eyes and think that this is the end. It is all very strange. I'm smothered with a penetrating odor, like acid, and do not dare to open my eyes.

4

HOW LONG, O LORD?

I hear harsh voices speaking a language I do not understand. I am not dead, and I dare to open my eyes.

What has happened is that Lux, our little dog, ran at the intruder, who fired his gun at the dog, not at me, but missed him and hit the big glass bottle of pine spirits behind me. Its contents are running out onto the floor—what a penetrating smell!

The Russians are here!

More Russian soldiers come down the steps and search the cellar; upstairs we hear footsteps stamping around, apparently searching the house.

I look at them.

They look tired, dirty, and not at all vicious. In sign language they motion to us what we believe is a question—do we have cigarettes?

We give them almost all we have. They thank us and sit down for a few minutes to smoke. They do not loot, murder, steal, or rape. We rejoice, thinking how lucky we are that this is the end, and how well we have all come through it unharmed.

How wrong we are! It is not the end—it is the beginning.

The beginning of the most terrible time in my life. . . .

What we have not realized is that these are the fighting troops, and they are just as weary and just as glad to be alive as we are.

But following them are the disciples of hell.

For an hour after the fighting troops have left, we stay unmolested. Actually the troops have not left; they are upstairs, and we hear machine-gun fire from our windows. It is an eerie feeling to think that from our windows our own people are being killed.

Before the Russian troops can proceed, they must cross the other canal, so that for quite a while we are the front line at which the troops gather. A lot of activity goes on upstairs. Footsteps back and forth, now hurried, then slow. Machine-gun fire mixing with the explosion of shells . . . tanks roaring . . . foreign sounds from voices heavy and guttural . . . inferno. . . .

The cellar door opens again. Boots appear on the steps, followed by the rest of the soldier, gun in hand. Behind him are several others. Uncle Carl is standing, they push him roughly back into his chair. They motion to us something that we cannot quite understand; we do not know what they want. It is made clear in one instant: Omi is wearing a pair of gold earrings, and one of the soldiers gets hold of one and pulls it right through her ear. A small trickle of blood runs down her face. She does not say a word. Mutti puts Monika into my arms and with trembling hands gives her watch to the soldier. Her face is like stone—I know what the watch means to her. Papa sent it to her; he had saved for a long time from his small army allowance to buy us our gold watches.

But Omi is left alone for a while.

The soldiers motion to us for more.

Uncle Carl has a gold watch on a chain; one of the soldiers takes it—and I don't believe he said "thank you."

They are making rounds.

In a few minutes there is nothing left on us or about us of any value—they have taken it all.

Most of the things that they have taken do not bother me too much. In times of war, with all the air raids going on, you learn to detach yourself from material values. But the gold watch from Papa and an antique necklace of gorgeous garnets—when they go, I have to swallow my tears. But I do not cry; I have

51

learned the meaning of pride in one instant, just as later I learned many more things in seconds. . . .

Laughing and most happy with their loot, the soldiers leave. We give a deep sigh of relief and sit down, still shaking.

Mama has started feeding Monika, who is crying. For the first time Monika's crying annoys me. I guess all our nerves are raw from the tension and fighting.

"Oh, my God," Uncle Carl says, "we still have that pistol! If they find a weapon on us they may kill us. I've got to get rid of it!"

"Well, for God's sake," Mama says, "what possessed you to bring a pistol along, Carl? Did you honestly believe that one little pistol could save us from a horde of Russians?" She is angry, but when she sees his unhappy face she regrets it, saying, "Well, you could throw it into the toilet next door. That's the only place I can think of where it would be safe and not found. Give it to me, I'll throw it away."

"I was going to use it for something else, anyway," Uncle Carl mutters.

"What way is that to talk?" Mama interrupts. "Have you lost all your senses? At this point we are still alive—and believe me, we are going to stay alive!"

"But you shouldn't go," Uncle Carl says. "It's too dangerous. I got us into this, I have got to get us out."

Silently, I admire him. It is not an easy task, and it must have taken Uncle Carl a lot of courage to do it, but he leaves, goes to the adjoining building and somehow, in the turmoil, he is able to fulfill his task with no trouble. When he returns, he looks relieved. "It's okay," he says.

"What does it look like outside?" Opa asks him.

"The sun is shining as if it does not know what's going on," Uncle Carl replies.

The sun is shining? Is it really day already? It seemed just like a minute ago when the first Russian troops had come and then the looters. . . .

I think of my pretty watch from Papa. I console myself with

52

the conviction that he is alive, he has to be, and that he can always get me another one. And if he cannot, what does it matter, as long as we all stay alive?

―――――――――

That thought reminds me of another incident when material values had no meaning to me and I counted my blessings that Mama and my two sisters were alive. . . .

During the last few months before the final attack I attended a course at the Rackow-Schule for French interpreters. I loved the French language and hoped that if I did not succeed in journalism, I could always fall back on interpreting. So three times a week after work I stayed in town for supper and then went to school. Mama did not like this too much because of the air raids, but she also felt she could not hold me back in my plans for the future, and she reluctantly agreed.

One night I had finished my class and was in the underground on my way home when the train stopped. Air raid! We left the train but did not bother to leave the station, since it was beneath the ground and just about as safe as anywhere else.

I always hated to be in the midst of big crowds, but this time it was especially frightening. More than half a dozen times the ground shook from the impact of bombs hitting somewhere nearby. Dimly we could hear the bombs falling and the antiaircraft guns. I had heard some gruesome true stories of people who were caught in underground stations during an air raid and were hit by bombs. Next day people found, after a lot of digging, the mass graves of people who were drowned because the water lines had been hit by bombs and flooded the area. I could just picture what went on before all of them were finally dead by drowning, and I shuddered.

But nothing happened to us and I sent a prayer of gratitude to heaven. Once outside, I found pure horror. Flames over flames, people running back and forth, crying desperately for a sign from the loved ones they could not find. Some had started digging amid the rubble. Now and then I could see some hoses splashing water into the flames. All transportation was out of order, and I had to walk home. It was, of course, "black-out," but I could see very well; the flames illuminated more than enough. The air raid was over at about eleven o'clock—at three o'clock in the morning, I arrived home. It is not the nicest feeling for a seventeen-year-old girl to walk home through a flaming inferno, alone, at three in the morning—but I guess I only knew one purpose: I wanted to be home with my mother.

The street on which our house stood was dark. I thanked God for that—it seemed to indicate that nothing much had happened here.

I heard hammering coming from some of the apartments, which was nothing unusual; almost every night windows were shattered, and most of the time you just gave up and boarded them up with wood. There was not enough glass in the world to replace broken windows every night!

As I walked towards our apartment entrance, I saw Mama standing at the top of the stairs.

"Oh, thank God, you are home," she said, and although I could not see her clearly, I could hear tears in her voice. "My darling Inga, I am so glad you are here."

Her words were somewhat unusual. Although we loved each other very much, we were not given to flowery endearments.

"Is anything wrong, Mama?" I could not keep the anxiety out of my voice.

"Don't come up here," Mama said.

Now I wanted more than ever to go up there and find out what was wrong. I walked towards her.

"No!" Mama said, and she stopped me cold. "You cannot go there—simply because there is nothing there!"

"What do you mean 'nothing there'?" I said. "You're standing on the staircase, everything looks all right to me."

"Inga," Mama said emphatically, "we were hit. We have nothing left but what we are wearing on us. And we are lucky to be alive."

54

She finally reached me and led me gently towards our apartment door. Where our little apartment had been there was nothing but a big dark hole. Somewhere in the darkness down below I could see some of our belongings.

I sat down on the steps. "What happened?" I asked Mama.

She sat down beside me and put her arm around me. "Oh, my God," she said again. "Am I glad you are alive! For a while there I thought that you, too. . . ." Then she could restrain herself no longer. She cried bitterly—and seeing her like this made me unhappier than the thought of being homeless, so I broke into tears too.

We finally both calmed down a little. "No one is hurt?" I asked her just for reassurance. "Where are Chris and Monika?"

"They are over at Omi's place, they are safe," Mama replied. And then she told me how lucky they had been.

Once in a while a bomb was dropped which we called "the blockbuster." It blew out the insides of a building but left the walls intact, somehow like a tornado. People were sometimes found sitting peacefully in their chairs, but with their lungs burst and just as dead as if they had been shot.

In the little air raid shelter we had built, my family was not exactly safe from something like this, but a quirk of fate, or call it what you may, had saved their lives. The blockbuster had come down about ten yards from the shelter, but it had hit the edge of the canal at such an angle that most of the impact went right over them—they were that close—and a lot of the blast went into the canal. If it had not been for that, I would have come home and found my family peacefully sitting in the shelter but not answering me, ever. . . .

I shuddered. "What is going to happen now?"

"We will stay with Omi for a while, and then maybe we can get another place, somewhere."

Again I considered myself lucky; my family was alive, and thank God we had Omi. Several weeks later we had reestablished ourselves with the most necessary belongings, and somehow Mama had managed to make a new home. How she did it I'll never know, but somehow she did.

Now here we are again—losing all we own. I look at Mama and her beautiful, tired face—and I swear to myself then that if we ever get out alive and I grow up and have things, she will never be in need for anything. And all I can think is how much I love her. . . .

My chance is here now, sooner than I had really expected. All I can do at the moment is not show how frightened I am, not let her know how it hurts to see things go— what she needs now is an ally, a helper, not a frightened little girl who wants to run and hide somewhere.

Again we hear footsteps approaching the cellar. What enters now cannot possibly be described as human beings—just a horde of drunken, dirty, and ugly animals. Their pistols are waving back and forth, and we know that they want jewelry. But how do you make a drunken devil, whose language you do not speak, understand that those before him have already taken all, that we have nothing left, that this is the truth?

Of course they do not believe us!

They angrily motion to us, over and over, something that could be interpreted as, "If you don't give us what we want, you are going to be shot"—emphasizing that they mean what they say with threatening gestures and pistol-waving.

I do not know how we finally convince them and get rid of them—it does not really matter. For a little while we sit down again and try to think out our situation.

We know we are in deep trouble.

We realize that this probably will not be the only occurrence of its kind. There will be others after these, and others after those.

We may be lucky, and be convincing enough so that they will believe we have nothing left. On the other hand, one trigger-happy irritated Russian may well lose his temper and just shoot.

Our slow, creeping feeling of panic grows. We also know by

now that the horror stories we have heard from the refugees are true. What else is in store for us? What about rape and murder—both of it en masse? I do not dare to think much further and try to get back some of the optimism that previously has always helped.

It does not do much good, for the next bunch is already on their way down to the cellar.

The same thing happens over again.

One Russian has seated himself in front of me and is looking at me. I feel very uncomfortable but suddenly I remember that I had learned to speak some Croatian. Since it is a Slavic language a little like Russian, I decide to take a chance and start a conversation.

"Dobar dan—káko ide tébi?" I say to him.

He looks up at me, startled. Before he has a chance to recover from the shock, I continue: "Ja som njemica."

"German?" he asks back, in disbelief.

I nod, and say a few other meaningless sentences.

Somehow these words seem to have some effect and possibly save us from a lot of nasty things—at least for the time being. As it turns out, he does not believe I am German—he thinks I am Polish! He probably figured that I was setting a trap for him and would report him to the Kommandant if he misbehaved! I learn another lesson: the power of language and communication. Frankly, my knowledge of the Croatian language is extremely limited; these are just a few phrases I had learned from a friend—but whatever I learned I always learned well, and it now comes in handy.

For quite a while he sits in front of me, looking at me, throwing his pistol from one hand into the other, undecided as to what to do. I am frightened. It is not all clear what it means to him that he does not believe I am German—it could work either way, for me or against me. After what seems like an eternity, he motions to the others to leave and he follows; with a sigh of relief, we watch them go.

From then on we feel just a little bit more secure. We have a secret weapon: the truth, in the enemy's own language! But of course, it is just a slight comfort, it could work the other way around too. We might just meet a Russian soldier who will think I am a spy or something.

We spend the following hours in constant harassment, anxiety, and the most nerve-racking circumstances.

Some of the hordes that come are worse than others. Some of them are Mongolians with harelips and mean-looking slit-eyes; the stench from dirty clothes mixes with that of vodka or some other alcohol. All in all we have had our fill of the conquerors.

But the worst is yet to come.

All of a sudden we hear women's voices upstairs, speaking in Russian. Then the sound of wood being hacked to pieces, and a lot of shuffling and commotion going on.

Mama says, "I am going upstairs to see what is going on up there."

"Please, don't go" I beg. But my plea is weak; at that time our nerves are already so shattered from the constant tension, uncertainty, and insecurity that none of us are able to protest too much about anything.

Mama comes back.

"Do you know what is happening?" she says. "The Russian women from across the canal (foreign workers whom Hitler had brought to Germany to work) are here. They are taking everything they can lay their hands on. I asked one of them why she was doing that, and she said in pretty good German, 'Ah, gutten Tagg, wirr wollen klauen!' (Ah, good day, we want to loot.) Can you imagine that? When I told her these things were mine and she had no right to take them, she got very angry and talked to the Russian soldier, and he came and threatened me with his pistol!"

"Let it go, Lisa," Omi says. "It really doesn't matter much right now."

"Omi, Walter and I worked a lifetime for everything we have. Haven't we lost enough yet? How often can we go on rebuilding?"

"As often as we must.'" Omi says.

I wish Paula were here—she would show them! I do not have a chance to ask Mrs. Stromberg where Paula is because another horde comes in.

Again we are lucky, and again they leave, angry, but without hurting us. For a few hours we have peace.

We sit waiting for the things to follow, but for some unknown reason we are left alone for a while, so we begin to think that possibly it really is all over.

"We ought to eat something," Mrs. Schulman says. "Why don't I go upstairs and cook some potatoes. It seems to be fairly quiet out there now. It will do us good to get some strength." We are all grateful for her suggestion. We have some firewood in the basement, and upstairs we have a stove that can cook both ways, gas or open fire. Of course there is no gas, but we can make a fire.

I don't know what happened to those potatoes. We never had a chance to eat them.

While Mrs. Schulman is upstairs waiting for the potatoes to start cooking, the cellar door bursts open and Uncle Fritz and Aunt Evi, her four-month-old baby in her arms, come running in, out of breath and terrified.

"Hide!" Uncle Fritz yells, and pushes his wife and baby into the adjoining basement where we used to have tools, potatoes, and other odds and ends. He throws a blanket over her and tells her to be quiet.

Then he sits down, panting, and tells us what has happened.

All of them, over in the air raid shelter, had come through the whole ordeal in about the same way we have. They too had no trouble with the fighting troops, but then much the same happened as did to us. For a while everything went well. Then just a short while ago, one young Russian soldier, drunk, motioned with his pistol to Aunt Evi to follow him. Both Aunt Evi and Uncle Fritz knew what he wanted. Uncle Fritz was just not the man to stand by and see his wife raped and then possibly murdered. He started towards the Russian, who aimed his pistol and was just about to shoot, when an older Russian soldier knocked the pistol out of his hand, and the shot missed Uncle

59

Fritz. They started running, grabbing the baby, and here they are.

We are horrified. If it happened once it can happen again. This is the fate intended for all of us. . . . We have a little time before it hits us, one by one, or maybe all at once—what is the difference! We are the only civilians in an area of about two square miles, and there are thousands of Russian troops. . . .

I start crying.

"Mama, please, let's leave here and go where the fighting is over—we may be safer where everything has already settled down a bit. There has got to be some normalcy somewhere!"

Chris, seeing me cry, joins in. Monika has awakened and whimpers and everybody starts talking at once—either for or against leaving.

"Please, listen to me, all of you!" Mama tries to make herself heard. "First of all, Inga, stop crying. The little ones can sense you are upset, and we must keep our minds in order. I think we should stay. It is the only safety we have; we don't know what we may run into when we leave here. Here, at least, we are still alive."

"Safety?" I shout. "You call this safety? We are caught here like mice in a trap, just waiting for them to do with us as they please!"

I am near hysteria. But I do not have time to calm down or do anything, because at that moment we hear a cry coming from upstairs and freeze in terror.

It is Mrs. Schulman, screaming "No, no, please come and help me, Hans!"

Mr. Schulman is up on his feet in a second and races upstairs. It is the last we see of either one of them—alive, that is.

"We have to help them," someone says.

"How?" someone else asks. "Do you have weapons for all of us? Or do you think we could just go and attack a few thousand Russians with our bare hands?"

Nobody answers. What is there to say?

In the meantime I have calmed down, but it is the quietness

60

of the Dead Sea. I feel nothing for the moment, not even fear or terror.

"Mama," I say, "if these filthy pigs touch me, I will kill myself, just to save them the job. I know where the pistol is hidden, I can go and get it."

"For God's sake, Inga, don't I have enough to worry about without you making such horrible statements?"

Mama is right, of course. Nevertheless, in my seventeen-year-old emotional state of mind, I mean it.

"I can't stand it any longer," Uncle Fritz says, "I have got to go and see what is happening out there."

No one protests. We sit silently, and Uncle Fritz leaves.

After a few minutes he comes back.

"Well?" we ask.

For a while he says nothing.

"It was the Russian who went after Evi," he whispers hoarsely. "He must have come after us when we came running here. Upstairs he found Mrs. Schulman and grabbed her."

"But what is happening to them—where are they?"

Uncle Fritz looks sick. "The Russian is still with Mrs. Schulman, she is bleeding. Mr. Schulman is sitting beside her, holding her hand, crying."

I feel like throwing up. It happened about forty-five minutes ago that the Schulmans were taken away, which means that the Russian is still. . . .

Uncle Fritz has not used the word "rape"—but I know what he means.

Half an hour later he goes outside again to see what has happened in the meantime so that maybe we can take care of them, carry them back in and help them.

When he comes back, he is ashen. "My God, my God. . . ." he mumbles. He is trembling all over.

Then he kneels and prays.

When he has recovered a little, he tells us: "I saw Mr. Schulman being carried away by a Russian soldier and a Russian woman. They threw him into the canal and kept his head under water until he was dead. Mrs. Schulman was shot in the mouth by the Russian who raped her. She is bleeding all over, but she is dead too."

After a few moments of terrified silence, he puts his hand over his face. "It would have been Evi." His voice is only a whisper.

So that is the way the end is. . . . I know that this is the first incident only—when will the next one be? And who will be the next one? Would it not be better to end it all before it happens?

I sit down to smoke a cigarette.

It is obvious that day by day one or two of us will meet much the same fate. Eventually there will be no one left, or maybe just me, alone? That thought terrifies me even more. I wish myself dead, just to have peace.

Is it right to end your own life? The answer, of course, is "no" regardless of the circumstances. Somehow God had planned this to happen to us, but why?

The "why" is important.

I try to picture God as I saw Him in my childhood days—a kind, gentle figure, always smiling, always forgiving, loving us. Sometimes He appeared in the shape of a cloud in the sky, until it gently and mysteriously took on another form, but never angry, never revengeful, never threatening. Where is He now? What terrible thing have we done that He thinks it necessary to punish us so much?

Here in Germany are Protestants and Catholics in planes, dropping bombs on Protestants and Catholics in other countries, killing. Yet every Sunday they go to church, pray, and know as Christians that they were taught "Thou Shalt Not Kill." Why do they kill? Do they believe their cause is just? If it is just, is it right to kill? Who would decide whose cause is just? On the other side are people, also Christians, who go to church and pray. They too know the Ten Commandments. Do they believe they are right in dropping bombs on us, or raping, or murdering women and children? Maybe they are more in the right than we are—Germany fired the first shots. But who is right and who is wrong? And what does it matter when it is so often the innocent who pay the price for the guilty?

And above it all stands God. And if He looks down on us and sees all the murdering, all the disaster and heartache man has created for himself, why does He not put an end to it? Do we not call Him the Almighty?

I know that no one in this basement has committed a crime so bad as to deserve this punishment. Maybe others in our country have, but why are we punished?

God, who has always appeared to me as fair and just, has suddenly turned into an angry figure, a power who permits all this and does not do anything to stop it. I was told to do right when I was little and everything would be well. In my opinion, I had done right in life with the exception of a few minor child's sins. Sometimes I gave Mama a hard time growing up, but was that unusual? All in all, I had been raised with the typical Girl Scout attitude, but most important of all, I had loved God and all His creatures.

Sinners we all are, I know that. There were times when I was not at all nice, but so was everybody else in the world. Then why are we singled out in this way and punished?

Is everything I have been told a lie? Even what I was taught about God? If not, how does it all make sense? Where is He? And most of all, why does He permit this?

Somehow I know I have to find answers to these disturbing questions, but now temporarily, I have to give up.

"Where is Omi?" I hear Mama say.

All of a sudden we realize that Omi has not been with us for quite some time. I vaguely remember her saying that she was going to feed the goat a little hay and I saw her go up the cellar steps. That was quite a while ago.

Again we have a feeling of foreboding. What more tragedy is to come?

"I'll go and see if I can find her," Mrs. Stromberg says. "I am a sixty-year-old woman. I don't think anyone is going to hurt me."

We thank her and she leaves.

The rest of us try to eat some dry bread, saving some for Mrs. Stromberg, but it tastes terrible. The bread had been lying underneath the bottle of pine spirits. When the bottle broke, much of the liquid had poured right over it. We washed it off right away, but it still tastes awful.

Since I cannot answer all my burning questions, I have to continue in another way.

Is there hope for us to get out of this alive? If we do, will life after that be worth living?

I think back to the past years. It is strange, but they seem like a dream, unreal and vague. Reality is here, and it is a cruel reality. It seems to me that we are the only Germans left in Germany who are still alive—there is no sound, no news, no sign anywhere that there are others. There are only Russians. And in my mind it is pretty clear that there is no real end in sight; this is the end, and it is never-ending, like being in hell. . . .

I would give a lot for just one stranger to come by and give us some news, anything that would tell us that there is hope, somewhere, that life one day will be back to normal. . . .

No one comes. No one speaks, and even God, the Almighty, is as silent as the darkness in space and gives no answers.

Leaving the city
one saw nothing, for the horror of the surroundings
blotted out all else; everywhere
the white bones of the dead were
scattered and on the roads were starving women
putting the children they could not feed
into the grass to die.

Wang Tsan, 177-217 A.D.

5

THE DAY THERE WAS NO ROOM AT THE INN

Outside, ironically, it is still a pretty day. The sun is shining, the air is soft and gentle, almost a loving quiet caress. . . . After eight days in the basement with the feeling of confinement, of being trapped, the mustiness, the candlelight with its dimness, it is a relief at least to taste the day. But fifty steps behind us lies the chamber of horrors. . . .

It had not taken us long to make the decision to leave the basement; of the original ten people, eight are left. The rape and murdering has already started. . . . To stay would mean certain death, we are now sure of that. Out here, in the light of day, regardless that we have no safe destination, regardless of the unknown perils that may await us, out here at least we have a chance.

For a few moments I close my eyes so that the illusion that nothing is wrong will linger for just a moment longer. . . .

Then in a split second that ends.

The "Stalin Organs," which had been quiet for a while, for

some reason have started off again, and as though that is the signal to continue the war, all other infernal noises join: machine-gun fire, shells exploding, tanks roaring—all the deadly noise of war.

My God, my God, how are we going to get through this?

"Come on, what are you waiting for?"

Uncle Fritz's voice shows impatience, mixed with panic. I don't blame him. To linger would mean suicide. . . .

Besides, there are these sounds again, these sounds . . . more threatening, more frightening than the noise of cannons, guns, and shells—the guttural sounds of the Russian language. . . .

They are all around us. Thousands of them: in tanks, behind guns, holding machine guns, running back and forth.

We walk, but we don't run.

Behind us is the house, to the right stretches the canal that separates the city from us. On its banks are the Russian troops, trying to get across. Here is where the cannons, the machine guns, the majority of the fighting troops are located. To the left of us is the newer canal, which was eventually to replace the old one. On its banks are also Russians, but not the fighting troops. These Russians are trying to get supplies and reinforcements across.

In the middle are we, walking. There is only one way we can go, straight ahead.

What awaits us ahead we do not know. All we have to do is walk, away from here. . . .

Beyond the old canal to the right lies the city, or rather what once was a city. It lies clouded in smoke and flames, now and then an explosion bursting into the air. Death-roars. . . .

Something strikes me as strange. If the Russian troops are fighting from the right of us, at the banks of the canal, and the reinforcements are coming over the canal to the left of us, and in the middle are we—then how can we have shells exploding around us? Surely the Russians are not shooting at their own people?

The answer is simple. These are our own shells! A last, desperate attempt by German troops to defend an already

66

doomed city. . . .

We walk.

Funny, really funny. If we are hit by a shell now, then it will be our own defense weapons that kill us. . . .

Well, I for one like that better than being raped by Russians and then shot.

I wish Opa would stop saying, "Where is Mother?" I want to get away from here.

Ugh! That smell—what is it? Is that the way death smells? No, just now that smells like smoke. Smoke from the city . . . but something else too. It must be death. I have never smelled death before . . . sweet, ugly sweet.

Momentarily my stomach cringes.

Come on, we have got to get away from here. . . .

Opa! Will you stop saying "Where is Mother?" It gets on my nerves. No, that smell can't be Mrs. Schulman. The one who was raped and then shot. They say that it takes a few days for decay to set in. Or is it only hours? I should know, we learned about that in school. No, no, it can't be here. It has to be something else . . . but what? Are we going to find it when we go further? Is it ahead of us?

I can't go! I don't want to go! Stop, all of you! Stop walking! But I keep going. We still are not running, just walking.

Hello shell, welcome. You are a German shell, aren't you? Ha ha! The Russians would not like that one damn bit! That would really be funny; the Germans killed by German shells—right in front of the Russians' eyes. . . .

Opa, stop turning around looking for Omi! I can't stand this much longer. . . . I am going to be real mad at you, do you hear? Still, maybe she is right behind us. Maybe one look back won't hurt. . . .

The house is standing behind us like a sick person who wants to come along but is frozen in shock, paralyzed.

The flower boxes in front of the windows with the remainders of Omi's geraniums seem to wave a sad and weak good-bye.

Where the window glass had been there is now nothing but dark and empty space—an open wound.

The roof shows some holes—like a silent scream.

The linden tree in front of the house is devoid of leaves, and its bare branches stand silhouetted against the sky in a gesture of surrender, reaching up into the heavens like a pagan statue imploring the gods to come down to earth. . . .

Just one more look. For a moment I feel a short sharp stab in my left side, then it is gone, there is nothing. It's almost a relief to feel so calm.

"Fritz, for heaven's sake, can't you walk a little slower?" Mama calls. She pushes the baby carriage angrily one step faster, then stops abruptly and turns around, looking for Opa.

He is walking slowly and painfully, once in a while he stands still and looks back.

"Where is Mother?" The urgency in his voice makes us feel guilty; we have left her behind! I don't like to think back to the last few moments in the basement—who wants to recall a nightmare? But Opa's distress hurts me, and I try desperately to recall what had happened before we made our decision to leave: after we realized that Omi was missing, Mrs. Stromberg decided to go look for her. When she went upstairs, she saw all the rooms crowded with Russian soldiers. She realized that it would be best not to linger too long, so she went outside hoping to find some trace of Omi. There, too, were hundreds and hundreds of Russian soldiers. Mrs. Stromberg, knowing Omi, had the brilliant idea to look in the goat shack. There was blood on the floor, a lot of it. She felt very sick, but then realized that next to the blood lay something else: the goat's hide neatly and expertly skinned. She thanked God silently that at least it was not Omi's blood.

When she went to return to the basement, she heard a soft hissing noise.

Running parallel to the shack was a high wire fence. Between the fence and the shack grew a thick tall hedge. The small space left was hardly wide enough for someone to hide there.

"Pssst! Mrs. Stromberg," came a whisper. There, between hedge and shack, was Omi!

"Thank God, you are alive," Mrs. Stromberg said, "but why

on earth are you hiding there instead of being with us in the basement?"

"Mrs. Stromberg, you won't believe this," Omi whispered, shaking her head. "I find it hard to believe myself."

Mrs. Stromberg pulled Omi gently towards her. "You can tell me later, but first let's get back to the basement."

"No!" Omi pulled away from Mrs. Stromberg's grip. "No, I am not going back there—ever!"

Omi had never given any of us the impression of being easily frightened. Mrs. Stromberg was surprised to find her in such a state of fear.

"What happened?"

"Well," Omi said, "I went upstairs to look after the goat. As I walked through the kitchen, a drunken Russian grabbed me. It is hard to believe, but there was no mistake as to what he wanted! I tore myself away—I don't think he had expected much strength in anyone so small. I ran into the hallway. He came after me, so I ran into the next room. I knew the only way out of there was through the window—when he appeared in the doorway, I jumped! Fortunately, as you know, it's not too high, so I didn't get hurt badly, but I sprained my ankle a little."

"These stupid pigs," Mrs. Stromberg said, disgusted. "For God's sake, can't they even let a seventy-five-year-old woman alone? Anyway, you can't stay here forever, you better come along with me."

"No," Omi protested, "let me stay here just a little while longer, I have got to get my wits back together first."

Mrs. Stromberg finally realized that it would be futile to coax Omi any further, and left. Omi always had had a mind of her own, and possibly she was embarrassed to explain the happenings to us and needed time to get over the shock.

Meanwhile, we in the basement were getting more panicky by the minute. We felt utterly trapped. All that kept us from leaving right then and there was the fact that Omi was missing, and that we were not sure where to go.

Where could we go? We knew the best place would be an area

where the fighting had been over for some time, where some normalcy had been established, but was there such a place?

We were desperately trying to think of any areas of Berlin where the fighting might be over when in stumbled Mrs. Stromberg, her hair disheveled, her dress torn, breathing heavily. She was pale, and for the first time since I had known her I saw her really upset.

"I am sixty-five years old," she muttered. "Please, give me some water."

Mama gave her a cupful of water, which she hastily gulped down. Although she was still shaken up, her voice had regained some of its normal tones. She looked at Mama and with an urgency in her voice that had never been there before she said: "Mrs. L, you must go. Leave here. No one is safe from these beasts. If your children's lives are dear to you, you better leave, and quickly!"

"But we can't leave without Omi," Mutti was close to tears. "Where in God's name is she?"

"She is all right!" Mrs. Stromberg said, and she told us what had happened to Omi. We all felt relieved, to a point, but it was just a temporary relief. What would happen next?

"Come on," Mrs. Stromberg urged us. "If none of you are going to leave here, I am. I am not going through something like that again. . . ."

We had been so concerned about Omi's fate that we had not thought of asking Mrs. Stromberg what had happened to her. Now she told us. On her way back into the basement, she saw a Russian soldier who looked like a higher ranking officer. Since she spoke a little Russian, she felt that maybe she could help us all by approaching him and telling him to hold his troops in check, or else she would report it to the Kommandant when the fighting was over.

He just laughed at her and told her that he was the Kommandant, and he would possibly consider leaving us alone if she were willing to. . . . When she angrily refused, he became nasty.

He threatened to shoot us all if she continued to refuse. Having seen what had happened before, she knew that he meant what he said. When it was all over she came to us in the basement.

It was now completely clear to us that we had to leave. Once the decision was made, there was no delay. We had very little left to take along. The big question was Omi.

"I will go and see if she will come along," Mrs. Stromberg again volunteered. "As far as I am concerned I am over the shock. It has already happened to me, so what's the difference. . . ."

"All right," Mama agreed, "we will walk slowly so that you will have time to catch up with us." Before we left we agreed to meet at my cousin's house in Tegel should we get separated on the way, and with that we said good-bye to Mrs. Stromberg.

We made up our minds that we would try and get to my cousin's home in Tegel. There was a possibility that the fighting had been over in Tegel for about four days, and in that time some normalcy might have been established.

Tegel was a suburb, located in the extreme northwestern part of the city. Our home was located in the western section of Berlin. From our home to my cousin's house in Tegel it was ten or twelve miles. We were fairly sure that the city's eastern section was the first to be occupied. The Russian troops in our area had come from the north, and we had no idea what the circumstances were to the south of us.

We have not much choice in regard to the direction which we should take. South of our house is a canal leading to the "West-Hafen." The bridge crossing this canal, which would take us south, is totally destroyed. Behind us, leading west, is a breakthrough to the new canal north of us, running parallel to the old one, and this breakthrough has no bridge at all. We must go east at first, then turn north. There is one more bridge to the east, crossing the river leading into the West-Hafen, but that bridge, too, has been totally destroyed. If we turn north, walking parallel to the river, we will find another bridge across

71

the river, and if that one is passable, we can go to Tegel. Otherwise. . . .

And on we walk—one foot left, one foot right, face straight ahead. There is the bridge. The one that leads across the canal to the right, south into the city.

Of course it is destroyed. Well, we can't go there. Anyway, the city is the worst place to be right now, from the frying pan into the fire! No thank you . . . I'd rather walk straight ahead. There will be another bridge.

The Russian troops around us are too busy fighting the war to pay attention to us. Good for us!

Hey there! Another shell . . . how about that . . . our guardian angel is really working overtime . . . and another one . . . how about that? I must remember to say a special thank-you prayer for that dear little angel . . . my, my, how he has to keep busy . . . next time I have a chance to pray, that is. . . .

Duck the shells? Not on your life! We must walk. Walking is good for you. Keeps the muscles in shape. Straight through, that's the way to do it. . . . But for heaven's sake, are we the only people walking?

Isn't there anyone else in this world but us? Where are all the people?

It is a weird feeling, as if we are the only ones left alive, only we and Russians. . . .

There, over to the right, there is something.

A dead horse. Blood, all dried up. Broken eyes. Maggots crawling around. Why is its belly bloated? Well, never mind, dead is dead . . . maggots. . . . Death is ugly. . . .

There is that smell again. The death smell. At least now I know where it came from. . . . See, just a horse. . . . But I love horses. Poor little horse.

What are the others? The other shadows lying in the road? Maybe I better not look. . . .

Out of the corner of my eye, although I try hard to look past it, I see the outline of a body. A blue uniform, torn to shreds. Air force? Something red, a lot of red, on that blue uniform. . . .

Further away there are more figures. They lie quite still. Without going closer, looking closer, I know the shape of death. The toll for the bridge has been paid . . . I am glad I am not going across that bridge.

What is an Air Force uniform doing on the ground? Well, never mind. We have to keep walking. There will be another bridge. . . .

Zzzzzzzinnnnng . . . there is my friend, the shell, again. Missed us! Ha-ha, missed us! I hope you won't get tired, little guardian angel. . . .

And still we are the only people walking.

It is really not too surprising. At the moment we are in no-man's-land. Water to the left, water to the right, water ahead of us, water behind us. I never realized that we were so enclosed by water. . . . But the left canal stops at one place, they never had a chance to finish it. If the bridge ahead of us is also destroyed, then we can turn left, walk for a while alongside the river, and hopefully find one bridge leading across that is not destroyed, or at least not completely.

The occupants of the few weekend houses here and there most likely left some time ago to go deeper into the city. Maybe we should have done that too. . . .

Still, who knows what is going on in the city? . . . Maybe we were lucky after all to have stayed home as long as we did. It is surprising that every member of our family is still alive, what with being caught in the crossfire of German and Russian shells and bullets around our little house and family in no-man's-land.

All alive . . . except . . . where is Papa? Is he still alive?

I am glad he is not home now. He would have fought the Russians invading our home and they would have killed him. Yes, I am glad he is not home now. But I would like to know

73

where he is. . . . Suppose he comes home soon? Will he find us? How could he find us? Ah well, he will find a way. He knows how to do things.

———————

There is another shadow in the road. We cannot help but look, for we have to walk around it. Somehow it looks familiar. To the right of it, between road and riverbank, is the little old hut where we used to buy flowers when we went to the cemetery to visit the graves of our relatives. The old lady who owned it was always well liked—a fairly toothless, but friendly smile would greet the customer, and she would never let anyone depart without a few words of interest about either the deceased or the living relatives, yet she never talked about herself. Now her flowers have outlived her. She is the figure lying in the road near her hut.

Two or three of her plants are still green and undamaged. The cut flowers are strewn about, wilted and sad.

She is lying in the dust, her face hardly recognizable beneath the deep wound. The dried-up blood has formed a mask of protection. Her right arm is stretched out beside her, the palm of her hand open, as if she wants to collect payment for her flowers. Her left arm and hand are placed below her breast as if someone had tried to fold her hands across her body but left in a hurry without finishing the task.

This time I stop. My throat feels dry and I can't swallow. Somehow, quite unaccountably, a phrase from Goethe's *Herman and Dorothea* comes to my mind: ". . . das Alte stürzt, es ändert sich die Zeit, und neues Leben spriesst aus den Ruinen. . . ." ("The old will fall, times change, and new life will sprout from the ruins. . . .") But it is just a flash and I do not spend more time on it. When I leave the scene, a feeling of bitterness goes along with me.

We should have buried her, I find myself thinking, and then: what with?

Until then I had not thought about death as being ugly—the promise of life ever after had precedence. Now, having seen the

74

maggots on the horse, I cannot help but think about other aspects of the physical form left behind. It disturbs me, but my thoughts will have to wait till later. Now we must hurry to catch up with Uncle Fritz and his wife and children.

Far in the distance ahead of us we see them. My bitterness increases; does he care so little about what happens to us? Then I remember how I myself hesitated to look back. . . .

All this time, I have not taken much notice of little Chris. What a little trooper she is! Her cute, funny face is still messy, her blonde hair stringy; her knee-high socks have slipped down and formed rings on her ankles; she looks so tired and so forlorn but also so brave that I feel like running up to her and hugging her. Along the whole trek, which lasts several hours, I never hear a word of complaint from her. That is Chris!

I leave Opa to walk alone for a few moments; he has recovered a little—maybe resigned to fate—and I catch up with Chris.

"Walk with me for a little while," I say.

"Okay." She puts her hand in mine.

It feels good to be close. As with all older sisters, until now Chris has represented more of a responsibility to me than a companion; the age difference is just too great. I am seventeen, she is nine. But now that has suddenly changed: at this moment we are just sisters, regardless of age.

"Are you scared?" Chris asks.

I do not quite know how to answer this—if I told her the truth, would it upset her? But Chris is Chris, she is not much of a crybaby.

"Yes."

"Me too!" she says emphatically with her deep voice. "Do you think we are going to be there tonight?"

I do not quite know what she has in mind by "there," but I feel it is best to reassure her—whatever!

For a while we walk together, then she decides to go back with Mama and the baby, and I make sure Opa is all right.

In the meantime we have met people coming from other areas, but they all walk in the same direction. Apparently all of them hope there will be some safety in Tegel. No one speaks to

75

anyone else—all are just walking. In the distance we can see the bridge; it has been partly destroyed, but enough of it is left above the water so that a crossing can be made. That makes us feel better.

"It's so sad about the old flower lady," a familiar voice says beside me.

"Oh hello, Mrs. Peters!" I am delighted. She is another next-door neighbor, about thirty, dark blonde, pretty, petite, a widow with a daughter Chris' age.

She has been twice widowed. Her first husband, who was drafted in the very beginning of the war, was killed and left her with a very young daughter after only a few short years of happiness. She married again—happily.

I remember the day she became a widow for the second time. She was at home in her apartment when two policemen came knocking at her door. Her husband and another one of the tenants had taken a large pushcart to transport some building materials when a car hit them both from the rear. Her husband had been at the front pulling the cart, which had a long bar going forward from the center, and the other man was pushing at the back. Mrs. Peters' husband was killed instantly—the bar went right through him. The man in the back was badly injured but lived through it and eventually recovered.

Mrs. Peters struggled on through life. She received a small widow's pension, which did not enable her to lead a merry life, but with a good amount of shrewd housekeeping she managed to get along. Her apartment was always spotlessly clean and her daughter was always well dressed. Mrs. Peters was a good seamstress and sewed her daughter's clothes herself, sometimes her own as well. It was a well-known fact that Mrs. Peters, in the beholding eye of many a bachelor or widower, was a good catch. But the many proposals of marriage she received were left unaccepted. I believe the two experiences of becoming a widow by the age of twenty eight (about two years ago) had left her with a feeling of ill-fatedness.

Now here she is with her little girl, walking right beside us. They had spent these last days in the earth-bunker with Uncle

Fritz, his family, and the other tenants. Looking for male protection, Mrs. Peters had decided to walk along with him, but finally had to give up. "He walks so fast, nobody can keep up with him," she says, slightly irritated.

"Mama, are we going to stay with Chris and Mrs. L?" The question comes from Gitta, Mrs. Peters' daughter. I sense that she would like nothing better than to stay with us. Chris is her age and she is hoping for a companion and playmate.

In the meantime we have caught up with Mama, who invites both of them to stay with us if we are able to make it to my cousin's house at Tegel. They are glad for the companionship, just as much as we are, and happily accept. The two girls jump up and down singing, "We are going to stay together, we are going to stay together." They walk along holding hands.

Gitta takes after her mother—pretty, petite, neat, a little shy, with dark blonde hair coming down her shoulders in braids.

The sun is still shining, warm and comforting, the river on the right flows gently along, now and then a little ripple, and if it were not for an occasional corpse floating by, one could pretend that it is a normal spring day and nothing terrible has happened. But the illusion does not last long when one looks a little further. There is the destruction; the endless trek of people; still the sounds, though distant, of exploding shells; and ahead of us is the bridge. It is the bridge we must reach and we must cross—and the other side is uncertainty and not hundreds, but thousands of Russian troops.

The street seems endless. I have walked it before, in better times, and it had always been a pleasant walk.

We finally reach the bridge. Like us, thousands and thousands of people are waiting to cross, but there is no impatience. We all do have the same thing in common—time. . . .

Slowly, one person at a time, we can go over. It takes hours before it is our turn, and we have seated ourselves in the grass along the riverside. It gives Opa most of all a chance to stretch his sick and weary feet. We are worried that once he sits down he will not be able to get up again.

When the time finally comes, he has no problem getting up;

77

he is as anxious now to cross as we are. But getting Opa across the bridge is a problem. How are we going to do it? There are areas where it is impossible to hold onto anything, and it is a matter of walking freehand about twenty feet above water on a path approximately thirty-six inches wide. . . . For us it is not difficult, but Opa? The two little ones have to help if we are to succeed, and we arrange it somehow like this. First I go with Opa behind me holding on to me; then come the two girls, Gitta and Chris, giving me a hand with Opa; then comes Mrs. Peters, helping Mama with Monika and the baby carriage.

It is slow progress. Now and then the path has been disrupted, and we must cross a gap two feet wide. That is not easy for Opa, but somehow, urging him to go slow, we manage. Mrs. Peters helps Mama lift the baby carriage, and we count our blessings that she is there.

I have mixed emotions about our crossing, especially since I will be first to touch the ground on the other side. What possible guarantee is there that we shall not leap from the frying pan into the fire?

All of a sudden, despite the warmth of the sun, I turn cold. Ahead of me I see the thousands of Russian troops. I have to stop; I just cannot walk any further . . . I don't want to see them. . . .

The water looks as ever—dark and yet gentle, here and there a lonely leaf floats by, once in a while a jumping fish is a silver spark in the darkness. . . .

I turn around. Opa is standing behind me, one hand is holding on to a piece of steel serving as a railing, the other is stretched out towards me. It is not quite clear to me whether the gesture is one of help or a request for help—at that moment it does not matter.

What are we doing here? How did we get here? I don't want to go into nowhere—a girl belongs home!

Vaguely, from somewhere far away, I hear Mama saying, "Inga, what's the matter? Can't you go any further?" but even the anxiety in her voice does not make me move. I want to go home!

Then suddenly I seem to hear Mrs. Schulman cry, "Help me, please help me!" and there is Uncle Fritz, ". . . it would have been Evi, . . ." and there is the brute, waving his pistol, ". . . Uri, Uri!" and there is Omi, blood coming down her leg, ". . . shell . . ." and there is the machine-gun fire from our window, and the two Volkssturmmen, ". . . we want to be with our families . . ." and Mrs. Stromberg, ". . . I am sixty-five years old!" Dear God, where is safety?

Behind me everybody has to stop because I have stopped. Even if I wanted to, I could not go back now. . . . What is there to go back to anyway? Childhood memories? Was I ever young? If I was, what happened to that child? Where did it all go? Is this the way people grow up and mature?

I feel anger arising in me. Who is responsible for all this? Who has done all this? The anger brings me back to reality. I don't want to go back! And if I don't start moving soon, there will be a panic—people will start pushing each other and fall—I have to go on!

Opa's hand is still outstretched, but now it is trembling.

"Inga, please, we must go," he says, his blue eyes full of understanding.

And so we cross the bridge.

Across, safe and sound, no terrible things happen. The Russian troops are busy; they are not paying any particular attention to us. It seems that they are trying to make a camp. They hurry back and forth, leaving us alone.

I had not paid any particular attention to Lux, our dog. I don't even remember how he crossed, whether he swam across the water or crossed the bridge, but here he is. I'm glad to see him. He seems to be the only sign of normalcy, of constancy, and I bend down to hug him. He responds with a happy tail-wagging and then runs off ahead of us, always making sure we are right on his heels. From then on we try to watch him to make sure he does not follow the smell of food coming from the Russian camps.

But for a moment, when we are not looking, he slips away and reappears suddenly with a piece of chicken. I feel slightly jealous; we have not had chicken for months, and I am beginning to feel very hungry. There he is, chewing away on his chicken wing! But I quickly check myself and am ashamed; who knows when he will ever eat again, when we know we hardly have enough food ourselves to survive. . . .

Right now I am not hungry as much as I am worried. Will we find my cousin Hilda's house intact, undamaged, at least enough so to live in? And if we do, will she give us shelter for a while? She has a family herself, and if you have just a little food left and in comes a crowd of other people, you feel obligated to share. But who can afford to share in times like these? And who has the heart to eat when he is surrounded by other hungry people, especially if they are relatives? Well, first we must get there.

"Mama, what time is it?" I ask.

"Inga," Mama says, annoyed, "you know that we have no jewelry left." Then she comes to a sudden stop. "Wait a minute—I forgot." She fumbles excitedly around in the baby carriage, then holds something up, triumphantly. Her eyes light up with the first smile in a long time. "Look here, they didn't find it, they didn't find it!"

In her hand she holds the gold watch Papa had bought me for my birthday. In a last-minute decision, instead of hiding it in my clothes, she had put it in the baby carriage, and the Russians in their search somehow missed it. At least we have one valuable possession left, although I am sure the value to us is more sentimental than material.

She glances quickly at the watch, then hastily puts it back where she found it.

"Quarter of five," she says. "It's still going, I now remember winding it this morning."

My feet have started to hurt, and if I hurt, how must Opa feel? I can see he drags himself along, and I am very much afraid that the strain will be too much for him.

"Just a little while longer, Opa," I say.

80

"It's okay," he says, trying to smile.

We walk, and walk, and walk.

In front of us we see a crowd of people bent towards the ground, busily doing something.

"What's all that about?" Mrs. Peters inquires.

As we get closer, we see what it is. The carcass of a horse is lying there, and people are trying to cut it up. Each one is trying to get the biggest and best piece. Knives flash back and forth, up and down, silvery glints in the sun, touched with red. . . . Within a short while there is nothing left but a very ugly-looking bloody mess and some bones, while people are running in all directions as if they were holding crown jewels.

I feel very nauseated.

Is that what hunger does to human beings? It turns them instantly into butchers? It deprives them of all dignity? It takes away compassion and feeling?

If it does, then we have not yet reached that point. But some day soon, we may be there too. Then what? What will we do? How will we react? Will we fight among each other in order to survive? Slowly and gradually a sickening awakening to the realities of life, of being human, begins to shape up inside me, and I don't like what I see.

Some Russian soldiers have observed the incident. One of them says something which causes the others to laugh while they are all looking on.

Mama, silent, serious, and sad until now, says, "Let's get away from here—quickly."

She pushes the baby carriage hastily ahead of her and we follow. Again I discover mixed emotions inside me. People have to eat to survive, so what is wrong with what these people did? What is the difference between going into the butcher store and buying some meat or cutting up a dead horse for meat? Is there a difference? Somehow, instinctively, I know that there is, but at this point I am too tired, too exhausted, too emotionally numb to analyze it. But I make a resolution: I will never let myself be that hungry, at least not for meat. How long am I going to be able to remind myself of that. . . ?

81

In the meantime, we have reached the other part of the city. Until now our walk has led us through a suburban area with more woods, parks, and quiet roads than houses. Now we have reached the typical city—buildings close together, each four or five stories high. Some are still in good shape, right next to others completely destroyed.

What strikes us as strange is the fact that there are not many people on the street—are they all still afraid to come out?

We see a man standing in a doorway staring down the street, mumbling, "Where is she?"

"Excuse me," I approach him, "do you know the shortest way to Billerbecker Weg?"

"Do you live on the moon?" he answers, attempting to be funny. "Don't you know there is a curfew here? Anybody found on the street after six o'clock will be shot on sight!"

"We'll never make it!" I want to say it loud, but it comes out only as a whisper.

"What's the matter?" Mama can sense something is wrong.

The first reaction after I tell them the news is, I believe, normal—we all start running. Mama is pushing the baby carriage with one hand, with the other she is dragging along Chris, who has started crying with the full deep power of her voice. Gitta has joined Chris and is sobbing with her, less powerful in sound performance. Mrs. Peters is holding on to Gitta, trying to keep up with Mama; I am dragging Opa along something terrible, he is half up, half down.

"I can't go on!"

Opa has torn himself loose from my grip and just stands there, holding his chest, breathing heavily.

"I just can't," he says almost apologetic. "You go on; I am an old man, maybe they won't shoot me. . . ."

We realize the foolishness of our action.

"Opa, we will not do any such thing," Mama says firmly. "What in God's name are we doing, running like this? We are not going to make it anyway. Let's rest a moment and see what else we can do."

"Well," Mrs. Peters puts in, "we could see if we can get shelter in one of these houses here for at least one night."

"Why didn't we think of that right away? Erna, you are marvelous!" Mama says.

We all start breathing more freely again—the obvious solution, so simple! And here we acted like chickens with the fox in the henhouse! So we proceed towards one of the houses, whose entry hall is boarded up with wood. (As a matter of fact, the buildings all are barred like this.)

After about eight or nine very loud knocks, we hear someone approaching.

"Who is there?" a deep voice inquires.

"We need shelter," Mama says. "Would you please let us in?"

"We cannot let anybody in," the voice behind the wood says. "The Russians have counted everyone, and if they recount and find that there are more than at the last count, they think we have been hiding someone."

"But sir," I protest, "we were just told that there is a curfew on, that anybody on the street at six o'clock is going to be shot on sight. . . ." I am close to tears.

"Weeelll," the voice comes through the wood; then, "No, no, I am sorry, but we cannot let anyone in!" And after a short pause, "You better go back home."

"Home?" I shout. But he has gone. I hear his footsteps dying away.

We have all heard. No one speaks. This time we do not run; we slowly walk to the edge of the sidewalk and sit down on the curb: one old man, two mothers, two little girls, one small baby, and one teenager—me.

At six o'clock we will all be dead. We have fifteen minutes. . . .

Mama searches in the carriage for the watch. She holds it in her hand and looks at it, silently. She has put her arm around Chris, who is now crying quietly. Mrs. Peters and Gitta are sitting huddled together, just staring.

"Mother," Opa mumbles.

I want to cry. But if I start now, I will never stop—and I don't want the Russians to think we are sniveling cowards. If it has to be, I hope it will be soon.

Maybe it would help to pray. But I don't know what to pray for. Anyway—does God exist? At this point it does not seem so.

Not quite two thousand years ago, ". . . and it came to pass in those days that there went out a decree from Caesar Augustus. . . ." Long, long ago. . . .

And just as long ago it seems that the story of the birth of Christ was retold each Christmas in my life, and long ago it seems that I cherished it and found joy and peace in it. Long ago. . . . ". . . and she brought forth her firstborn son, and wrapped him in swaddling clothes, and laid him in a manger; because there was no room for them at the inn. . . ."

We are not Christ, we are not sinless, we are not pure, but we are Christians, and we are human beings. What is our crime? What have the seven of us done that we should die for it now?

Mama has put the watch back. She is bending down to Monika, the baby. For a long time she looks at her and then she says softly, "What kind of world did I bring you into?" Her voice is gentle, but the sadness of thousands of years of man's history is mirrored in her eyes.

6

RESPITE

"Hello," says the man on the bicycle, his mouth showing a trace of a smile, his eyes friendly and warm.

Twelve eyes look up at him in disbelief. Where did he come from all of a sudden?

"Don't you have anywhere to go?" he asks—and we know that here is salvation.

He is about thirty-five or forty, with graying hair, dark eyebrows, blue eyes, tall and slim. He leans casually against his bicycle as if there has never been a war and as if neither the Russians nor the curfew exist. It is his eyes that impress me most. They radiate a kind of quiet intelligence, a human understanding.

"No!" We all speak at once.

He asks no further questions.

"Come along," he says, and he starts to walk.

Obediently we rise and follow him, still somehow disbelieving that there is hope.

"But," Mama says to him, "you have your bicycle. Without us you could make it home in time to beat the curfew. Here you are going slowly with us—aren't you afraid they are going to shoot you, too, if we are all found on the street at six o'clock?"

"Oh," and again there is the gentle smile. "Don't worry

85

about that—in a few minutes we will reach the city limits and we will be in the suburb. There is no curfew in that area."

We accept his answer as the truth, without even the slightest inkling that it may just be the kindest lie in the world. . . .

He starts telling us about himself. He is married and has a little daughter, and he owns a small one-family home in the immediate area where my cousin Hilda lives.

"You know," Mama tells him, "we were trying to get through to my niece's house on Billerbecker Weg—but I am not sure how welcome we will be—after all, well, you know how it is. . . ."

"Yes, I know how it is," he says calmly.

After a few moments of silence, he continues, "I have a friend who left Berlin to spend the rest of these horrible days in West Germany with his family and friends. He owns a house like mine, and right at this moment it is empty. I don't believe it is a good idea at this time to have a house unoccupied. There is a lot of looting going on, as you probably well know. So I thought it might be a marvelous idea if you would live there until they return, which will probably be quite a few months from now. It will help keep his home in shape, and you will have a home until you can return to your own."

We all stop short at his words. Only Opa, whose hearing is not so good, keeps on walking, and I run after him and stop him.

"Opa!" I shout. "We have a place to go, we have a place to go! Do you understand? Do you hear? We are safe!"

Opa says nothing. He turns around and walks the few steps back.

The young man and the old man look into each other's eyes, and neither of them says a word. Still I have the feeling that some kind of conversation is going on between the two, only we can't hear it, at least not with our ears. . . .

"My God!" Mama says. "Do you really want to do something like that?"

And Mrs. Peters adds, "How can you trust us like that? After

86

all, we are strangers to you, you know nothing, but nothing about us. . . ."

"I know people," he replies serenely.

From then on we walk fast. We look neither left, right, nor back—only ahead.

Only one thought is in my mind: we have somewhere to go, we will not be shot, we will most likely not be molested, and we won't have to be beggars asking for asylum . . . it is a miracle!

We reach our destination in no time at all. There it is: pretty, comfortable, inviting, and hardly damaged. Miraculously, the windows have glass in them and seem to send out a friendly smile with the clean, white curtains showing. There is a little flower garden with daisies, lilac bushes, tulips, and a rosebush, all embraced by a wooden picket fence. Never has any house looked so beautiful to me.

"Here we are," says the man with the bike. "Please wait just a few moments; I live right on the next street, and I have to go and get the key."

He doesn't come back right away. I begin to get nervous. Where is he? It seems like ages! Suppose he was just telling us a story to save us from desperation, and nothing was true, and we would never see him again . . . we would never be able to go in. . . .

Every minute I expect to see a face appear from behind the curtains, peering at us suspiciously, someone motioning us to go away from their property. . . . I just want to fall to the ground, bury my face, and shut out the world . . . I feel weak and dizzy and tired.

There he is!

He is holding up the keys and they dangle from his hand. It is a beautiful sound.

"Here," he says, and he smiles. "I just realized that I have not introduced myself to you. My name is Franz Stillman. I live at. . . ." He gives us his address, and then he starts to open the front door.

"Wait a minute!" Mama says. "Are you sure we are really not

going to present a problem, that your friends will really be in favor of what you are doing?"

He nods. Mama continues, "Then I pledge to you that I will take care of this house as if it were my own. And only God knows how much we are in your debt, and only He will be able to return your kindness, because I don't think anything I ever do in my life will be able to repay you."

"That's all right," he says, "but I do have one request. Sometimes in a situation like this it is hard to leave on a moment's notice. You must remember that this is my friend's home, and when he returns with his family you must leave immediately, and that is not always easy. . . ."

"We most certainly agree with you," Mama says. "But hopefully, before your friend's return, we will be able to go back to our own home. Maybe in a couple of weeks things will be back to normal. Anyway, whatever the situation, we promise that the moment you want us to leave, regardless of the reason, we will go."

And so we enter our temporary home.

Mr. Stillman shows us around, points out where everything is, and what we can use and what we had best leave untouched. As he is ready to leave, Mama says, "Wait a minute, Mr. Stillman, we have forgotten something!"

"Yes?"

"We forgot to introduce ourselves. You still do not even know what our names are, where we live, and so on. I apologize. . . ."

She starts putting down on a piece of paper our names and our address.

"Oh, that's all right. I knew sooner or later you would remember," he smiles. He wishes us good luck and departs, telling us that if we need help to let him know.

Opa and the two girls are just about ready to collapse. Chris has thrown herself down on the carpet, taken the seam of her dress into her mouth, nursing it, and is already deep asleep. Her face is dirty from the dust mixed with her tears, but she looks so peaceful that we do not have the heart to wake her up to wash. Mama takes a face flannel, wets it, and carefully wipes off the worst dirt. Then she picks her up and carries her upstairs to the bedroom.

The otherwise clean and neat Gitta looks no better than Chris today. Mrs. Peters follows Mutti's procedure and lays Gitta on the couch in the living room downstairs.

The upstairs has one large master bedroom with two beds in which Mutti, Chris, and I can sleep, and it has one smaller room with a bed which we designate for Opa. The couch downstairs sleeps two, just perfect for Gitta and Mrs. Peters. Monika's sleeping quarters are no problem; she feels secure in her baby carriage, and we think it is best to let her sleep there for reasons of familiarity and security.

Right now Opa is sitting in the kitchen, his head resting on the kitchen table, and it is hard to tell whether he is asleep or not.

"I hate to wake him," Mama whispers.

"We have to, Mama," I whisper back. "He is not comfortable that way. . . ."

We nudge him gently, and he raises his head immediately; he was just resting.

"Would you like to go to sleep, Opa?"

"Yes, Lisa," he says, and we show him his room upstairs. After we are convinced that he is comfortable, we go downstairs and sit at the kitchen table for a few moments.

Now the exhaustion comes all of a sudden. All three of us—Mama, Mrs. Peters, and I—are just about ready to collapse, and so we say good-night to each other. Mrs. Peters joins Gitta on the couch, Mama and I go upstairs, and after a quick wash, we collapse on the bed. I feel Mama gently kissing me on the forehead, and that is the last I remember of that day.

Something cold and wet is pushing against my hand. It is Lux. His soft brown eyes are asking me if I am going to play with him.

I am still half asleep and don't really feel like waking up yet. Last night's sleep was different from that of a great number of preceding nights—a soft, snug bed, no air raids, no shelling or bombing, no Russian boots, no disturbance at all! I don't think I have slept that well in years. . . .

It has never taken me long to wake up and immediately know where I am and what took place the previous day. I guess constant nightly air raids give a certain amount of training in instant alertness.

So here we are. Safe and sound, in a home that is not ours, but is shelter nevertheless. We are alive and so, God willing, we will stay alive until Papa comes home. Then we will be a family again, and life can be normal for a change. . . .

I look around me. Clean, white curtains at the windows, Monika's pram is next to one window, close by, a little dust is showing on the furniture, and to my left is the door leading to the staircase down. And the sun is shining!

Today I can feel its warmth . . . some rays peep through the curtains and settle on Monika's pram—a shadow, now here, now there, like dancing butterflies in the breeze outside.

Mama's bed is empty. She and Chris are early risers and are probably already downstairs in the kitchen.

I take a look at Monika.

She is sleeping peacefully. Light brown curls, rosy cheeks, eyebrows delicately lined by nature, dark and curved eyelashes, lips pink and heart-shaped. She is so pretty . . . and she is still so small and so helpless.

I want to pick her up and cuddle her, but waking her up would most certainly interfere with Mama's schedule. So I settle for a quick little kiss on her forehead, which makes her stir just slightly. She turns her head to the other side and continues to sleep.

Well, I guess I have to go down.

The nice cold water in the bathroom wakens me completely, and I take my time. It is a long time since I had a bathroom and running water!

Downstairs Mama and Mrs. Peters are sitting at the kitchen table talking. Mama has made a cup of ersatz coffee, and the two women are enjoying the tranquillity of the morning. From the adjoining room I hear some giggling and commotion—Gitta and Chris are having a pillow fight.

"What's for breakfast?"

"Oooo," Mama says with a dry smile, "scrambled eggs and ham and rolls and delicious real coffee. . . ."

"Mother!" I reply, half laughing, half scolding, "do you have to make fun of our situation?"

"You are lucky she can joke about it, Inga," Mrs. Peters says. I have to agree with her.

I sit down at the table and drink my coffee. One slice of bread, dry—is that all?

"Can I have another slice of bread, please?"

"I am afraid not," Mama says, and this time she does not smile. "We have only a few loaves left, and we don't know when we will be able to get more food."

"Ah well. . . ." I am young, and at this time it does not bother me too much. There is a great deal to be thankful for instead of griping about food! What I don't know yet is the fact that I have never experienced real hunger before. It will not be too long before I will. . . .

For the time being, though, I thoroughly enjoy what I have—shelter, and a certain amount of peace.

I do not pay any particular attention to the furnishings inside the house. That is taboo; it does not belong to us, so it is unimportant. But the sunshine, the birds, the flowers, and the trees, they belong to everyone, and so my first exploration trip is directed to the outside area.

Yesterday I had not realized that there was a backyard too. It is small, but neat, with some flowerbeds and some huge sunflowers, in which the birds had been finding a most welcome source of supply. There are a few fairly old trees, and some grass. Each piece of property is divided off by a picket fence, and most of these have another border of a hedge for privacy.

91

All this makes a cozy and inviting refuge. All in all, it looks as if the war went by here without leaving a trace—how lucky we are to be here!

But the best thing is that we have not seen a single Russian uniform since we arrived! As a matter of fact, we have not seen anybody at all. The houses on either side and in front of us look deserted—curtains drawn, doors locked, not a sign or trace of life. I guess everybody is either in West Germany or in hiding.

Whoever among our neighbors is home prefers not to show his face. The streets are just not safe yet, and although we are fairly sure that there is no Russian camp in the near neighborhood, it is best to be cautious. A strolling Russian patrol may see people (especially women!) and report their find to their comrades. I personally prefer not even to look outside the window to the front. What I don't see won't hurt me!

The only safe place is the backyard. It is inaccessible from anywhere but the inside of the house, and the surrounding gardens block the view from and to the main street.

Lux comes up to me, tail wagging, a stone in his mouth. He casually drops it at my feet, then looks up to me, daring me to take it. I dare—and throw it into the yard. He runs after it and thinks that this happy game is going to continue, but I don't feel like playing. Disgustedly, he gives up and lies down beside me but not without giving me a dirty look.

It's time to think a little.

What a difference from yesterday to today! Yesterday we did not know if we would still be alive today—and today we are in a place that comes close to paradise. Yesterday we were still sitting at home in the "mousetrap" . . . but no, I cannot permit myself to think about all the events that took place.

Maybe today is the time to think ahead, not much, just a little . . . for instance, what am I going to do for the rest of the day? And tomorrow? No, I cannot think about tomorrow, that is too far ahead; let's take each day at a time. . . .

So, today . . . the best thing would be to sleep a lot to make up for all the nights without rest. And then maybe there is something to read inside the house.

I decide to go inside to find some reading material. I remember that I have not made my bed and decide to take care of that immediately. Then a few old magazines provide a temporary source of interest. Before I realize it, it is lunchtime.

"I have some rye flour," I hear Mrs. Peters say to Mama. "I cannot expect you to share what you have with us without contributing something myself. We could cook a soup from it, you know."

"That's marvelous!" Mama gets out the cooking pot and starts immediately.

What a horrible thought—soup from rye flour! I shudder, but secretly, so that no one notices how appalling the thought is to me.

While Mrs. Peters finishes cooking the soup, Mama prepares the meal for Monika.

Now here is something I would like to eat! In a small suitcase Mama has saved (and would have been willing to defend like a lioness her young!) the rations of Nestlés baby food and some dry milk. The suitcase is under lock and key, and rightly so, because I could not have guaranteed that I would not have taken a little taste here and there—it is so delicious!

Well, at least the baby is taken care of for a while. And, sooner or later, someone will have to give us some food too. After all, nobody lets a whole nation starve to death! Or. . . ? A terrible thought starts growing inside me—suppose they will let a whole nation starve to death as a plan of destruction? Maybe that's a part of war that follows when you lose the battle?

The sight of the people cutting up the horse comes up before my eyes. Oh God, please don't let me be so hungry, not ever!

If before the thought of the rye-flour soup appalled me, it is now a pretty good proposition, and I quickly and silently ask God's forgiveness for my sinful thought. It does not taste too bad after all!

Opa has come down and is also sitting at the kitchen table.

"I don't want anything," he says.

"Opa, you have got to eat something," Mama scolds him gently.

93

"If only I knew if Mother is all right," he says sadly.

"Opa, Omi will be all right, we will go and find her as soon as things have calmed down more," I encourage him, and Mama and Mrs. Peters agree with me. "But suppose we find her and then you are half-dead with worry and lack of food. How would you feel then?"

That seems to convince him.

One and a half ladles of soup and two slices of rye bread, dry—that is the portion we each get. The first day it is all right, but after three weeks the situation is not quite so easily solved. However, the first day I don't know it will be so long, and longer, before we will have one decent meal, and so I enjoy it as much as possible.

That day goes by without much of anything happening. We are all still weary, and none of us want to think about the future. For instance, what will we do if the family who owns the house decides to come back within a day or so? Mr. Stillman has assured us that they do not plan to return too soon, but people do change their minds, and the threat is there. But somehow we have come through so far and so, God willing, we will be safe a little while longer.

My thoughts turn to Papa, and I wonder if he is alive. It has been so long since we last heard from him. . . . Surely, if he were alive, he would be a prisoner of war. When would he be released? What would it do to him to be imprisoned? Would it change him, and if so, in what way?

Papa was never a warm-hearted, outgoing father. He was strict and very much demanded what he considered his rights as the head of the household, but he was a good father, despite his lacking ability to show affection. We all knew that he loved us. He was also proud and loved his freedom—being a prisoner must be rather unbearable for him. . . .

I think of the days when we visited him at the base, the second time of our school evacuation, when he was stationed within Germany. This time we had been sent to East Prussia, near the Lithuanian border. Evacuation during the last years of the war was the rule rather than the exception.

The first evacuation of the school at the beginning of the war was horrible—we children were only twelve years old and so homesick, especially since we never knew if the next day we would be orphans or not. Never have twelve-year-olds listened to each night's news so intently as did we. Another air raid—where did it hit tonight? And then we would sit in agony waiting for the next letter to arrive from home.

Our teacher, who was very good, started teaching us Italian and Russian in order to occupy our minds to the fullest. She herself spoke German, English, French, Russian, and Italian. We already knew English and had just started French, which were the languages of our school schedule. Italian and Russian were taught by her on her own, but somehow it was stopped soon—she must have had orders from higher up to do so!

That evacuation only lasted nine months. Then we returned home and sweated out the air raids and all the other things of the war at home, which we all preferred!

When our group was fifteen, the second and last evacuation took place, and this time we were sent to Heinrichswalde, near Tilsit, East Prussia. In contrast to the first evacuation, which had our whole class together in one camp, the second one was more pleasant. We were distributed among the residents of Heinrichswalde and were mostly treated like members of the family. I remember the day we arrived.

It was a little bit like the placement of "Little Orphan Annies." The train arrived; the station was filled with people looking us over, and leaving the train we had "please take me!" expressions on our faces, so that—oh horrible thought—we would not be left over with no place to go.

As a matter of fact, one or two girls, in contradiction to the so vehemently advertised efficiency of the Germans, were left over. Finally some kind soul was found who was willing to give them shelter, and as it turned out they had just about the best home of any of us. But what a feeling!

Life there was not bad. The families were mostly kind to all of us and we had no complaints. School continued at a hectic pace. Much was demanded of us, and we had to study hard. I

95

don't regret it; I learned a lot. It was better to occupy one's mind with study than with the fear of losing our loved ones and our homes. . . .

My girl friend Ursula (I called her Ursel) and I had decided when we left Berlin that we would try to stay together in one home, and we were lucky—we did. We shared the same room. The head of the household was a German officer away in the war. His wife and two small children—one boy and one girl— were taking care of a rather well-established home. The woman was a nice person, educated and refined.

There are more pleasant memories connected with Heinrichs- walde than unpleasant ones. We were close to sixteen years of age; soon we would have our high school certificates and then life could begin! At this point, apart from the constant air raids, the war had not yet struck home too much, and we had learned to live with it. We felt that life held hope.

Mother would send some cake coupons from home, and with the help of a little pocket money we could go to Tilsit into a café and have delicious ice coffee (a mix of coffee, ice cream, and whipped cream), and pretend that we were grown-up and sophisticated and just spending a lady's leisure time. It could not be done too often, since it was a forty-five-minute train ride to Tilsit, and we had to have permission from our principal, which was not easily given!

Ursula and I were lucky again. Our landlady's little boy had been sick with whooping cough, and we were quarantined at home and could not go to school. At first we enjoyed the forced inactivity: no school, no homework—hurrah! But then we got rather bored. We were getting on each other's nerves, and also on the nerves of our poor landlady, so that finally she sent us to her sister in Tilsit for a few days.

We rejoiced. Finally we could get to see some life!

Fate favored us again (or so we thought!) and sent the sister away for two days to visit her husband, also an officer in the German Army, who for a few days was stationed nearby.

The lady had placed a lot of trust and confidence in us. She left in our care her little two-year-old boy. I am not sure whether we deserved her trust completely. We did take care of the little boy very well, and fulfilled our duty to the fullest, and possibly more, as far as he was concerned, but at the same time we saw a chance to get into some mischief.

Mischief took the form and rather handsome shape of two young lieutenants, who were quartered in our landlady's sister's home temporarily, and on whom we had cast a very interested eye.

With the lady gone, we saw our chance to practice grown-up entertaining, and in lieu of something better, we did this in the form of an invitation to try our homemade candy at eight o'clock one evening. Then we waited in agony to see if they would accept.

In our sixteen-year-old minds we had decided it was time to bring some romance into our lives, and the two unsuspecting chaps were to be our victims. Of course our idea of romance went no further than seducing them to a little eye-to-eye flirtation, and if things got really serious, possibly a kiss. The thought that the two, who were about twenty-one, might get other ideas did not for one minute enter our minds!

Well, we were lucky again.

The two young men were gentlemen, and after a polite hour spent in pleasant conversation (we were even too shy to go through with our eye-to-eye flirtation, possibly due to lack of practice!), they said good night, thanked us for a nice evening, and departed.

We gave a sigh of relief. After our rather daring invitation, we did get just a little scared at our boldness and the thought of what might have happened. We felt that we had some kind of guardian angel watching over us.

Since our success in the romance department proved to have been very negative, we decided to try our luck in the entertainment department, meaning not that we would do the entertaining, but that we would let ourselves be entertained. It seemed easier!

97

This was to take place by going to see a movie classified as "suitable for persons over eighteen years of age." We were not quite sixteen, so we were confronted with the difficult task of disguising ourselves to look like eighteen-year-olds.

In those days it was not too easy—youth under a dictatorship government was not encouraged to be vain or seductive. The motto was: "Be bright, be smart, be a Party member, be plain, have lots of children. . . ." Whether this philosophy is positive or negative is a matter of opinion. As far as I was concerned, I did not want to be a "plain jane" all my life, and I did want children, but not lots of them, and I did want them in wedlock, although the government was not too particular about that. As long as you populated the Reich, you were all right, whether you were married or not. Somewhere there, among other things, the Reich's philosophy and mine parted company.

To this day I fail to see what there was about the movie that was so delicate that it could not touch the eyes and ears of a sixteen-year-old! It was called "Münchhausen" and was the story of the "Lying Baron"—and in color! It was the first time that I was to see a color movie, and the thought fascinated me, but first we had to make preparations to get there.

We raided the wardrobe of our vacationing landlady. She had beautiful clothes, and we spent a breathtaking few hours just looking through, probing, testing, putting on make-up, and doing other intriguing feminine tasks.

Finally, we both decided on suitable outfits. It was not as easy as it sounds—Ursel was rather on the chubby side, well-developed for her age, and had a problem fitting into the clothes. I was skinny and tall and had the problem of making believe that there were curves where there weren't any!

So, dressed like peacocks, we departed, with fluttering hearts. We knew that at each cinema soldiers or police were posted mainly so that no minors would be entering the sacred halls. Now and then they would spot-check, and more than once caught a very embarrassed under-eighteen-year-old. Then after the film had started one could expect another spot-check, and so, even if one was lucky enough to gain entry, the forbidden fruit could not wholeheartedly be enjoyed.

We did get into the cinema without any problem, but I must admit that I hardly remember what it was all about; I was too nervous to enjoy it.

After Ursel and I had been seated for about a half hour, the expected footsteps of the authorities were heard, and they stopped right next to our aisle.

A flashlight shone into our eyes, and a voice said, "May I see your identity card, Miss?"

I looked straight ahead, pretending not to hear. Ursel, who sat closer to the voice than I did, felt obligated to show her identity card and she had to leave.

I sat horrified! I was very unfamiliar with the procedure and was not sure what the consequences were. Would our principal be informed? Would Ursel even have to go to jail for violating a law? If the principal was told, would Ursel be thrown out of school? If all this happened to Ursel, then I was just as guilty and could not possibly sit back and do nothing!

In a way it was funny. Ursel looked much more mature than I did, yet it was Ursel instead of me!

I felt like running out of the cinema and chasing towards home, but that would really have looked suspicious. I sat through the movie, but it was not much fun, it was just agony. I breathed a sigh of relief when it was over and I could start running home. The venture was so much different from what we had dreamed it would be!

It was "blackout," of course, and it was hard to see anything. I was scared to death, but I finally got home. Ursel was in bed, reading and munching our homemade candy. "Well, if you aren't lucky!" she said, slightly envious.

I sat down on the bed, took a piece of candy, and while munching with sheer joy that the escapade was over, demanded, "What happened? Is there going to be any trouble? What did they do to you?"

"Oh, nothing much." Her brown eyes were still a little envious. "They just told me to go home and better not try anything like that again. How was the movie?"

"To tell you the truth, I didn't enjoy it—I was too worried."

"A penny for your happy thoughts!" Mama's voice is taking me out of my memories.

"You know, I was just thinking about the time in Heinrichs-walde and Tilsit. There were times when I wished you could have been there."

"I can well imagine that the two of you got into quite a bit of mischief there," Mama says, and she is also smiling a little. "Maybe it's just as well for me that I wasn't there!"

It is best to change the subject.

"I'll go outside and pick some flowers—we have not had flowers in a vase for quite some time. It will cheer us all up a little."

The door is already open, and Lux sees his chance to chase some butterflies. He is out in a jiffy and roams around the garden. Apparently he suspects a buried bone in one area and starts digging.

"Lux, stop that!"

He gives me another dirty look but obeys and decides to lie down.

The flowers are not in good shape. They are in the last stages of bloom, and I know that if I pick them, they will be wilted by tomorrow.

I go back inside the house; Lux stays outside for more sunshine. Just as I am telling Mama about my disappointment over the flowers, we hear Lux barking outside.

Then a shot. . .

Opa jumps up from the table, runs towards the window, and I see that he raises his right arm in terrible anger and shakes a fist at someone.

100

"You dirty bastard!" Opa says, his voice hoarse. I have never heard Opa talk like that.

Mama and I run to the window to see what is going on. Outside is a Russian soldier . . . that Russian uniform again. We see that he puts an ugly black pistol back into his holster, gives Lux one last cold look, turns around, and walks away.

Opa is holding himself up by the window sill. His face is white, he wants to go towards the door to go outside, but he is shaking so much he cannot walk.

Mama gently leads Opa back to the kitchen chair, and I run outside.

Lux is lying on the ground, quiet and motionless.

"Mama!" I scream, "Lux is dead, our Lux is dead. . . ." Blood is running down from his head, and I dare not touch him. Between sobs, I hear myself saying, "I hate you, I hate you, I hate you. . . ."

"Inga!" Mama is shaking me gently. "Lux is not dead."

She picks him up carefully and carries him inside the house.

"Are you sure? He is really not dead?"

"No. Look, the bullet hit him from the front, then slid along his skull and came out the back. He is just in shock, I think."

Mama has beside her a dish of water and washes off the blood.

"See here. The second hole in the back of his head is much larger than the one in front. I may be right."

"Thank God for that," Opa says. "Do you really think he will live?"

"Well, I am no doctor, but I think there is hope."

"I did not realize how fond I was of the little mutt," Opa mumbles, his mustache trembling a little. "I just hope you're right."

We make him a bed from a big carton we found in the attic, with some rags in it.

I still am very doubtful; so far he has not given any obvious signs of life, but his heart is still beating.

101

I spend the rest of the day reading in the garden. After a while Mama calls me in for supper; it is rye-flour soup and one slice of bread. We have decided to bring a little change into our lavish meal, and therefore we will eat the soup spiced up with saccharin for lunch and with salt for supper from here on.

So, with no more occurrences of any special meaning, ends the second day.

7

HUNGER DAYS

I am wide awake. Beside me Mama and Chris are sleeping restlessly, but they are asleep.

I look at them enviously. Can they take it better than I can?

It has now been four weeks since we arrived here in our refuge. Our nerves have calmed down a little, and if it were not for the hunger, we could almost feel as if we were at peace. Has peace really come? I wonder.

At first there were rumors over rumors. From the bits and pieces of information picked up here and there, we can assume that the whole city is now occupied by Russian troops, a very disturbing thought.

So the English or Americans never made it to Berlin!

One of the rumors said that Hitler and Eva Braun and several other "faithfuls" had killed themselves in the Reichskanzlei.

Naturally, after bringing the nation to disaster, they would not be able to face the realities and consequences. I can still hear and see the slogan "WE WILL NEVER CAPITULATE" crudely painted and written all over Berlin on walls, on doorways, on roofs, on trains.

If they are all dead, then we are now a nation without government. What does this imply? And what are the consequences?

I am too young to know very much about politics. Frankly, I

don't really care. There is a problem in our life right now that is predominant—hunger.

The first few weeks of our stay here it was bearable—the three or four slices of bread a day and a couple of ladles of rye-flour soup held us over the worst, since we still had reserves from the "better" times of war in our bodies. Who would ever have thought that people should think back to a war as "better" times!

On May 7, 1945, Mr. Stillman came over to see us, and we thought he was going to tell us that we had to leave.

When I had been thinking of peace, I had pictured it as the finality of war, the ending of hostilities, the beginning of a new life: people would start rebuilding, food would be available, work would begin again; life would be back to normal.

When Mr. Stillman informed us that as of today, peace was here, that Germany had surrendered and the war was over, our first reaction was indescribable. We hugged each other, and we cried. Our thoughts went to Papa, and that he would probably be back soon, and we thought of going home. How else would he know that we are still alive?

Mr. Stillman did not participate in our joy. "I would not leave just yet," he said quietly.

We were shocked. "Why not? The war is over, you said!"

"On paper. There is a lot more going on though. . . ."

No matter how hard we tried to coax him to tell us more, he would not say another word. We had enough confidence in him and his judgment to hold our expectations very much in check from here on. We decided to just wait and see what would happen next.

As a matter of fact, nothing happened. No fanfare, no big celebration, no church bells ringing peace, but maybe that was because there weren't any churches left. There was no more hope for the future than there had been before, no more food than there had been before, no definite news about the German prisoners of war coming home—just nothing.

I believe that all the adults in Germany certainly had not expected much along these lines, but for a seventeen-year-old optimist the revelation was utterly depressing. Day after day I would wake up, hoping for something to happen. Something nice had to happen—the war was over, wasn't it?

But nothing changed.

By now, that too has become part of daily living. That too one learns to live with, like a cancer that will not heal. . . .

We have begun to look like skeletons, and sometimes I feel like one.

Opa's face is haggard, his Kaiser Wilhelm mustache is drooping, and his hands, which never shook before, have started a certain rhythmical tremble. He hardly ever walks anymore. When he gets up in the morning he just makes it to his chair in the kitchen, and sits there almost all day without moving.

The once so pretty Mrs. Peters has now a hard-looking face. What made her beautiful was the soft roundness and glow of her cheeks. That is now gone and there are sharp lines instead. The two girls are cranky and ill-tempered most of the time. There is nothing for them to do, and we have exhausted our imaginations to coax them into different games. They have played them all.

None of us has as yet dared to go anywhere, and certainly we will not let the children go outside to play except in the backyard, and that is too small to hold any attraction for long.

We have begun to get on each other's nerves.

Mama is the worst off. She has the responsibility for one old man and three children, for despite my seventeen years I still sometimes act like a child. Each of her three children is in a different phase of life: one baby, one child, and one teenager, and therefore each presents a different emotional problem for her to cope with. There are times when I know I am unbearable and make it hard for her, but I can't seem to help myself.

I look at her now beside me sleeping, and momentarily I feel the old love and gentleness in me—my brave, lovely, loving mother. . . .

But oh God, I want to sleep!

I have started to itch terribly. It has been like this for several days now, but each day it gets worse; tonight it almost drives me crazy. I toss and turn. What would I give for a decent meal!

105

Roast beef, chicken, rouladen, pork chops, potatoes, cake . . . the thought of food is unbearable. Right now I would settle for Monika's baby food. . . . What? How can I even think such a thought? Yet each day when I see Monika's food prepared I get angry. She gets the best food, but I am Mama's child too, even if I am seventeen! Don't I have a right to some decent food also?

The itching gets worse—I have got to sleep!

Maybe it will help if I try daydreaming. Until recently it has always helped to get my mind off things I don't want to think about. But lately it does not work too well.

Well, let's see now. . .

When Papa gets back, we will have something to eat. He has always provided for us; we never had to be hungry! Papa . . . where is he? I can feel he is still alive. I know that I could sense it if something had happened to him—I cling to that thought desperately.

———————

I remember when we went to see him in Danzig, where he was stationed for a while. He had asked Mama and Chris (Monika was not yet born) and me to come and spend some time there with him.

He had rented a little attic apartment five minutes away from the North Sea. It was adorable, like a doll's house; everything was so small, and it had the most beautiful view towards the ocean. What a delightful time that was!

We would get up in the morning and eat breakfast. Then, dressed in our bathing suits, we would rush down to the ocean to spend the whole day swimming, loafing in the sun, reading, and relaxing. At dinner time Papa would come to the fence around his barracks at a lonely and hidden spot and hand us a mess kit full of German Air Force dinner. He had found out that he could ask for seconds and took advantage of it. He always had seconds, and I am sure the cook must have acquired an inferiority complex, because despite the large amount of food Papa ate, he never gained weight! It's a shame we could

106

never tell the poor cook that he fed a whole family with his dinner!

It was the nicest summer vacation I have ever spent. Danzig was a most interesting town. It had a great number of very old houses. I spent one afternoon in a home that was four hundred years old, with people still living in it! These old houses had a charm all their own. The town hall was also centuries old. What I remember most of all of that town hall were the ceilings covered with beautiful paintings. Then there was the boardwalk with the restaurants facing the ocean. Having dinner there was a delight, but it was expensive and we did not do that too often. Instead, we preferred little cozy places facing the harbor; they were not only cheaper but also had more atmosphere.

Danzig's main economy consisted of fishing, and so, overlooking the harbor, we saw every type of fishing boat. Some were old and interesting, others new and sleek; some sailboats also added to the romantic view. Young as I was, I have always appreciated beauty, and I was not alone in that. Here and there would be an artist with an easel, painting and forgetting everything around him.

The dish we ordered most of the time was fish in every shape, form, taste, and style. It was freshly caught and was always delicious. Besides, it was very economical—it only cost us five grams of our fat-ration coupon.

But all good times have an end, and the day came when I had to say good-bye.

Mama and Chris stayed there a while longer; actually all the time Papa was stationed there. All too soon Papa's unit was sent to Russia.

Upon my return to Heinrichswalde, I heard rumors. The girls told me that late at night they could sometimes hear heavy guns, maybe cannons. The native population had begun to show worried faces, and some families had gone on a "vacation."

Naturally it concerned us, but we were too busy trying to prepare our graduation papers and studying hard for that important day to spend too much time thinking about it. For our graduation ceremony we had written, composed, and directed a musical that was, in style, international. We were allowed to use every language and all the things we knew about each country to show what we had learned. I enjoyed it thoroughly and was chosen to take the French part. All of us had contributed to the play—it was born of combined effort, and though we did not know that we were doing it, we did actually prove that we were good subjects for a democratic way of life!

Like everything in life, though, our enjoyment was marred by one bitter drop in the wine—our parents were not there. It was hard to take, but maybe it taught us to enjoy the reward of effort and work for its own sake, for achievement, instead of praise. I guess it was much harder on our parents. What parent would not give anything to be present at the day of honor in the life of their child? As it was, we were taught independence the hard way.

For a while it seemed as if it never would, but finally the big day did come, and we sat in class with pounding hearts waiting for the results of the test and the verdict on our papers. If the paper was marked "excellent" the chance of graduating at the top of the class was also excellent, regardless of the mark on the other tests, as long as they were "good."

When my paper turned out with the mark "excellent" I almost jumped up into the air with joy. The paper was the final and decisive factor, and if no one else had an "excellent," I was at the top! As it turned out, there were only three "excellent" marks given; one in English, one in French, and one in German. I had the one in German!

My goal had been reached—now I wanted to go home.

The graduation ceremony was lovely, even though our parents were not present. We just made believe that they were sitting there with us, and in thought and spirit they were. Our teachers sat there beaming with pride, and our foster parents showed no less enjoyment. After all, they too had contributed in some way to our achievement. When it was all over, we thanked all of them for what they had done for us and with us.

Our foster parents, knowing that most of the time we had spent there with them had been hard work, wanted us to stay on a little while longer to enjoy their home town, but only a few of us agreed to do so. We knew that we would be safer where we were. We knew that going home meant nightly air raids and destruction and all the turmoil that came along with being in the middle of a war—but our hearts were always in Berlin.

We said good-bye, not completely without regret, and departed. About three months later, Heinrichswalde belonged to Russia.

If only that terrible itching would stop!

I decide to go and drink a glass of water, hoping it will do something for me and that itching.

I must have fallen asleep over the conclusion of my reminiscence of the past; looking out the window, the first sign of dawn shows. It is still too early to get up, and I go back to bed hoping for some more sleep.

It is impossible. The itching has become unbearable, and I toss and turn, toss and turn. In frustration I finally start crying, and my sobbing wakes up Mama.

She reaches over to me. "Darling, what's wrong? Is something bothering you?"

"I feel like tearing my body apart!"

"Is that itching back again?"

"It's agonizing, Mama! I'm sorry I woke you. . . ."

Mama is already out of bed. "Let's have a look at it." She lights my bedside lamp.

"Oh, dear," she says, concerned, "tomorrow you will have to go and see a doctor. You are covered all over with bumps."

I look at myself. Mama is right—swellings, each one the size of a quarter, cover my entire body.

If I have to go and see a doctor, it means I have to go downtown, back into the Russian jungle! That thought frightens me terribly. I have not set foot outside this house since we came here, other than into the backyard.

"Mama, I don't want to go!"

109

"Well," Mama says calmly, "I doubt whether we will find a doctor who makes house calls. We will be lucky if we find a doctor who has an open practice at all under the present circumstances. But a doctor you must see. I don't know what it is; it is neither measles, nor mumps, nor scarlet fever, nor anything else of that kind, that much I do know."

"But how do I find a doctor?"

"As soon as possible I will go and see Hilda. She could give us the name of her family physician. In any case, she is familiar with the neighborhood. I am sure she will know where we can go."

With that Mama brings a dish of water and a cloth and puts a cold damp cloth over my heated body. She does that for the rest of the night, and it gives me some relief. I doze a little.

During the day, when I am up, the itching is at least bearable, and in order not to think about it, I read a book.

After breakfast, Mama leaves to see Hilda. Since she has to walk, it takes quite a while before she returns, but that same afternoon I am on my way to the doctor's office. Before I leave Mama hugs me and says, "Don't be afraid; Hilda has told me that everything is already fairly calm in that area, hardly any Russians visible. There is even a streetcar in use, it can take you almost halfway there."

If a streetcar is running, then things must be fairly normal, and so my fear diminishes a little.

I get to the doctor's office without incident—everything is just as I have been told. But the office is crowded. It looks as if it would take till tomorrow before the doctor can see me!

Finally, it is my turn.

It is a lady doctor, and after she has examined me she looks at me with compassion.

"What you need I cannot prescribe for you," she says sadly.

"Well, what is it I need?" I am a little impatient and irritated.

"Butter," she says. "You have hunger edema."

She puts me on the weighing scale.

"How much did you weigh six weeks ago?"

"One hundred eighteen pounds."

"You now weigh ninety-eight pounds," she says, "so you have lost twenty pounds."

I must admit it shocks me. I know I have lost weight, but I did not realize it was that much.

"Put a dish of cold water near your bed at night, and if the itching starts, cool yourself with a damp cloth. It's the only thing I know to tell you for relief other than to advise you that you should eat a decent meal—and soon, by hook or by crook."

"That's a lot easier said than done!" I am a little bitter.

"I know," she says.

Well, if I ever am in a position where I have to lose weight, I know just how to do it!

On my way back home, I have to walk past gardens filled with fruit trees. I look at the apples and pears and cherries. None of the fruit is ripe yet, but my mouth waters.

For the first time in my life I have thoughts of stealing. I could climb that fence—easily!

The phrase "Mundraub" comes to my mind. The law says that anybody stealing because of hunger, and stealing only to eat, will not be punished severely. So the thought of punishment does not stop me from climbing that fence. What is it then that makes me go past without doing it?

I don't quite know myself. Maybe pride? Throughout the turmoil all of us have kept one thing that nobody could take away from us—dignity. Whatever it is, something inside me still fights for something—but how much longer will it last?

Mama looks worried when I get home.

"I thought you would never come back. I was worried half out of my mind."

I explain that the doctor's office was crowded like a sardine can.

"Well, what did the doctor say?"

"She says I need butter; I have hunger edema."

Mama stands stock-still, her face is white and motionless.

"Oh dear God, how much more . . .?" she says, and then she

puts her hands in front of her face, turns her back, and I can see her shoulders moving up and down.

I could kick myself. I could have lied! How stupid of me—have I lost all power to think? Why did I have to blurt out the truth like that? Didn't I realize what it would do to her?

Well, the damage is done.

"Mama, things can change," I say, but there is no enthusiasm in my voice. All I can think of is to change the subject.

"You ought to apply for a doctor's license—you did exactly the right thing, Mama. The doctor told me so."

"That's good to know."

I decide after my first stupid mistake not to tell her my thoughts about stealing. It's time I grew up and learned to cope with certain things myself!

I make another decision: from here on in, I am going to go outside when Mama is feeding Monika—the sight of that delicious baby food is more than I can bear. . . .

———

From last night to today I have had a fairly good night's sleep. When the itching started, I would just reach over to the water dish, cool the cloth in it and wring it just moist, then wash my whole body with the soothing cool cloth. Of course, I have to sleep in the nude, but fortunately it is summer.

So I am feeling rather good today and decide to spend most of the day outside. It is beautiful out there; the sun shines, the birds are busy with their nests and with singing, there is a happy hum of bees in the air.

When we came down from the bedroom this morning Lux, our little mutt, was up and about greeting us, his tail wagging, very much himself again.

Oh, that makes me happy!

He was not too badly hurt after all. Mama was right, the bullet had slid right along his skull but did not get through, and he had just been stunned.

At the breakfast table, another surprise is waiting—a glass of milk, made from Monika's ration of dried milk.

"There may be another supply for small infants soon," Mama says, almost apologetically. "Besides, Erna and I will try and get through to home today. We want to see what it looks like, maybe we can even save a few things here and there. From all we have heard, the situation is fairly calm most everywhere by now, and I don't think there is any danger."

Now it is my turn to look pale.

"Mama, you are not serious, are you?"

"Don't worry, we will be back before you know it." She tries to calm me down.

Home, the place that is supposed to create a feeling of longing in people—to me it represents a nightmare. And my mother wants to walk right into that nightmare!

Why does she want to go there? I think, though, that I know the answer. Maybe, somewhere there, where we used to live, is some food.

We know the goat was killed by the Russian soldiers, and when we left we did not know how many chickens were still alive, or how many rabbits, but there is a chance that they may have overlooked some. And we need food.

So Erna and Mama leave; it is still fairly early in the morning. I know that the rest of the day is going to be extremely difficult. Walking back home will take three to four hours, plus three to four hours to get back, plus the time it takes for them to look around. All in all, they will be gone at least ten hours. It will be a day filled with nervous tension until they get back. . . .

But there is another difficult task ahead for me—I will have to feed Monika. Mama does not know how that baby food tempts me, and so she leaves me the task with no misgivings. But I myself am not sure how far I can trust myself—honesty and honor are one thing, and hunger is another.

One little voice inside me is telling me that a seventeen-year-old has as much right to eat as a baby, but when I am holding Monika in my arms, and she looks up at me with her beautiful blue eyes, and her little fat fingers touch my cheek, my hunger is momentarily forgotten.

Opa, the two girls, and I are having our usual supply for

113

lunch. Strangely enough, today I do not feel too hungry; I think the nervous tension is stronger. Opa and I keep looking at the clock, but as is usual in times of stress, it does not seem to move.

After lunch, with Monika back in bed for her nap, I decide to go outside. It is really nice to lie in the chair there and daydream. I wonder how my teacher is getting along . . . would she have ever dreamed that all her efforts would end up in this?

She had such high hopes for me. She wanted me to study journalism, she felt I would be good in this field. And another scholarship was in sight for me. . . .

Now, here we are, a battered, shattered, torn-to-pieces country with no government, no law and order, no food, no hope.

When we were still together in Heinrichswalde, it was not even close to our minds that it could end up this way—but then we were only sixteen . . . a lot of things can happen in one year.

It would be nicer to be back there right now than to be here in our present situation. But enough of my daydreaming; the tasks of the present are waiting. I have to go inside and feed the rest of my companions. Mama has left each person's portion neatly and accurately assigned: one slice of bread, the soup already cooked, and each one is entitled to one-and-a-half ladles full.

By now, of course, eating has become a necessary evil. We eat to stay alive, and even that is questionable with the amount of food we are getting. So it does not make any difference what it tastes like.

"Inga, will you play a game with us?" Chris has her blue eyes fixed on me.

Before I have a chance to answer, Gitta enthusiastically throws in, "Yes, let's play 'doctor.' "

"Doctor" is a game they never seem to tire of. I am the patient, they are nurse and doctor, and they take old rags, usually some baby powder, and any kind of cream they can get hold of, and bandage me up.

"We have no powder and no cream." I am trying to get out

of it; I just don't feel much like playing. I am too nervous about Mama and Erna.

"We can take sand and water," Chris says.

I resign myself to my fate—after all, the two little ones subconsciously must be tense also. It is only fair that I should help to divert them.

"Hey!" Gitta has a bright idea. "We are going to operate on you!"

Good grief—what next?

After I have been placed on the couch (the operating table), they take a pencil with which they give me an injection.

Both of them have handkerchiefs around their faces; Gitta is the nurse, Chris is the doctor. I just pray that they won't get the idea of taking a real knife!

I have a piece of rag placed on my face, then Gitta puts a few drops of water on it for anesthesia. Since I am supposed to be under chloroform, I am also supposed to be asleep, but I do peek for a few seconds to see what they are going to operate with—just in case!

Opa is observing this whole procedure with a grin. It's the first time in many weeks that I have seen him smile—that makes it all worthwhile. . . .

He must have read my mind.

"Chris," he says, and he has a very mischievous glint in his eye, "I have the right knife for you to operate with!"

He holds up the big kitchen knife. The two girls start giggling so hard they have to stop the "operating" for a minute.

Of course, I have jumped up. "Now wait a minute! Here, take this." I have discovered that a spoon handle will serve the purpose just as well!

"Inga, you are supposed to be under anase . . . under anes-teeee . . . well, you are supposed to be asleep!" The two girls are indignant and push me back on the couch.

Opa has put the knife back into a safe place and is still grinning; his mustache is bobbing up and down.

I must admit the two little ones are quite efficient! When it is all over, I have my arm bandaged, having had sand, taking the place of powder, placed between arm and bandage. It rubs, of course, and I decide to take it off as soon as the opportunity arises.

"Now the patient needs medicine, Nurse Gitta," says Dr. Chris.

Gitta has a glass of water and pours it down my throat.

"Take temperissure," Dr. Chris demands.

"Yes, doctor."

Another pencil is put into my mouth.

"Temperissure okay, Doctor Chris." Nurse Gitta is matter-of-fact.

Dr. Chris, benevolently, "You can go home now, patient."

I thank them very much.

"You got to pay us!"

"Oh, of course, of course! I am so sorry!" I write a big "1000" on a small piece of paper.

"Will that cover it, Doctor?"

Dr. Chris and Nurse Gitta nod graciously, and I am released.

I suggest to them that they take a nap. It is far beyond midday naptime, but who knows how long the two mothers will be gone . . .?

They comply with my request without giving me any trouble—strangely cnough!

Opa is lying down on the bed upstairs, napping; Lux and I go outside. I look at the watch; it is three o'clock—they should be home soon. Oh, God, I hope nothing has happened to them—what would I do?

Outside, at least, I always get diverted. There are the trees, the flowers, the birds; now and then a beetle or an ant, working hard at transporting a dead bug to its home base, crawls by.

Make-believe, my favorite game, has to help once again. I pretend to be a famous opera star with a magnificent voice, and right now I am standing on a stage singing, and when I am finished everyone will start applauding, bringing down the house. . . . Then I will get showered with bouquets, and re-

116

porters will come in and want my life story—my life story? Why is there always a flaw in a pretty picture?

My life story. Ha ha! Some story . . . how would you like to hear it, Mr. Reporter. I was born on the fifth of February, 1928, in the beautiful city of Berlin, except that it is not beautiful anymore. Look around you: destruction, death, hunger, despair . . . we will never capitulate! . . . Who is my father, you ask? My father is a hard-working, ordinary man, just like you. . . . Where is he, you ask? I don't know. I don't know if he is still alive even. . . . My mother? My mother, Mr. Reporter, has gone to dig up (not only literally speaking) some food for us, because we are slowly starving to death. . . . Where is she looking? In a place that I once called home. . . .

No! I am not going to think about it, I am not! You ask why not? Very simple—it hurts! Let's talk about my childhood, it was a very nice one. Oh yes, it was pleasant . . . until we were evacuated when I was twelve. Oh God, I was so homesick. . . .

The trouble started before that—in September, 1939. I had only one playmate, a boy whose name was Rudi. He was twelve.

Our first reaction to the news that Germany was at war was a mixture of fear of the unknown and excitement: we could do something for our country! We were not quite sure what, but do something we would.

We ran outside, expecting foreign airplanes to appear instantly, and we were ready to defend our country. We looked up into the sky; but the sky had not changed one bit, it was peaceful and quiet.

We were relieved and disappointed, all in one. It did not last long. During the next few days, one of the other tenants was appointed to be Air Raid Guard Warden, and when he noticed our eagerness he directed us to help him build an air raid shelter. Ah, finally we were needed!

One of the more strongly built basements was selected to be the air raid shelter. The two of us worked like little beavers to make it not only more secure, but also a little more comfortable. We had a hunch that we would probably spend a few nights there and, being our age, planned to make the most of it. Imagine, we would be up talking like adults at night!

So we carried sandbag after sandbag to be placed in front of the basement window, set up a drinking-water canister with a supply of cups, scattered a few candles around and matches, collected chairs and a table from the tenants, and thoroughly cleaned up the basement. It was hard work, and when it was all finished, not only all the tenants but we, too, were surprised at the result! The final touch was a couple of games we decided to sacrifice for the country by placing them in the basement, just in case we got bored!

Well, we never quite got out of it what we put in. During the first few years there was hardly ever an air raid, but there were many false alarms. Later, when all hell broke loose night after night, and a few times we were very close to being hit, we decided that that basement was not the safest place to be in.

This time the adults had to do the work—it was beyond our capacity. Approximately one hundred yards away from the house and twenty or thirty yards away from the canal, the tenants dug a huge hole in the ground which was to replace the cellar shelter.

My grandparents had on their grounds large stacks of railroad ties, placed there by the Magistrate of Berlin and intended for future building purposes. The war interrupted these plans, and the railroad ties were just waiting to be used. We were able to convince the Magistrate that they were best applied to build a deep, secure, outside shelter. Within a few weeks it was finished; and all of us felt very much relieved to be out of the basement. It was better to think of instant death if we suffered a direct hit, than about a death trap where we might be buried alive under a heap of walls, pipes, bricks, and furniture. . . .

By that time Rudi and I had become a little older and also a little wiser. It was not a game any more—we had become aware of the reality of war. . . .

One more incident that took place during the first years of the war stands out in my memory very vividly.

118

I was about twelve years old then. Mama and I were listening to the news. After it was over there was to be a broadcast of one of Adolf Hitler's speeches given in the Olympic Stadium. I cannot remember what it was all about, but Mama was listening very intently, and as the speech went on and on, her face grew more worried every minute.

Finally I, too, could not help but pay attention, as Mr. Hitler's voice became louder and louder, and I heard him scream at the top of his voice," . . . and so I ask you, people of Germany: Do you want total war?" And the thousands in the stadium were screaming back, as if hypnotized en masse, "Yes! Yes! Yes! Heil! Heil! Heil! Heil! Heil!" in a devilish rhythm of frenzy.

"My God!" Mama said. "Are these people out of their minds? They cannot possibly be sane. Don't they know what that means?"

You see now, Mr. Reporter, how a few thousand people can ruin the lives of millions . . . or does it take just one person? If you look around, you can see that Germany got its "total war." It could not have been more "total." . . . Except, where do I fit in? Or my parents? Or the millions who did not want this? But most of all the thousands of children who are always, in times like these, the real victims?

Anyway, I don't want to talk about that, I want to talk about pretty things. . . . Now why did you have to ask me that question? Of course I can't tell you what I plan to do in the future! But I know what I am not going to do: I am not going back to that place! I don't even want to think about it. . . .

Good-bye, Mr. Reporter. No, don't mention it. Oh sure, I'll sing a song. Let me see now—I do know some nice songs, I had happy times, too, you know. Okay, here is a song of happy times.

> *Wind and ocean waves sang me a lullaby,*
> *And the seagulls took my dreams up high into the sky.*
> *Noticed, when I'd wonder if I'd ever see*
> *All the magic beauty far beyond the sea.*

119

And though life fulfilled my dreams and showed the
  world to me.
All I ever think of is my home across the sea,
Where my heart was happy, where the seagulls fly,
And the ocean waves sang me a lullaby. . . .

It's funny—most people sing when they are happy. I don't have to be happy to sing: a pretty song always distracts me.

So here I am sitting outside singing. It is getting close to evening, the birds are busy gathering their supper. The sun has dimmed its light to a gentle orange shade. Inside the house, the two girls are playing noisily, and here Lux is busy digging in the ground, barking at something invisible. I guess he plays make-believe too!

What am I griping about! The world is not too bad. Peace, real peace will be here soon; we will have something to eat, life will be back to normal, Papa will come home, and any minute now Mama and Erna will be back . . . will they? . . .

I decide to check on Monika. Mama has taken the pram along with her to carry whatever goodies she comes up with. There is bound to be something left at home that we can use. Anyway, we put Monika in our bed, after we had secured it with furniture so she would not fall out.

The two girls have already picked up Monika and are playing with her. But I do wish Erna and Mama would come home soon.

I hear some movement outside and rush to the window. Thank God! There they are!

But something is wrong—Mama is pushing the pram in which Erna is lying limp, with her eyes closed.

I run to the door, the two girls right behind me.

Gitta sees her mother. "Mommy, Mommy! What's wrong with Mommy?" she screams.

Erna opens her eyes. "Nothing, darling," she says. "Please don't worry, I just don't feel good, I am just a little nauseated."

I look at Mama. Her face is not white but almost yellow, so is Erna's.

Mama, Gitta, and I help Erna out of the pram and lead her towards the couch. She lies down and closes her eyes again. "Please leave me alone for a while."

"What happened?" I whisper so that the two little ones won't hear me.

"Later," Mama whispers back. She turns to Gitta. "Your mother is sick from the long walk we had, Gitta. She needs rest right now, so why don't you two girls go outside and play for a while. When we go to bed tonight, you will sleep with us, Gitta, just for tonight."

That satisfies Gitta; she hugs her mother, and then the two girls go outside to play.

Mama is sitting down now, and she is shaking.

I get her a glass of water, she gulps it down.

"Erna was raped!" Mama says.

"Oh God, how dreadful! Is she going to be all right?" The question may sound inane, but whether a woman who had been raped would be all right or not depended upon how many Russians had participated. Also I could not help but remember what happened to Mrs. Schulman. . . .

"I'll tell you more later," Mama says. "Right now, I have some good news for Opa."

Opa sits up, eager.

"You heard from Mother, Lisa? Tell me, did you hear from Mother?"

Mama hugs him. "Opa, Omi is all right!"

She tells us that they had no trouble getting back to our house. It was a terribly long walk, but they were not molested. But what a shock to see the devastation in our home! Inside there was nothing left at all, no sheets, no curtains, no towels, no dishes, not a single spoon, no mattresses; even some of the furniture had disappeared. All Omi's chickens were gone, all the rabbits, not a single living animal remained except one lonely little rabbit, hopping around trying to find some grass. They caught it and put it in the pram. They were going to bring it home and then ask Mr. Stillman to kill it for us. We had never done anything like this before, but we did need food.

121

After they had done this (and I had to smile a little when I pictured the two ladies trying to catch that poor little rabbit) they went over to see if Mrs. Stromberg was possibly back home. They were lucky—Mrs. Stromberg greeted them enthusiastically.

"Oh, wait till I tell your mother! Wait till I tell her you are all right!"

She calmed down a little.

"She has been almost out of her mind, not knowing if you were all alive or not. Opa is all right, isn't he?"

"Oh yes," Mama replied, "but where is Omi?"

Mrs. Stromberg told them that after we had all departed, Omi finally left her hiding place behind the hedge and the shed. She decided to go and see if she could stay with a relative further down in the city. On her way she met Mrs. Stromberg, who was standing in front of the destroyed bridge, undecided what to do. The two ladies decided to go back and hide in the basement for a few days, then try again.

After a few days a temporary bridge was built across the canal, and they went to see Aunt Grete, the relative with whom Omi wanted to stay. Aunt Grete had been lucky—nothing in her home had been destroyed or looted, and she was more than happy to have Omi stay with her. Mrs. Stromberg, knowing that Omi was well taken care of, decided to return to her own home, though, lucky for us!

Of course, Mama was tempted to go right away and see Omi, but both women were afraid that they could not make it there and then back to us in the same day. Mrs. Stromberg promised them that within the next few days she would try to visit Omi and tell her where we were.

So, with good news, a little rabbit, and in better spirits, they decided to return to our temporary home. When they arrived at the bridge that led to Tegel, a man in a rowboat came towards them across the water.

"It's faster this way, ladies," he volunteered. "You go across

122

the bridge with that pram, and it's going to take you twice as long." He pointed to the other side of the river. "See, I have taken all those people over there across already. A few more won't make any difference."

Mama and Erna were pleased. They were very weary by now. They gladly accepted the man's offer and thanked him.

It was a dirty, ugly trap! As they landed on the other side, they joined others like themselves standing on the bank. The group was suddenly confronted with a handful of Russians: one officer and several soldiers.

Erna and Mama both felt like running, but at that moment a Russian with a gun motioned to the group to follow him. He smiled, and everybody heaved a sigh of relief, hoping that maybe it would be just some kind of routine check. They were led into a kind of barracks, where the Russian officer was waiting.

Everybody was carefully scrutinized. Mama noticed that the officer's eyes were fixed more often on Erna's face and body than on any of the others. The officer said something to the other Russian, who motioned to all the men in the group to go with him.

From the refugees coming from the eastern section of Germany we had heard of incidents where the men were separated from the women and shot, and the women were raped. We also knew that these were not just propagandistic horror stories, but cruel plain facts. The people who told us these things were still in shock. . . .

Now here was a similar situation.

The men turned pale, the women started crying and holding on to their husbands. But the Russian with the gun calmed them down temporarily; the Russian's smile seemed fairly sincere.

After the men were outside, the Russian officer left and the soldier with the gun came back into the room. He motioned to Erna to follow him.

123

Erna knew what would happen.

Mama bravely followed them; once outside Mama cried, "Erna, come on, let's make a run for it!" and started off full speed with her pram. She soon realized that Erna was not with her, so she went back. Erna was moving like a sleepwalker, her face expressionless, pale, eyes open but not seeing anything. She followed the Russian soldier into another barrack. A few moments later the Russian soldier came back out, alone.

Mama was close to screaming; she wanted to run, but she could not leave Erna to her fate just like that.

After an eternity, Erna appeared in the doorway.

Mama rushed towards her. "Are you all right?"

Erna nodded and held on to Mama.

"Come on, let's go!" Mama urged her.

"I can't," Erna gasped. Mama had to strain her ears to hear her. Suddenly Erna started vomiting, her body shaking almost in convulsions.

When she had finished, Mama put Erna into the pram and pushed her all the way home.

"I asked her on the way back home, 'Erna, why in God's name didn't you run with me?' " Mama's hand, picking up the cup of ersatz coffee I have made for her, is trembling. "She said 'Gitta has already lost two fathers. I could not risk leaving her an orphan. . . .' and I can see her point. We all know that they do kill women and no one ever knows when. . . ."

There was no need for me to ask about the little rabbit—it got its freedom.

"But Mama, you said the Russian soldier came out again after a few moments. . . . Who did it?"

"It was the Russian officer. He had waited in the barrack after he had ordered the soldier to bring Erna to him."

So it's still going on; no safety yet . . . I hope to heaven that the family who owns this home is going to stay in West Germany for a long time to come yet. . . .

124

"Let's go to bed, Mama."

"Yes."

We call in the children, who protest a little, but when they see how tired Mama looks, they oblige. We don't bother tonight to tell them to wash up. We are glad when they are in bed.

Slowly, wearily, Mama walks up the stairs.

Another day is over.

8

TODAY YOU MUST RETURN!

I decide to sleep late.

After Mama's return last night she told us, hurriedly, that today in a grocery store in the neighborhood, there would be a supply of milk for anyone with a child under twelve years of age and five hundred grams (one pound) of bread per person. Also, we were supposed to get some lard. Of course, in cases like this, one would have to get up very early and be at the store hours before it opened, for there would be hundreds of people standing in line waiting their turn.

Mama must have left at five o'clock in the morning.

My decision to sleep late does not work out too well. The thought of a slice of freshly baked bread with some lard on it, and possibly a kind of milk and flour porridge, is nearly driving me out of my mind. I can almost taste it. Our own supply of bread had not lasted very long. The later supplies of bread and milk for the children were small and erratic and getting them always involved hours of waiting in line. The mathematics of our rations are very accurate: each slice of bread weighs about twenty-five grams, each loaf of bread can be cut into twenty to twenty-five slices of bread—with four slices of bread a day, that loaf lasts about five days.

Of course, one never knows when the next supply will be available. All in all, it is too much to die and too little to live—so people merely exist. . . .

No sound comes from Opa's room. Well, it is still fairly early—he is better off sleeping. Today, after the good news about my grandmother, he will probably sleep better and longer with the tension about her fate taken from his mind.

The two girls are still asleep too. They were awake until quite late last night. The newness of sleeping together was intriguing to them and they made the most of it. Now they are naturally tired. Just as well.

I wash and get dressed and go downstairs.

Erna, who is usually up early, is quite understandably asleep after yesterday's ordeal. She probably did not sleep all night and is now exhausted. Usually she went along with Mama for supplies.

When I get downstairs, only Lux wakes up and greets me, tail wagging. It is bad enough in normal times to be the only one awake when everyone is still sleeping, but when one is hungry it is even more distressing. Why on earth isn't Mama home yet? We could be sitting here eating. . . .

I take a book to try and read, but I have read it before. I can't concentrate.

If Mama gets a supply of milk, we can make that porridge with flour and saccharin, since she still has some dried milk left for Monika. But it will take time to make it!

I think when she comes home with that bread I'll grab it and bite into it without asking. . . . I don't think I can stand to wait for the porridge. . . .

Of course, there is one more thing I can do.

I could open the suitcase with Monika's baby food in it and eat that. I know (although Mama does not know that I know) where she has hidden the key. . . .

What a terrible thought!

How can I do something like that when I know how vital it is for Monika to have that food. But Mama is going to get milk for her . . . and I don't have to eat it all, just a little bit, just a few spoonfuls, just a taste. . . .

Nobody will let a baby starve, not even the Russians. There

127

will always be some food for a baby. Besides, who has the hunger edema? Monika or I?

I do! Didn't the doctor say, "by hook or by crook"? Is it my fault that we don't have anything to eat? Who has the right to decide who should go hungry and who should eat? And I am hungry.

It is not very hard to open the little suitcase. The baby food is in a container that has the picture of a round-faced, smiling, rosy-cheeked baby on it. I ignore it, and Monika's face is a faint, floating image for only the flash of a second.

Lux looks at me. Is he interested in what I am doing? Is he looking at me with disapproval?

Ridiculous! He is just a dog.

Anyway, out you go! I don't need any witnesses. . . .

I open the door and let him out.

I must say the food tastes better than I remembered it. But I find it extremely hard to stop. I cannot eat it all! I cannot! . . .

Well, it is done.

The suitcase is back where it belongs, the spoon is washed and put back into place, and I have left most of the baby food.

At this point I don't feel guilty.

Again I take the book I have already read, and again I cannot concentrate. A question has come up that I had not anticipated before: shall I tell Mama what I did, or shall I keep it secret? I did not eat so much that it would be noticeable at first glance (at least so I think), so why tell her?

But all my life I have told my mother the misdeeds I committed when I was little, and I always told her the truth. In this case, she would not scold me if I told her; she has much too much understanding for human failings . . . but it would hurt her. It would make me feel better if I went up to her and said, "Look, I did this, I could not help myself, or did not want to help myself," or whatever, and the air would be clear and it would be forgotten soon.

Not telling her would mean that I would never forget it.

But I did it, and if the penalty for it would be that I alone would have to live with this, then it would be necessary for me not to tell her.

Still, I would not lie to her. If she asked me, I would have to tell her.

There is nothing like being busy when one has problems, and so I decide to clean up a little. Erna is awake now; she still looks pale and withdrawn, but she seems all right otherwise. We do not discuss yesterday's events, and before we know it Mama is home.

She looks very disappointed.

"I did get the bread and the milk," her voice is tired, "but I did not get the 'Butterschmalz' (lard). The third person in front of me got the last. . . ."

"Don't be too disappointed, Lisa." Erna tries to comfort her, although it is not too easy for her to conceal her own feelings. "Maybe there will be another ration soon. Then we can take turns. I will leave even earlier, stand in line for a few hours, then you can come and relieve me and wait till it's our turn. That way we could make it."

"That sounds good," I put in, but I feel very uncomfortable.

Mama, after she has given us our supplies, is beginning to prepare Monika's food. She looks at the can and its contents longer than she normally does. Before she dips in the spoon to take out the right amount, she hesitates for a few seconds. She does not look at me, says nothing, and continues in her preparations, but I know that she knows. . . .

I don't want to think about my misdeed. Punishment or reward comes in ways different from the way we expect it. As if to prove that point, later on in the afternoon there is a knock on the door.

"Hello there!" It is the friendly voice of Mr. Stillman, and he is holding in his hand a fairly large bag.

We are always glad to see him, except that until the first few moments are over we are tense, fearing that he will say we have to leave, that his friends are coming back. . . .

Today he says, "I have something for you. Here, look."

He gives Mama the paper bag.

She takes one look and then she runs over to him and hugs him.

"Oh, Mr. Stillman, oh, you are an angel. Thank you, thank you so much!" Then she turns to us. "Guess what! We have potatoes—a whole bag of potatoes!"

Well, Mr. Stillman, whether he likes it or not, gets a hug from all of us, although I personally feel guilty and don't feel I deserve this unexpected fortune. In my mind I debate whether I should tell the others that I don't want to eat any potatoes, but they would think I was deathly ill if I did. So, with the optimism of youth, I decide that maybe God wants to show me He has forgiven me. . . .

Oh, what a feast!

We have boiled the potatoes, and since we have a bottle of cod-liver oil that has been guarded by Erna like a crown jewel, we can make fried potatoes. Of course the oil has to be used sparingly—we have a little brush with which we put the cod-liver oil into the frying pan. And then we eat!

The rest of the potatoes are used slightly differently. We peel them after they have been thoroughly scrubbed, and boil them. Then we make a gravy from a little cod-liver oil with flour browned in the frying pan with water, salt, and pepper added. After the potatoes are used up we put the peelings through a mincer and make little patties which we fry in cod-liver oil in the frying pan.

Our menu for three days is planned—three days of joy!

Thank you, Mr. Stillman!

One more week has gone by.

Life has been fairly peaceful, if one can call it that. We are back in the same routine of mathematical assignment of food, and are getting even thinner, nothing else has changed from the first day we arrived. . . . We are waiting, although no one quite knows what we are waiting for—for a tremendous bang with which we will be informed that finally things are changing? For a mailman coming to the door with a letter from Papa saying he is on his way home? For Father Christmas with a big bagful of food? Or, oh horrible thought, for Mr. Stillman coming to the door saying, "You must leave now. . . "?

The worst part in our situation is that we have no tasks. Work would help, but finding work means finding the Russians again. Besides, is there work available for anyone yet?

Sometimes we feel as if we are living in confinement. The whole country is one large open prison, surrounded by a sea of hostility, indifference, and hopelessness. . . .

From the house next door on our left, for the last two days have come sounds of activity, and once in a while we can catch the disturbing and tantalizing fragrance of cooking food. Have the owners come back? In that case, the war must be over completely, or how had they managed to get back home? Also, it means that the people who own the house we are living in could be on their way back. . . . It's best not to think about that. I will never go back there—never, never, never. . . .

Up to now we have not seen the people next door. But outside it is pretty; outside I can pretend it is all mine. Outside I can daydream all I want to, I can sit and dream and shut out the world. After all, the sky, the sun, moon, stars, trees, flowers, animals, the wind—God created them for all people, and so they do belong to me. Some day I will go and see other countries . . . some day? I still have hope for the future? Why not? Nothing lasts forever, not even the bad times. . . .

First country to visit . . . Italy . . . Venice of course. I always loved the water. How wonderful it must be to live near the water, especially at night, when the lights shine and glitter, like a beautiful lady dressed up for a gala evening with diamonds and pearls and emeralds and rubies. . . .

131

. . . And Naples. Don't I know a song about Naples? How does it go. . . ?

O mia bella Napoli, du Stadt am blauen Meer,
O mia bella Napoli, mein Herz ist sehnsuchtsschwer. . . .
In mir tönt eine Melodie, wo ich auch sei—
O mia bella Napoli: Dir bleib ich treu. . . .

I am singing it with the full power of my not too beautiful voice, and as always when I am singing, I do not notice anything going on around me.

So I do not notice that two eyes are watching me, and when the voice of my next-door neighbor finally comes through to me, I stand still, frozen. I cannot run, although I want to—the voice is not German.

They are the sounds, the horrible, hated, feared, ugly sounds of the "liberators"—they are Russian. But the voice is that of a woman. She is standing on the doorstep of the adjoining house.

At first I am relieved, but then I remember that Mrs. Schulman's husband was killed by a Russian soldier and a Russian woman together, and I also remember that it had been Russian women who said, "We want to steal!"—and when Mama objected, they had complained to the Russian soldier with the machine gun, who in turn pointed the gun at Mama. . . .

I still have not been able to move. I am confronted with the enemy, and the enemy is my next-door neighbor!

Here is my chance to throw into her face what I think of her and her Russian countrymen!

I think I will shower on her everything that I have held bottled up for weeks. I will tell her what kind of so-called "human beings" her country has sent into another country. I will throw into her face what crimes have been committed, I will. . . .

"War nix gutt" she says with a smile that momentarily disarms me.

132

I look at her more closely: Blonde hair, blue eyes, round face, chubby figure. She looks a little bit like a blonde Paula, my Ukrainian friend from other times. Her slight resemblance to Paula makes me forget what I want to tell her. Besides, I realize she would probably not understand me!

She holds something in her hand, which she now offers to me. It is a beautiful red polished apple.

All of a sudden she is not the enemy anymore, but her resemblance to Paula and her friendly gesture make her slightly familiar.

I am beginning to relax a little.

"You, from Ukraine?" I ask her.

She nods, "Kiev."

"My papa, Kiev," I tell her.

"Ah, da, da!" Her voice sounds cheerful, and it is not because my father has been in Kiev, but because we have realized that we are, somehow, communicating.

For about an hour we try to talk to each other, and it is not always easy. Several times, even with the help of sign language, we do not get the message right, and we end up laughing.

I find out that her name is Ljuba, she is twenty-three (although she looks slightly older), and she is waiting to return to her country. There is more she tries to communicate to me, but the language difficulty is too great.

Somehow I get the impression that there are other people living next door with her, but I don't get the relationships: uncle, or father, or brother, or friend!

The fact that there is a Russian male living next door does not exactly add to my feeling of security—although I do not believe that she would just stand by and watch a young girl being raped. But my past experience is still vivid in my memory, and her friendliness cannot quite overcome my mistrust.

I go back into the house with mixed emotions. "Who was that out there with you?" Mama asks.

"A Russian girl. She is living there temporarily with some other people."

133

"Oh dear . . . well, there is nothing we can do about it. But maybe it would be best from now on if you stayed in the house."

"I have already thought about that, Mama. You're right."

That takes one more thing from me; the thought of being cooped up in the house is not too pleasant.

I share my apple with the two little ones, who are quite delighted. If anything, eating the piece of apple makes me more hungry than ever before. . . .

Our bread ration is in a disastrous situation. We have only enough left for today and half of tomorrow, and there has been no word about a new issue. The future looks gloomier than ever before.

The only clothing we possess is what we were wearing when we left home. I wore my best dress, but right now it looks terrible. I have worn it every day for weeks. Washing it has always been a problem. I walk around in my slip late at night while I wash it, hoping that next morning it will be dry. I get up early and iron it before anybody else is up and put it back on. Underwear is not that much of a problem. You wear your dress while the underwear dries. Wear and tear is slowly showing; in addition to that, we were all several pounds heavier when we bought our clothing! As a result, it fits neither here nor there, and all of us look as if we are wearing someone else's clothes. I am very tired of that once so pretty and well-liked dress. . . .

And still no definite news about Germany's future and fate. Once in a while, when Mama and Erna go to get the few rations issued, they pick up rumors—but some of these are so contradictory that we do not pay much attention to them.

Peace is supposed to be here, but what kind of peace is it?

The biggest question is: Will Berlin stay indefinitely under Russian control, or will the other Allies, America and England, claim a share?

The biggest part of my prayer every night contains a request for the Americans or the British to come to Berlin. . . . They are

134

civilized people, they would not permit raping, looting, and killing. But at this point no one knows anything.

We shall just have to wait a little bit longer.

"Inga, will you go and see who is at the door?" Mama is feeding Monika, and she looks surprised. Who would come to see us?

For a moment I hesitate—suppose it is a Russian? But they don't knock politely!

I go to the door. As I open it, I am so stunned that I cannot say anything. I just stand there, staring, until finally the beloved voice of Omi says, "Well, aren't you going to let us in?"

In all the turmoil I have not cried except for the night when the itching almost drove me insane—now, as I am hugging Omi, we are both crying.

Mama has heard the familiar voice. She puts Monika down and comes running. Opa is holding himself up at the kitchen table and all he says is, "Mother, Mother, it's you, oh, thank God." In his eyes are tears; it is the first time in my life I have seen him cry. The tears are collecting in his mustache and look like dewdrops in wilted grass. The two little ones have come running and hang on Omi's skirts, and everyone talks at once—it's quite a commotion! There is a lot of hugging, sniffling, and shuffling going on, and no one quite hears what the others are saying.

Suddenly I catch a glance of someone else standing in the open doorway. At first I see nothing but a huge bouquet of tree branches; lindentree branches. There is a big box standing on the floor, and from behind the tree branches a voice says, "Hello, Angel!"

"Paula! Mama, Paula is here too!"

Paula is no exception; she is crying also.

We embrace, laughing and crying at the same time. At last we settle down and start talking.

"Wait a minute!" Paula says, and she pushes the box towards us. "I have something for you!"

135

We open up the box, and we almost crush Paula to death when we see what it contains—FOOD!

Butter, cheese, sugar, dried milk, some bread, a few cans of meat.

Life is changing after all!

The food that Paula has brought along is, of course, the life-saver in the truest meaning of the word, but an emotional life-saver is the bouquet of lindentree branches Paula has picked for me. She remembered how I loved trees, and especially my old linden tree in front of the house. I did not dare ask her if they came from home (I know it could not be possible; I saw the branches of our tree all charred), but does it matter?

I pick the prettiest vase I can find in the house and arrange the branches in it; as my fingers touch the wealth of green, the velvety softness of the leaves, life itself is saying, "I am!"

But life also has a strange way of making itself known. It starts at birth: pain delivers us into this world, and it is grief that delivers us closer and more inseparably than anything else into the hands of God. . . .

Suddenly and quite unexpectedly a multitude of feelings shoot up—grief over all the victims that war (or man?) has created; the uncounted and countless tragedies that have occurred; the torn-apart families; the children who do not understand why they have no parents or why they have to go hungry; the men who have borne indescribable hardships in countries they would rather have entered as visitors, not fighting men; the soldiers who came home to find their families dead, killed in an air raid; the senseless destruction of centuries-old beauty; and the millions of people who are wandering about aimlessly, looking for only one thing: a home and peace . . . just like us. . . .

I had promised myself not to think about home. Now, with the leaves so close to touch, a door opens that I thought was closed. I am homesick!

There I see our house: warm, inviting, friendly; the flower boxes in front of the windows where the birds came to eat; the pretty red bricks; the veranda where Omi and Opa used to play cards and where Opa and I would play "cheating"; the lilac bush outside. On summer evenings, when the bittersweet fragrance of freshly cut grass and the delicate perfume of lilac blossoms softened the cool evening air, Papa used to play the accordion and I would sing along with him. I remember the fruit trees giving me a choice: cherries, plums, peaches, apples, or pears. I remember the canal, which always reflected the evening sun, and my linden tree, decades old, with a kind of treehouse in its top whcre as a child I used to sit and sing. . . .

> *Outside, where road and fence meet,*
> *There grows a linden tree.*
> *It held within its shadow*
> *So many dreams for me. . . .*
> *Then through the world I wandered—*
> *But everywhere I roam,*
> *I hear its gentle whisper:*
> *"Come home, my friend, come home. . . ."*
>
> *Storms, bitter cold and icy,*
> *Opposed me on my way.*
> *Go on!—Can't you forget them—*
> *The linden leaves' soft sway?. . .*
> *Now, everywhere I'm walking,*
> *No matter where it be,*
> *It says: "Return, old fellow—*
> *You'll find your peace with me. . . ."*

And now, that is all gone—forever. Dead. Destroyed. Stamped on. Gone.

I don't want anyone to notice that I am disturbed. I have never liked to make a display of my feelings in front of others. I manage to say a quick "excuse me a minute" and I run upstairs. There on my bed, I am not only crying because I am sad and hungry for a glimpse of normalcy, a touch of gentleness in this

wicked and tortured world, I am crying because the picture of
Christ, saying "Father forgive them, for they know not what
they do," stands before me as big as the world. . . .

Mama's good, tender hands touch my hair.

"My darling," she says, "I know why you are crying; it is
good that you do. . . . But life goes on, someday it will be
better. You must look into the future with hope. Life is never
at a standstill. Every second something changes, God has arranged it that way. . . . Sometimes it's for better, sometimes it's
for worse; what is good about it is that it changes. Only when
the world and life stand stock-still, and there is no change at
all—then it is time to despair, because that is the final death.
Wherever you are in life, whatever situation you are in, whatever fate may do to you, never forget that as long as there is
change, there will be hope."

I have to stop crying so that I can hear what she is saying.

"Mother, I want to go home, but I'm afraid, I'm terribly
afraid. . . !'"

"We all are," Mama says. "But we must face reality. We have
got to go back some day. Nothing will happen. Look at all of
us, we are all still alive! Isn't that already a miracle?"

I nod.

"All right, no more crying now. Wash your face with cold
water and come down. We are going to have a feast!"

The beauty about being young is that grief is short-lived.

We are indeed having a feast. I don't think any meal has ever
tasted better than the one I am eating today. For weeks on end
we have not even seen butter, cheese, sugar, or meat.

Paula is the "Queen of the May" and is enjoying every
minute of it!

We ask Paula how she found Omi.

"Simple," she says with a big, beaming smile, "I go look for
Angel. War nix good, I know. Me frightened for Angel. Mrs.

138

Stromberg says you all okay. She tell me where Omi is. I visit Omi, Omi says we go visit all. Me say okay—and here we am!"

We have to rearrange our sleeping situation.

Paula and I sleep together, Mama and Omi sleep together, little Chris is fairly comfortable on two lounge chairs put together. Opa, Mrs. Peters, and Gitta are left unchanged.

Frankly, I would not have minded sleeping on the floor. With Paula around, nothing is going to happen to us; she speaks Russian, she is brave, and she is loyal.

What was it that Mama said about change? Of course everything does; with that thought and for the first time in weeks without hunger pangs, I go to sleep.

For a while, life is not too bad. I have companionship in Paula, who is closer to my age than anyone else around me. We have a little more food than we had before; Opa has started to show some signs of life and being happy again since Omi's return. All in all, the world looks brighter than it has for some time now, except for Omi's tales.

She brings us up-to-date with the present situation in the city. She has been told of some awful events by the occupants of the apartment house where she had found temporary refuge. Looting, raping, and murdering were common during the first days of the conquest. If the husbands of the wives or the fathers of the daughters who were the victims of the raping Russians tried to defend their families, they were just taken away and never heard of—fate unknown. . . . In many cases it was not only one Russian raping one woman but several standing in line waiting for her, until the victim was half-dead. One woman told Omi that some of her relatives underwent an indescribably sordid ordeal: when the husband of the woman who was intended for rape went for the Russian with his bare fists, they were kind enough not to kill him. They tied him up in a chair and forced him to watch the whole procedure. . . . After the sixth Russian was finished with the woman, the husband was half-insane. As for the wife . . .

139

Family suicides were not uncommon.

The physicians were busier than ever before. They had to take care of raped women with their insides torn; and injections and medication were given en masse, at least as much as was available.

Most of the time the women had to cope with the situation alone; their husbands or fathers were away somewhere else in the world in prison camps or dead. . . . The young girls who had never had any sexual intercourse were the worst off. . . .

It was not a rumor, but apparently an official fact, that the Russian "Kommandantura" (High Command) had issued a statement that the Russian troops were permitted to do as they pleased with the population: there would not be any punishment for looting, raping, or murdering. . . .

". . . We, the people. . . ."

We were not treated like people, we were "game" that could be hunted and killed.

If you live in the jungle, you learn the rules of the jungle, and the most important one is to hide from your enemy. We, the people of Berlin, learned that soon and well.

We learned how to protect ourselves. We learned to hide in attics, in hidden corners in basements, behind walls, inside wardrobes, under beds. I would never make a good hunter because I know what the wild animal feels when it is being hunted.

But we also learned one more thing, and we will never forget it: we will never be believers in the so-called "Paradise" of communism!

So far our family has been lucky. We count our blessings that we left home when we did. We know that had we stayed, none of us would be alive now.

We also know that some day soon we will have to return.

———————

"Don't worry, though, Lisa," Omi is reassuring us now. "That part about the 'open city' was in effect only a few days. Things have calmed down considerably since then. There are still incidents taking place, but it is not one-tenth as bad as it was."

"If only Walter was home," Mama replies. Her voice is a little shaky.

"Man okay!" Paula puts in with optimism. "Man come home soon—you see!"

"Let's go outside a while, Paula," I coax her. The conversation is getting too emotional. I don't want to cry again.

She and I are lying on a blanket in the grass and look up into the sky.

"Pretty." I have caught a ladybug. I let it walk from one hand onto the other.

Paula leaps up. "You pretty too, Angel," Paula says. "You watch; Russian soldier nix good. Me watch for you, me hit them, bang, bang, bang!" She makes a slapping motion with her hand: left to right, right to left, left to right.

I have to laugh a little. Paula is tall and on the chubby side, and the way she is standing there now she resembles very much a goddess of wrath and revenge in her anger. I could imagine that a Russian soldier might think twice before getting her very mad. Besides, she is Ukrainian, and they would not dare touch her.

"Will you go back to Russia?" I ask her, and I hope she says no.

A cloud has come over her face.

"No," she says. "Me never go back to Russia. Me love Germany, me have friends here: Angel, Mamma, Ommi, Oppa, others. . . ."

We are interrupted in our conversation by our next-door Ukrainian neighbor, who greets us across the garden fence.

The two girls discover that they are both Ukrainian, and for a while they are talking and I don't understand any of their conversation. After a while Paula indicates to me that we have been invited to visit the girl next door.

I take that with mixed emotions. Paula is my friend, but I don't know the other girl. Still, Paula is with me, and so long as she is, she will not let anything happen to me.

141

"Mama, Paula and I will be next door for a few minutes," I yell quickly into the house, then we climb over the fence and walk into the house. The girl shows us around from room to room.

Most of the things inside are either already packed or being packed. I don't quite get the situation. The girl shows us certain items, which she apparently likes, with the pride of ownership. It appears to me as if she has lived here for several years, worked hard to acquire each piece, and is proud of all the pretty things she owns.

But how did she get all this without being able to speak German? What kind of job did she have that would pay such a nice salary, so that in a few years she was able to acquire all this?

She finally displays a whole wardrobe filled with good, fairly elegant clothing. It does not look like the kind of clothing Ukrainian women usually wear. In style, in cut, in material it is completely different from the usual preference of the Russian (or Ukrainian) women. Their style has always leaned more towards bright, gay colors, with frilly designs—this wardrobe is sophisticated in a quiet way. As a matter of fact, what the girl is wearing looks somehow odd on her, but I don't quite know why.

She picks out two dresses, holds them against my body, says something to Paula, who nods in approval, and with that she hands them to me.

There again I am confronted with mixed emotions. I am not used to being given handouts; my pride rebels against it. If I refuse, she may have hurt feelings, thinking that I won't accept because she is not a German. What shall I do?

My eyes meet Paula's. Paula again nods approval. If she says so, then I should accept.

I thank the girl very much, and Paula and I leave.

By the time we arrive back home, the vanity of a seventeen-year-old has taken the upper hand, and I begin to enjoy my unexpected wealth. At least now I have more than that one

142

dress I have been wearing constantly for almost eight weeks! It is bound to fall apart soon.

I try on the dresses, and they fit perfectly except for the length. That is no problem, though; I know how to hem.

I am happy as a lark and so is Paula.

"My goodness!" is Mama's reaction. "Where did you get that?"

When I tell her, she looks disturbed. "Wait a minute—where did the girl next door get the dresses?"

"Why, Mama, she lives there! They are hers, she probably bought them during the war."

"No, no, no. There is something wrong! Paula. . . ?"

Mama's eyes are demanding a thorough answer.

Paula squirms around a little. "Mamma, you nix ask! Angel no have dress, Angel look pretty. . . ."

"Where—did—she—get—them?" There is a pause in between each word, which indicates that neither one of us will get away with an evasive answer. When Mama asks like that, there had better be a truthful answer!

With that Paula tells us the whole story.

The house belongs to a German family who, like the people in whose house we are living temporarily, are in West Germany. After the Russian troops had conquered Berlin and found the Ukrainian foreign workers living in camps, they decided that these people should have houses so they assigned them either to empty ones or evicted German families to accommodate the Russians or Ukrainians. Therefore, it is quite apparent that the wardrobe does not belong to the Ukrainian girl but rather to the German family who owns the house.

It becomes quickly clear to me that I want no part of the "gift."

"I'm going over right now!"

Paula holds me back; she is serious and her voice is urgent.

"No, Angel!" She turns to Mama. "You tell Angel stay—no go! Nix good, give back. Girl be angry—bad!"

We both see her point. If I return the dresses, the girl will know that we know the situation and do not approve. She will feel threatened and might cause trouble, and trouble is one thing we cannot afford—our honesty could cause more harm than good.

"Well," Mama says, "put the dresses away, and when the family comes back we will return them—that's an even better solution." But that moment never arrives. Things begin to happen all of a sudden. From outside comes the noise of trucks, of shuffling and moving around. There are a lot of loud Russian voices. For a moment I dare not look out the window, but with Paula here I am not so afraid, and curiosity gets the better of me.

"Mama, Paula, come here and see what's going on out there!"

Outside are several Russian trucks, which are being loaded with furniture, household items, bedding, clothing, even a stove and the bathtub! All from the house next door!

"For goodness sake!" Mama says indignantly. "These people will not have a single item left when they return!"

"Well," Omi puts in, "it does not really surprise me. I forgot to tell you that the whole of Germany is being dismantled. Every machine, every tool, every car, or truck that the Russians can get hold of is being transported to Russia. All factories are being stripped bare, all workshops emptied. There will not be a thing left."

"Omi, you are kidding!" Mama says, unbelieving. "If they do that, then Germany will have no industry, which means we will not be able to survive. There will be no work, no money, no food, nothing! Without industry a country is dead!"

"Lisa, I have seen with my own eyes the freight cars loaded to the brim with machinery. You remember that Grete lives near the freight station, and you also know that everything coming from the Siemens factory has to go past there. I have seen the Russians riding on the trains. They have *USSR* written all over the trains. They have written it in German letters, almost as if to say, 'Look what we are doing!' I'm telling you, it is not a rumor. You wouldn't believe it if you saw it—freight car after freight car after freight car!"

"Ommi right!" Paula says, "Russian Kommandant say, 'Germans not must start war again, so all equipment go Russia.' Me no like Russia any more, me no go back, never!"

"My God!" Mama can hardly speak. "Then they are really trying to destroy us completely."

The revelation is so shocking to all of us that we do not even enjoy our meal; today it tastes fairly bitter. Where there was slight hope before, there is now renewed despair. How long will our supply last? What will we do when it is all gone? We cannot rely on Paula entirely to feed us—the source of her supply (whatever it was, we never questioned it) has ended.

In the depth of our gloom, Mr. Stillman comes over to see us. At first we do not think about his purpose. We tell him of the events next door.

"You did my friends a great service by being here. If you had not lived here, I am sure the same thing would have happened to their home."

He pauses, then says sadly, "I have bad news for you. My friends will be back the day after tomorrow. I think it is best that you leave here tomorrow."

None of us answer him.

My heartbeat is doing some crazy things: Go back . . . bump, bump . . . go back . . . bump, bump . . . go back . . . bump, bump . . . rhythmical, hollow, sinister. Empty space. Floating corpses. Dead trees. Shots. Cannons tumbling up and down, right to left. . . .

Go back . . . bump, bump . . . go back . . . bump, bump . . . What are these? What are these little spots in space? Stars? They are green. Green uniforms. . . Russians.

I don't hear anything. Everything is so quiet . . . why? Just these images, floating, waving, bizarre. . . .

Out of space comes Mr. Stillman's voice.

"Don't be afraid, little one." He pats me gently on the head. "Things are not so bad anymore. Nothing will happen to you, you'll see. And if you run into problems, just come and see me and I will try and help you—all of you. You've been wonderful lodgers, and I thank you for taking care of everything so well."

145

"Mr. Stillman, we are the ones who have to thank you. You will never quite know how much you did for us. We will never forget you." It is not easy for Mama to talk right now. I myself am incapable of saying anything; my heart feels as if someone has put a tight band around it, it is almost a physical pain. . . . That night I hardly sleep at all.

9

NIGHTMARE IN DAYTIME

My whole body is aching. I am glad when it is time to get up. I look at Paula, still sleeping peacefully beside me. How can she sleep on this? When we lived here before, my parents' twin beds, side by side, had sturdy metal box springs with comfortable soft innerspring mattresses; then on top of that a spread containing soft eiderdown, with finally the sheet and a feather-spread. The beds Chris and I used have disappeared. Paula and I share one of my parents' beds, but now the only thing left is the bed frame with the metal spring. I feel like an Indian fakir on a bed of nails. Yet we are glad to have at least that left. . . .

When we returned a few days ago, it was hard to believe that decent human beings had ever lived here. Mrs. Stromberg had told Omi that our home and property had been a camp for a few thousand Russian troops. It looked like a pigsty.

There was nothing left but badly damaged bare furniture. Knives, forks, spoons, towels, curtains, blankets, pillowcases, cooking pots, plates, dishes, mattresses, carpets, rugs, clothing, whatever is found in a household—it was all gone.

There were hundreds of empty food cans on the floor, flies were finding it most interesting to dig around in these. Old torn dirty clothing from heaven knows where, none of it ours, was scattered about. The occupants had often not bothered to find a toilet. The windows were completely shattered; notwith-

147

standing, the stench was sickening. Water or drinks had been spilled, and having mixed with the dirt, formed an ugly nauseating carpet of filth.

After we had lost our earlier home by the bomb, we had not been able to acquire much wealth, but we did have fairly good furniture and other possessions that make life more civilized. Most of all we had a clean, neat home.

Seeing this devastation was horrible for Mama. Only she knew the many hours of hard work that had gone into making our home. We just sat down on the few chairs that were not totally filthy and looked around without saying a word.

In the mess we discovered two dirty zinc buckets and in another room a large washtub, which could hold about eight buckets of water. The first thing we did was to haul two buckets of water from the canal; then we picked up a few rags, put them in the buckets, and made a fire in the cooking stove to boil them. Finding firewood was not difficult—there was enough splintered wood lying about. Now we had at least something to clean up with that we were not afraid to touch.

I do not know how many buckets of water we carried from the canal or how many days it took to finish the cleaning, but somehow we managed to get the place into livable shape. Later we dug outside, and found in the ground, run over by tanks or other vehicles, some clothing, some knives, forks, and spoons (on some of these it said Hotel Adlon), even some sheets and pillowcases and one or two blankets.

With these we did what we had done with everything else— they were thoroughly boiled, then washed and dried. Since we had no soap powder, we had to take some clean sand (if you dug deep enough into the ground, you found clean sand) to scrub the very soiled areas.

Nobody feels a displacement, an uprooting from home, more strongly than the very young and the very old. I believe they are the happiest of us all to be back home. The wound Omi had received on her leg from the shell splinter is healing very nicely. Thank goodness for that—if there were complications, where would we get medicine?

Paula is awake now. What a relief—it is boring to be up before everyone else with nothing to do. I want to go outside. It is getting close to the end of July. The sun is warming the ground in gentle comfort. This year there seems to be not much rain. . . . What will winter be like? Better not think about that now. . . . Some birds are back (miraculously), and a very touching attempt to continue growth has been made by the linden tree. Here and there, as if afraid it might not be quite safe, a tiny leaf has dared to break through in the most impossible place. . . .

Even the grass has started to come up. Man certainly has a hard time destroying completely. . . . Somehow that thought fills me with a kind of spiteful joy.

The food situation is no better than it was two weeks ago. The resources Paula supplied us with are gone. Again we have to depend on what is being announced as our rightful supply and that is not much. . . .

I fix a slice of bread, a ladle full of rye-flour soup, and there is a cup of "Ersatz" coffee for Paula and me. Paula sits down at the table with me, but does not eat.

"What's wrong, Paula? Are you sick?" I am alarmed.

Paula looks away. She nods her head sadly.

"Paula, come on, you have to eat! Something must be wrong. . . ."

"Me no hungry. . . ." she says.

"Come on . . . Paula, that is ridiculous!" And it is! In these days everybody is hungry all the time!

Paula knows I won't be satisfied with that explanation.

"Me must not eat," she says. "Me no ration card."

Oh dear, I had forgotten that all Ukrainians and other non-German nationals who have decided to stay in Germany do not receive ration cards. That is one way to force most foreign workers who for some reason or other take a liking to Germany or its occupants to return to Russia. . . .

"But Paula," I plead with her, "we have already talked about that. We agreed that we would all put together and share our food with you, just like you shared yours with us!"

149

"Me knows." Paula's blue eyes show love and tenderness. "But you all so thin now—me afraid you die. . . ."

"You're crazy! Me die? Ha-ha! Look at my muscles!" I pull my sleeve up and show her some tiny little muscle moving. I succeed at least in making her laugh, but she still won't eat.

"Okay." I pull the strongest string I know of. "Okay, then I won't eat either!"

As hungry as I am, I'm not sure I can go through with my threat, but lately, despite my hunger, I cannot eat with appetite. There is an odor outside which nauseates me. I do not know where it is coming from. It is a smell of decay and—death. . . . It frightens me, as if, should I look any further, I would come upon some unspeakable horror. . . .

I have tried to put it out of my mind, but it is not easy, since the odor is the constant reminder that there is something out there, somewhere. . . . Sooner or later, I know we will have to go and investigate it. Maybe tomorrow. . . .

Right now, I want to concentrate on Paula.

Hurrah, she is eating! Momentarily I forget the "something" outside.

"You know, Paula, when the war is over, I want to go dancing. Do you know that I have never been to a dance?"

"War is over," Paula says.

"Oh, I know. But you know what I mean; when things are back to normal. . . ."

Still, Paula's remark puts a damper on my future picture of joy. . . .

"Spoilsport," I mumble.

Activity has started in the household. Mama, Mrs. Peters, and the girls are also up by now. After they have eaten breakfast, we all get busy tidying up and doing some more of our wash.

I am hanging the wash up outside. I look down at the grass: fresh, green, and tempting. It has just sprung up through the ground and still has a new tenderness. If I were a goat or a rabbit or a cow, I find myself thinking, I would have no food problem. . . . Wait a minute—who says humans cannot eat grass? I take off in a flash.

150

"Mama! Mama! I just had a great idea. . . ."

"Okay, okay, calm down darling," Mama says. "What's your great idea?"

I am still panting, partly from running, partly from screaming my lungs out, partly from excitement over my discovery.

"How would you all like to have spinach for dinner?"

"Spinach? Where would you get that?"

"Well," I am tasting every moment, "we do have salt, and we do have flour, and outside is a whole lot of delicious fresh grass. . . ."

"By golly," says Mama, "the girl has something there, why not?"

With enthusiasm everybody takes knives and in a jiffy we have a nice supply of grass. It is boiled in salt water, chopped fine, and then we brown some flour and cream the grass with that. It is not too good—somehow it does not seem to get too tender—but it is a supply of badly needed vitamins.

Mama and Paula are doing the dishes.

"We need drinking water," Mama says. "Maybe you and Erna can go and get some."

I try to avoid Mama's direct look.

Getting water is one of the worst tasks anyone can assign me. It is not the fact that we have to walk one mile to get it and another mile to bring it home, but there is something else I have not as yet told Mama. Halfway between the water and our home is a little house which is occupied by Russian soldiers. On different occasions in passing, Erna and I have noticed the Russians observing us—questioningly, weighing. . . .

Erna sees the terrified look on my face.

"We'll be all right," she whispers reassuringly.

Well, we need water. The way we carry it is not too easy in itself. It is the supply for eight people, and we do not want to go more often than we absolutely have to, which is about every third day. We take the washtub, which is oval-shaped with a handle on each side. In addition we each carry a bucket. Getting there with empty containers is not too much of a problem. But getting back with all that water is a different story. Many times we have to stop and rest our aching arms and hands. We make it a point to stop before and after we pass the little house with the Russians, but it is always a nightmare.

The first time we went, there was another unpleasant aspect. The dead horse was still lying in the road: decomposed, decayed, and surrounded by the sickly sweet smell of death. . . . The next time we went someone had removed it, but the smell lingered in the air.

Still, we need water.

"Okay, let's go," Erna says. Outside and alone with me, she adds, "I don't think they are going to try anything in broad daylight. They are not quite that bold anymore—the 'freedom days' are officially over."

Erna is right; we make it to the water without incident.

The source of our supply is a public pump, which for some miraculous reason has not been destroyed. My back is turned towards the road. Erna is holding the bucket while I am pumping. I look up. Why is she staring at me like that? Then I realize she is not looking at me but right past me.

Before I can turn, someone standing behind me covers my eyes with his hands. I freeze.

Just as suddenly I'm released. I whirl about and see that hated uniform. It is a Russian soldier. He roars with laughter at my shocked and frightened face. He says something which I do not understand. Then he gently pushes me away from the pump and starts pumping. Erna and I are still speechless. When the buckets and the wash basin are filled, he picks up the two buckets and motions us to go on. Erna and I, the washbasin between us, follow quietly.

When he has carried our buckets for about a quarter of a mile, he puts them down and says something that we take to be good-bye.

We thank him (we have finally found our voices). He nods, turns around, and walks away.

Well, if that isn't something! A gentleman among the enemy. . . .

We still cannot quite believe our luck and try to get away

from the scene as fast as possible. But passing the Russians in the little house is today not quite as horrible as before. . . .

When we get home, we are both exhausted and decide to take a nap. Before I go to sleep, I thank God for protecting us once more—but how many more times will we be lucky?

"Where is Paula, Mama?"

The sleep has refreshed me, and I am now a little bored. I miss my companion, she is always fun to be with. Besides, with her around I feel a little safer.

Maybe I could dare to go outside with a book and try to get a little suntan.

"Paula says she wanted to go and visit some friends," says Mama. She is busy sewing some buttons on a dress. "That also means that you will have to go downtown alone tonight, and I am not too happy about you going there by yourself. . . . But I cannot leave Monika and Chris alone here. Maybe Erna can accompany you for a short while. . . ." There is a worried frown on Mama's face.

"Don't worry, Mama, it will be all right. I can run pretty fast," I brag.

"Yes, but I don't think you can outrun a gun," Mama says.

"Oh, they don't shoot so easily anymore." My optimism is bravado.

Frankly, I am worried. The idea of going downtown by myself is rather unpleasant. I am tempted to ask Mama to let me stay home overnight—but that would make things more complicated for her. . . .

After our return home, we found that at first it was very unsafe to stay overnight at our house—it was just too isolated, and straying Russians found it easy to break in. We had had some very frightening experiences, during which only Paula's presence, her ability to speak Russian, and her courage had saved us.

153

I remember especially one night of horror. The day had started not too badly; we were glad to be back home in spite of the filth and were hoping that maybe we were too isolated to be bothered by looting and drunk Russian soldiers.

I was outside hanging up some wash. Out of the corner of my eye I saw someone approaching—two figures slowly walking towards our house. It never took me long to recognize those uniforms—they were Russian. Up to now, I had been hiding from any person I did not know, to the point where I did not even go outside unless no one was in sight. This time I was caught unprepared.

Running back into the house would call attention to myself, I knew that. The only chance I had was to stay calm and unseen, and the only way I could figure to be undetected was to lie down on the ground. . . .

I have to chuckle a little now thinking back; how stupid one is when frightened! I sank slowly to the ground and lay there flat, hoping the grass would hide me from view. But the grass was only about one-half inch tall!

I remembered that some animals play dead when frightened; that is exactly what I did! I lay still until the Russians were out of sight, but naturally they had seen me. That was proven that night, when, after we had gone to bed, blocked up, boarded up, and locked in, there was a violent pounding on the door.

We did not make a sound.

Paula was not with us that night. She had gone to visit some friends and since the distances in a city as big as Berlin are great and had to be covered on foot, it never paid to visit and then leave the same day. The only way to do it was to stay overnight and walk back home the next day.

Here we were: alone, and far and near no one but us and some drunken Russians. We hoped that they would go away if there was no sound from within—but they knew someone was there.

Eventually, they were going to try breaking through the window. Their voices, guttural and threatening, indicated that they were bound and determined to come in. We heard them try their luck at the windows, which were covered with a layer of wire enmeshed in plastic. Since the windows were broken every night in air raids, this plastic was the best solution to that problem and had become high fashion during those days. It was fairly flexible, but not too easy to pierce or break.

Of course, it certainly would not hold out against someone trying hard to break in. . . . Our hearts were pounding so loud, we were afraid they could be heard.

"Mama, what are we going to do?" I whispered it, shaking.

"Darling, I don't know yet—just keep quiet, all of you," Mama whispered back.

Chris was awake now, too, and she started sobbing a little.

"Sssshh, Chris darling, you must be absolutely quiet," Mama said, just as scared as we were.

Monika was still asleep. Thank God—if she started crying now, our slim, but only chance was gone. . . .

The noise outside was getting violent.

"I'll be good, Mommy," Chris said, still whimpering.

I put my hand across her mouth.

"Listen," Mama whispered again, "we have got to get out of here. Let's see if we cannot hide somewhere else. Be quiet and follow me. . . ."

The door leading from the hallway to the outside was still locked. It was a very heavy door, and unless you had a hatchet, very difficult to pry open. Good for us!

Across the hall were several rooms which were arranged in a way that did not give any indication as to how many there might be. Before we lived here these had all been offices, which we had converted into living quarters. They had been quite pretty, too: white linoleum, bright windows, beautiful porcelain wash basins—everything had been neat and tidy. Now, of course, not much of that neatness was left: walls torn, windows and basins broken, linoleum ripped up, and so on. A shell is a shell, it does not care where it hits! (Neither did the Russians.)

We had started moving one bed into one of these rooms, since we had planned to give Mrs. Peters the front rooms. We were to take over the other rooms, but we never quite got around to moving completely. One of these rooms had two doors leading into it: one door from another room, and one door from the hallway. We had put a huge wardrobe in front of the door leading to the hallway, which covered this door completely. The door from the other room was visible, but we had also moved one of the kitchen cabinets into this room, hoping to finish the task of moving.

Now our aim was to get into the room that had the hall door covered by the wardrobe, then pull the kitchen cabinet in front of the other door and hope it would hide the room behind it.

After we had achieved all this, as quietly and as fast as we could, we sat down on the floor with a sigh of relief. Mama had taken Monika into her arms, still asleep with her pillow underneath her, and was saying a few silent prayers that the baby would stay asleep.

We had hardly finished the task of concealment when we heard the sounds of heavy boots outside in the hallway. It had not been a moment too soon!

The footsteps walked around for quite a while. Inside our hiding place, we held our breath; so far we had been lucky. . . .

Suddenly, maybe from the tension she could sense, Monika woke up and started crying.

We were almost paralyzed with shock. The Russians were bound to hear this—it was the end of our security. . . .

Mama threw Monika on the bed, pushed a pillow over Monika's head and buried her own head under the pillow, too. Now and then she would come up for air, then breathe it into Monika's mouth.

We could hear the muffled sounds of Monika's crying.

Weren't they ever going to go away? How long could the baby survive half-suffocated?

Under the pillow I heard Mama crying. "Oh my dear God . . . please, please, please. . . ."

I don't know how long this lasted, but finally, after what seemed an eternity, the footsteps disappeared.

Monika, even more upset by her ordeal, really started screaming now. Mama was rocking her back and forth in her arms:

"My darling, my darling, please be quiet now, please be quiet...."

Somehow it worked. Monika was exhausted, I guess, and finally calmed down.

We saw the Russians looking around outside a little while longer; there was still an element of danger. If they checked the number of windows and came across two more than there should be.... But once in a while, vodka seems to have its virtues! I guess they were just a little too drunk to count.

Thinking back to these moments now, I have no desire to stay here during the night. It was during that tense time that Mama decided it was best for me to spend each night at my aunt's house downtown. In all these thousands of apartments it was a fairly remote chance that any stray Russians would pay a visit to one particular apartment on the fourth floor.

The first night I went alone. Paula stayed with Mama and the others. But the night after our ordeal the same Russians who had frightened us before came back. This time, however, they met with a surprise—Paula. From behind the window she challenged them in a harsh voice, speaking Russian! Paula told Mama that they were looking for me: they insisted they had seen a young girl there.

Paula told them that they were just plain drunk, that there was no girl there, and that if they did not leave, they would regret it.

I don't think they believed her, but soon changed their mind. When Paula realized that they were trying to come through the window she broke the top off an old glass bottle, put herself into fighting position behind the window, and when the first hand came through, hit it with the full power of her young strong arms.

There was quite a lot of screaming in Russian and quite a stream of blood, but they never came back!

Paula knew that I was afraid to go downtown alone, so she accompanied me whenever she could.

157

Today I will have to go alone. Well, somehow I will take care of myself and just have faith that nothing will happen. I have some time yet; it is only afternoon.

I don't feel much like reading. Maybe today would be the day to dare a short walk outside. We have not seen any Russians for quite a few days.

I am longing to go to the canal, watch the sunset in the water, and make believe it is really peace. I can always picture sailboats gently floating along beside its shore, with people who are happy and singing, and maybe someone playing the accordion. . . .

Oh, how I long to hear some music again, to see people dance, and laugh, and drink some wine, and I myself among them, dancing and gay and lighthearted, and some nice young man looking at me from across the room. . . .

By the canal I find the sunset reflected in the water as I had pictured it, but the mood for make-believe does not come to life again. Instead, I find my thoughts going back to the day we left. . . . Somewhere here, somewhere nearby, was the spot where Mr. Schulman was drowned by the Russians. . . . The water gives away no secret; as always it floats by quietly, uninterested in all the human tragedies. . . .

There is that horrible odor again, and I look. . . . Suddenly, I feel cold, frightened.

Quickly, I turn around to run back into safety, into the haven of the house. . . .

And once again today I am frozen in terror, a terror much more powerful than the quick incident at the water pump, a terror so strong that momentarily it seems to be unreal, a nightmare. . . .

My throat turns dry, and the scream it wants to release into the sky is nothing but a gurgling sound within me. My skin feels as if a million sticky, ugly bugs are crawling up and down, and I want to run, run, run . . . but I cannot move. I have to stare at it. . . .

A hand . . . a black, decayed hand is growing through the

158

earth, like a flower of death . . . nothing else . . . just that hand . . . finally I can scream.

"Mama! Mama!"

But of course she cannot hear me. I must run away from here!

Inside the house I am still trying to scream, but each scream gets stuck in my throat.

"My God, girl, what is wrong!" Mama is shaking me.

"Out there . . . by the canal . . ." is all I can say.

Mama and Erna run outside at the same time.

When they come back they look sick too.

"It is Mrs. Schulman," Erna says. "Uncle Fritz told us that after the Russian shot her, he threw her into the hole that the Volksturmmen had dug—and there she still is. We'll have to contact those who remove bodies; we ourselves cannot bury her. . . ."

"I want to go now, Mama," I say.

"Of course, Inga. Stay with Aunt Grete until I send someone to get you, and that will not be until she has been removed. . . ."

———————

When I arrive at Aunt Grete's, I sink down on the bed.

"Are you sick?" she asks.

"No."

"You are early. Have you had supper yet?"

"No."

"Well, I will fix you some. . . ."

"No, thank you, I'm not hungry."

"Now I know you are sick," Aunt Grete says, slightly disturbed. "Well," she consoles herself, "If she gets hungry, she'll eat . . ." and with that I am left alone. There is no terror in me now. I am just very, very tired.

10

DAYS OF REVELATIONS

Somehow a certain amount of law and order has been restored. Rape and murder have changed from being the rule to being the exception. We do have electricity again, since work above ground could be done more easily than, for instance, restoring the waterlines underground. All the corpses have been taken care of: fished out of waterways; dug up from temporary graves; pulled out of collapsed buildings. Here and there some stores are in existence again, and now and then a bus drives along the roads. . . .

Old people and the very young are dying like flies. Typhoid fever, starvation, and other sicknesses that cannot be cured because of the lack of medication are taking their toll.

Now and then figures looking like living corpses appear, wearing green uniforms—ragged and dirty—German prisoners of war. . . . They wander around, slowly, unshaven and with hopelessness in their faces. They stand in front of destroyed buildings, looking for a sign of their loved ones. Now and then there is an inscription made with chalk: *Annie Mueller now at 10 Gartenstrasse. We are alive!* The lucky ones who find such inscriptions seem to find a temporary revival and hurry off. But not always is that hope justified; in many cases a family escaped, found temporary refuge somewhere else, and was killed there. . . .

160

Something like a newspaper has appeared; no one quite knows who prints it or where it is printed. Among its avidly read items is the list of people looking for their families, agencies representing children looking for their parents, parents desperately searching for their children, hundreds sought every day. The list of longing. . . . And still the tragedies go on.

Many prisoners of war, returning, find their wives sick, or pregnant with the child of rape, and not all can make the adjustment. Abortions are the rule, and not all women survive. In some instances the only answer some of them find is suicide. . . . In the newspapers, on the records, these are statistics.

I think that I shall never again be able to laugh or be happy. . . .

And day by day the list increases. Some families take the lost children and give them a home and love, only to go through horrible heartache when the original family appears from somewhere—torn between happiness for the children's sake and suffering from their own loss. . . .

How much longer do people have to pay? And why?

Soon there will be an answer to these questions. A horrible, devastating, depressing answer. . . .

But, for a while yet, we are spared.

I have decided to visit my girl friend Annie today. It seems like ages since I've heard from her. It takes me quite a while to get there. Well, at least the house is still standing—mostly undamaged. Her mother opens the door. "Yes, Annie is home," she says, and shows me into Annie's room.

My once so lively and happy girl friend is lying on her bed.

"Hello," she says, listlessly.

I have never had a greeting like this from her before; usually it was an enthusiastic, outgoing "Boy, am I glad to see you!"

Now she shows hardly any interest in my presence. Her once beautiful dark hair, with natural waves, full of highlights, is a

161

dull dark brown. It looks uncared for. Her eyes show shadows, a lifeless dullness; her face is thin with sharp lines.

"Annie, you don't look too good. Aren't you well?" I know it is a silly way to greet her, but I have not yet learned to be tactful.

"What difference does it make whether I'm well or not?"

She looks away, out of the window into nowhere. If at least she had said it with anger or any other kind of emotion!

"Annie, of course it makes a difference whether you are well or not!"

Maybe if I show some emotion, I can get her out of the lethargic mood.

"Oh, leave me alone," she says, and it sounds just tired.

Her mother enters.

"Would you and Inga like some tea, Annie?"

"No." Just that. She had always been a very polite girl, full of charm. Now there is not even the "No, thank you."

She turns her back to me. Her mother motions to me to leave the room. I follow her into the living room.

"You are shocked?" It is almost more a statement than a question.

I don't quite know what to answer and so say nothing.

"Why did it have to be my girl? . . ." Annie's mother is looking right past me. She is not really crying, yet tears are slowly running down her face, and her eyes are wide open.

"What happened?"

"I think that maybe she is blaming us. . . . But how could I know, how could I possibly know? . . ."

She presses both her hands together, as if she wants to squeeze a piece of wet paper dry.

"What happened?" I repeat my question.

"I suppose I should tell you," she mutters. She gets up and without asking if I want it, puts a cup of tea before me.

"When we realized that the Russians were coming closer, we were of course concerned mostly about Annie. She is our only child, you know. . . ." Of course I know. "Well, I suggested that she try to get through to my sister's place in the country,

162

hoping that she would be safer there. I couldn't go with her, my husband was quite sick. Someone had to take care of him. . . ." It is almost an apology.

"Of course," I say.

"At that time the Russians weren't close to my sister's place, so I had no misgivings about letting her go. She didn't really want to go. She kept saying a family belongs together in times like these. But we had heard all these horrible stories about rape and murder, and I felt she was better off where there was not quite so much vicious fighting.

"I thought the Russian troops would hurry through the small villages. We figured they were more interested in getting to the heart of the city. Besides, the Russians were coming from the east, and I was sending Annie to the west, the direction we thought the English and Americans would come. What we didn't know was that the Russians had already surrounded Berlin, and the English and Americans had stopped at the Elbe. . . ." She stops for a moment, the teacup is moving in rhythm, since her hand is shaking.

"I don't quite know how it happened—Annie did not say too much. Somehow she ran right into a convoy of Russian soldiers. They had stopped along the road, they were quite drunk. They pulled her into the truck, there were about ten of them. Annie screamed and fought and they laughed. Finally she managed to tear herself away, and she jumped off the truck and ran, but they fired a few shots after her. They missed, but she didn't have a chance; they soon caught up with her and threw her back in the truck. She still fought like a wildcat until a Russian bit her in the breast. There is quite a scar on her breast. . . ."

Annie's mother is now shaking all over. I go to her and hug her. "But she is alive," I say, the only consolation I can find.

"Oh, Inga, that's just it. We have told her that over and over again, but she thinks she should be dead. You see, there were ten of them, and all ten. . . ."

She covers her face with her hands, and it takes a while before her crying subsides.

"She was bleeding so badly," Annie's mother continues, "and

when they were all through with her they threw her off the truck and took off. Annie crawled away and hid in the bushes for a while. Then she wandered around the neighborhood trying to find help. Lucky for her, the first door she knocked on was the home of a country doctor. He somehow cleaned her up—she needed some stitches—he gave her some injections and also stitched up the breast wound. He told her that as far as he could tell now, she would not have too much trouble having children, except for the breast wound, which could give her trouble during a pregnancy."

"How did you find out where Annie was?"

"The doctor sent his wife, who told us the whole story. By then my husband was getting better, so I went back with her and brought Annie home."

She pauses for a moment to dry her face.

"Now she says that no man will ever marry her, that she is dirty. . . ."

"That's silly," I reply. "After all, it was not her fault."

"Oh, we keep telling her that over and over again, but we just can't get through to her. She says, 'Mother, if you fall into a mudpool, it is unimportant whether someone threw you into it or whether you fell in by yourself. You fall into the mud, you get dirty. . . .' Now what can you say to such a philosophy? I said to her, 'But, Annie, you can wash off the mud,' and she looks at her scar and says, 'Can I wash off that scar?' So what am I supposed to say other than that she is wrong, that time does heal wounds. To her these are just phrases, clichés. . . ."

"I don't know what else to say, either. I think I'd better not see her until I've absorbed the shock myself."

Annie's mother agrees, and before I leave I hug her again.

"God bless you, take care of yourself," she says, standing in the doorway.

————

I am glad to be on my way home again.

How very, very lucky we all have been so far. . . . It almost

164

makes me afraid to think about it, for fear that the devil is just waiting around the corner, biding time until his chance comes along to clobber us. . . . That brings me to the thought of protection, and of course to Papa.

Is Papa still alive? What will happen to us if he is not? Horrible thought. He *is* alive! Then why have we not heard from him yet? Surely they will let the prisoners write? But we know from prisoners who have returned from Russia that there were hardly any chances to send word to their families. At this point we don't even know where Papa last was—Russia, Denmark, Norway, Africa, Poland, France, Belgium—where?

It is quite a long walk to the bus stop. I have lots of time to think. Poor Annie . . . what will happen to her now? It could have been me. . . . How can people be so beastly? I remember the bright, sparkling, beautiful girl she was. . . . Never before have I realized more clearly that beauty comes from within. The Annie I saw today was a different girl. . . . That thought hurts and I have to figure out why. . . . It is not just that I have lost a girl friend; Annie is in no shape to want friends. Young as I am, I realize that she needs time to heal, and that can only come from people very close to her who give her a lot of love and understanding. What bothers me most about the whole situation is that a life can be destroyed through no fault of one's own—all you have to do is be at the wrong spot at the wrong time, and all hell can break loose. . . . Before you know it, you are down in the mud without ever knowing how you got there. . . .

It is an extremely uncomfortable thought. What little faith in life I have left is getting an even bigger shaking. I have always been an optimist, a happy girl, a girl who believed strongly and firmly that when you live right and do good, God will protect you. . . . Now life, or fate, or even God Himself, proves me wrong. What sense is there to believe in goodness?

I don't think I want to go home right away. Having to tell Mama about Annie is not what I feel up to just yet. I need some diversion.

Ahead of me I see the little baker shop—I think I will go in and chat a moment with the elderly couple who operate it. I

165

have always liked these two nice people. They are both shy and humble in a dignified way, never say anything bad about anybody, never miss church, would never knowingly hurt anyone. They took over the little bakery several years ago. Until then they lived in the country, and somehow city-living has not made them sophisticated. They are simple, kind, hard-working people. Their only child, a red-haired, fat little boy with a jolly face, came rather late in their life: the crowning of their destiny, and to them the only thing to live for. The boy was about fifteen when I had last seen them during the war's final days.

As I enter the bakery I realize it is a mistake. The sweet and tempting fragrance of the freshly baked bread drives me crazy. I am not sure I can concentrate on our conversation.

Thank goodness, they ask me into their living room where the fragrance still lingers but not as strongly. Business is very slow these days—three pounds of bread per person per week is just not the answer to a businessman's need for business!

"Please sit down, Miss Inga," Mrs. Gaertner says. Her eyes are swollen and red, as if she has just been crying. I look more closely at her husband. His eyes look the same. Have they had an argument? The thought is almost funny—not these two!

A cup of "ersatz" coffee is put in front of me, and then I hear another story of heartbreak, as if I had not had my fill for the day! Momentarily, I want to pretend to be in a hurry and leave politely, but I cannot bring myself to do it.

"Do you have troubles? Can I help?" I am saying it against my better judgment—I should have left well enough alone.

Mrs. Gaertner has her elbows on the table. She puts her face into her hands, and between sobs I hear her say, "It's Michael. . . ."

Her husband is standing straight up beside her; his face shows an expression I cannot describe, with tears slowly running down his cheeks, but he does not say anything.

Finally Mrs. Gaertner realizes that if she wants me to hear what she has to say she has to stop crying. They are always wearing white aprons that never look anything but sparkling clean; even now they do. She pulls a handkerchief out of her pocket and dries her tears.

"When the Russians came," Mrs. Gaertner begins, "they found that there were a few men among the occupants of this building. As you may know, there are about twenty families living here, and not all of the men had been drafted—some were working in ammunition factories or were exempted for various other reasons. Anyway, the Russians gathered together all the male occupants—and they claimed that shots had been fired from here. They were pretty mean. There had been some German soldiers around us trying to defend the house, but there were just not enough. A few of them were wounded, most of the others had to withdraw and tried to get back to their homes. When the Russians came, they shot the wounded in the neck. . . ." Her voice started shaking again. "All these poor young people, what horrible crime did they commit other than defend us? Anyway, they killed the wounded soldiers—I think there were three. Then the Russians rounded up all the other men and threatened to shoot them too, claiming that they had weapons hidden somewhere. But you know, Miss Inga, I don't believe that; the only people who shot from here were the soldiers."

She paused for a moment.

"They had rounded me up, too," said Mr. Gaertner, uttering a kind of disgusted laugh, "and I don't even know how to shoot a gun. I have not even held a gun, ever, in my life."

"Then they came for our boy. . . ." Mrs. Gaertner's voice is very unsteady, but she fights the need to cry again. "Suddenly they were just here, grabbing Michael, and saying that they believed he belonged to the 'Werewolf' group! Can you imagine, our Michael? We did not even want to let him join the Hitler Youth, because they didn't practice enough religion. . . . Then, of course, he was registered with the Hitler Youth whether we wanted it or not, but we did not let him go often. We had a good reason to keep him away, saying that we needed him in the bakery. Oh Miss Inga, he is such a nice boy, and he worked so hard. . . ."

"A good boy, a good boy," Mr. Gaertner is nodding his head three or four times.

Mrs. Gaertner fumbles in her pocket. She pulls out a photograph of Michael; although she knows I know him, she has to show it to me. It looks frayed and slightly crumbled—she must have been carrying it around in her pocket day after day.

"Look at him. Does he look like a boy who is mean?" Her eyes are pleading. I want to tell her that she doesn't have to tell me, I know . . . that the ones to convince are the Russians. Instead I ask, "Where is Michael now?"

"He was almost always with us—we knew where he was all the time. . . ." Mr. Gaertner throws in, ignoring my question.

"Where is Michael now?" I repeat.

"I don't know." Now there is not even enough strength left in Mrs. Gaertner to cry. Only her eyes tell. . . . She looks at the photograph. "Such a nice boy, the only child we have. . . ." Her voice is just a whisper.

"What happened?"

"Happened? They just took him away. . . ."

"Well, thank God, then he is probably still alive, Mrs. Gaertner," I try to comfort her.

"Do you think so, Miss Inga?" Her eyes are meeting mine in a flash of hope that almost crushes me. . . . Am I right to put hope where there may be no justification for it?

They are both coming towards me as if I just said "Thou Shalt Live. . . ." I feel like running. "You are the only one who seems to think that there is hope that he is still alive. The others have all said they think he is dead. But tell me, why would they shoot a fifteen-year-old boy? Why? You don't think they did, do you?"

I shake my head.

"Why do the others believe he is dead? What others?" I ask.

"Well, the other people in the house. They say that if the Russians suspected him to be a 'Werewolf' they would shoot

168

him, or, at best, send him to Siberia." She pauses for a moment, putting her finger to her cheek, pensive. "Yes, yes, that could be it, Friedrich, they might have sent him to Siberia. . . ."

I cannot quite tell if she figures this to be a hopeful thought, but by now I have realized something else: in general I believe in the truth, even if the truth is painful, but in this case I have my doubts. There is no proof that the boy is dead. As long as the two people can have some hope, their life will have some meaning and a purpose. . . . By the time the full truth is known, if it is a cruel truth, they may have been alone for enough time to be able to cope with it.

Mr. Gaertner wants to believe, but still can't.

"Well, if he is in Siberia, why have they not notified us? After all, we are his parents, and he is only fifteen. . . ."

"Oh, I know of quite a number of prisoners of war in Siberia who could not let their families know that they were alive." I have to swallow hard for a moment—all this is too much for me today, I just want to get away, but I cannot let these two unhappy people stay here alone without hope. "Besides," I continue, "there are rumors that soon the Allied Forces will be here, and then we can bring this to their attention and maybe they can find out."

"Do you hear, Friedrich? Do you hear what Miss Inga said?" Mrs. Gaertner's face is showing a radiance that proves to me my hunch was right. "She is so right; we can do that! The Allied Forces, the British and the Americans, they are human, they will help us. . . ."

By now Mr. Gaertner has given in to the temptation of hope. "Don't you speak English? You learned that in school, didn't you? Your mother was always so proud of you. She always told us about your good grades. . . . I bet you could talk to the Engländer. . . ."

"You could tell them that my husband is getting too old to take care of the business, that we need our boy home. . . ." Mrs. Gaertner and her husband are both trying to talk at the same time—it is as if someone has lit a small flame. . . .

Within myself, I am sending a silent prayer: Dear God, please

169

let it be that I did the right thing. . . .

"All right, that's what we will do. As soon as the Western Allies are here, we are all going to the Allied Kommandantura and will tell them what happened. They will try their best to help us." I don't know why I say *us*—the word spilled out. "At that time," I continue, "I will be back to visit you. . . ."

"Oh, no!" They both talk at once. "Oh, no! You must not wait till then to come and see us. Please come before then, won't you?" It is not the formal request for a visit—this is a plea. They have concentrated all their hope on me. It is a responsibility I am not sure I can handle, but I know I have no choice. I will have to come back. . . .

Outside again on my way back home, I give a sigh of relief. There is just so much a person can handle in one day. This day has been one I wish would be over soon. . . .

It is another fifteen-minute walk back home. My thoughts are with the baker couple. If the Americans and the British only knew how many people have put their last hope into their arrival. . . .

Will they ever come? Or has Berlin been sold to the Russians? Peace is here—has been here for some time now. What a peace!

I remember a sarcastic joke from the last days of the war, a kind of sinister *bon mot:* "Enjoy the war—peace wil be horrible!" At that time, of course, I did not know what it meant. Now there is hardly any doubt about its meaning. . . .

How did it all start? How does something like this start? I think back to my early teenage years, and even further back to my first encounter with politics (if the incident can be called that) at the age of nine, when I wanted so desperately to join the games of the girls of the Hitler Youth. At that time I could not quite understand Mama's reserve in letting me join.

That my parents were suspicious of Adolf Hitler's intentions was never more clearly shown than at the time when I had just reached the age of sixteen. I had been working in the Military Supply Office for about three months when I was approached by someone with the suggestion that I join the Nazi Party. I was told that by now I was of the age at which I could be of great

170

help to my country, each person would have to do his share, and so on. Being basically shy, and having worked at my new and first job after school for such a short time only, I did not quite know what to say. I saw no wrong in joining, but my parents' dislike of the Third Reich policies and all they stood for kept my answer very reserved. I simply told him the truth, that I would have to check with my parents first. The man seemed a little annoyed—was it not understood that my parents would agree?

I hastened to say that, oh yes, yes, of course they certainly would, but is it not the law that people under twenty-one, not being of age, must have the consent of their parents for important things?

I stressed the "important," and that seemed to please him.

I was uncomfortable for various reasons. First of all, looking back at my B. D. M. (Hitler Youth) record, it was not a very good one. At first I had gone all out for it. I enjoyed the company of the girls my own age, their games, the field trips, and some of the things we learned, such as first-aid, and so on. All in all, it was an organization much like the Girl Scouts. Once in a while we would put on a show and that I enjoyed tremendously. Once we put on a play in the Olympic Stadium, which held many thousands of people. I was about twelve years old then and my performance brought separate applause. I would have been a fool not to enjoy that.

But by the time we had reached the age of thirteen or fourteen, things changed; political indoctrination started. That's also when my problem started. I don't know quite what it was . . . basically, being a fairly bright child, I enjoyed the challenge of learning new things, but there was something artificial, forced, and at times hypocritical about the whole political subject. Since I was not only bright but sensitive, I perceived something I did not like. It was enough to dampen my enthusiasm to the point where I just did not attend meetings any more.

My parents did anything but object to that. Situations like these were very touchy. The government openly invited chil-

171

dren whose parents showed any form of opposition to the Third Reich policies and beliefs to inform on their parents! No parent in those days, under these conditions, could afford to let a division build up between themselves and their children. When the German population realized the criminality of their government's policies it was too late. Germany was already in the war and committed to the bitter end.... Those who tried to do something about it failed and paid dearly.

Another thing parents disliked intensely, was the so-called "Pflicht Jahr" (duty year). Every fifteen-year-old girl had to serve as a maid for one year in a household of four or more children— free! Now, basically it would not have been too bad— hard work has never really hurt anyone—but the conditions were difficult enough with the constant air raids, not much food, fathers away, and all the other things that go along with being at war, without also pulling young girls out of their homes for a year. Human nature also took its toll; these poor girls in many instances were taken advantage of to the point where some mothers just went and brought their daughters home! That was never looked upon with favor by the Party, of course. After all, families that had many children could do no wrong— they had done their part for the Reich! Unfortunate for you if you only had up to three. . . .

I was lucky. Since I was still in school, I escaped that fate.

Then there was the "Arbeitsdienst" (Work-Service) for the boys. At the age of eighteen they were either drafted into the Armed Forces or into the Arbeitsdienst. Girls could, at age eighteen, volunteer for the Work-Service. That was farm work—up at four in the morning, to bed at eight in the evening—for only twenty-five pfennigs (approximately eight cents) a day! Not enough food, hard labor, and little time or strengh left to write letters to their families.

Towards the end of the war it was the Work-Service first (for one year), then right away into the Armed Forces for the boys. The girls who volunteered for the Work-Service had a reason. They avoided being drafted into the Women's Signal Corps at age eighteen, purely slave labor.

Again I was lucky, just by the fact that I was born in 1928. Had I been one year older, it would probably have been the Signal Corps for me. Even then, towards the end of the war, they did draft younger girls. The fact that I worked in the Military Supply Office saved me. My uncle, who was a Personnel Director there, had a job open and I took it.

Since I had not been attending meetings of the Hitler Youth, we finally had a visitor, the leader of my group, to inquire why I had not been attending meetings. Mama said that since she was working in a factory (she had been assigned the job, since she only had two children), I had to help her in the house and take care of my little sister. It was acceptable as an explanation for the time being, but the lady insisted that I should at least try to attend a few meetings. Mama said she would let me go whenever she could spare me.

I never went. Finally, we had another visit—this time not quite as friendly. The lady said that they would have to strike me off the list (indicating that that was certainly not very good for my future) unless I attended some meetings. Mama told her that I had enough on my hands trying to get enough sleep with all the air raids, doing my school homework, helping her, and so on. She told her also that my grades in school were excellent, and that she felt that was more important for my future than anything else.

Good grades in school were always helpful, even in a dictatorship! After all, the Reich wanted educated people. So again the lady left, and to this day I don't know whether my name was stricken from the list or not!

Now that I had been approached to join the Party, all this might come to light.

As far as my joining was concerned, I had mixed feelings. I don't know any teenager who does not feel flattered by an appeal to be needed by the older generation. Here was my chance to show that I was really an adult, but I knew Mama and

Papa would not go for the idea.

"Guess what, Mama," I said, over dinner. Neither Mama nor Papa answered, they just looked at me, slightly apprehensive. Whenever I said "guess what," it usually meant something they did not approve of! They kept right on eating, and that irritated me.

"Don't you want to hear what 'guess what' is?" I asked, peeved.

"You'll tell us," Papa said, unperturbed.

Oh, parents!

"I have been asked to join the Party."

Simultaneously Mama and Papa put their knives and forks down on the table with a loud bang.

I was grinning to myself. The bombshell had hit! Now I was the one eating, while they just sat there!

Then, both of them at the same time: "Oh–no–you–don't!"

"What's so bad about my joining the Party?"

"What is so bad about it?" Papa was ready to explode. "I'll tell you what's so bad about. . . ."

"Wal–ter!" Mama looked at him, meaningfully. "Careful. . . . Words are not the answer now. . . ."

Hmm, this was beginning to be interesting! The opposition intrigued me.

"Lisa, I am telling you, she is not going to join any Party!"

"Of course, Walter, I agree. But there is no reason to make a big issue of it." Mama turned to me. "What makes you think you want to join the Party?"

Great! How would I answer that?

"Well, I. . . I. . . ." I was trying very hard to find the right answer.

"Well?" Mama never let go of a question. I had better come up with an answer.

"Well, if I don't join, what will my colleagues and my friends think of me?" I thought that was a good one and was very proud of myself.

"Have you ever heard such a silly reason?" Papa blasted off.

174

" 'My colleagues and my friends. . . .' " he imitated me. "Let me tell you something, you silly little green brat: your friends and colleagues won't care a darn if you are in the Party or not! How many of them are members themselves, anyway?"

"I don't know!" By now the issue was not whether to join or not—it was just plain teen-ager against parent. "But what difference does it make anyway? Do I have to have a reason? After all, I am over sixteen. I think I can decide for myself whether I want to do something or not. Suppose I tell you that I am going to join whether you like it or not?"

Papa was now standing in front of the table. He was furious! Mama looked at me very, very disapprovingly.

"In–ga!"

"Well, let me tell you something, young lady—you just wait and see what happens!" He was just about to let loose with another blast.

I decided it was time to call off the war. I was really not at all eager to join the Party. But what right did they have to decide that for me? Still, right now it was best to give in a little.

"You just won't let me do anything. . . ." I mumbled, peeved.

"Inga," Mama the Diplomat put in, "you are just too young to decide something so important. Once you are committed, that's it. It might be wise to investigate a little more if you really want it. Suppose we put the question off until you are eighteen, and then we'll reopen the case."

She gave me a chance to save my sixteen-year-old face.

Maybe it would be best to apologize to Papa. I did not really want him to be angry at me. He was home so seldom . . . soon he would have to leave again, and heaven knows whether I would see him again. . . .

"I'm sorry, Papa. I'm not really anxious to join. . . ."

"Well, okay," he said. By now the storm clouds had begun to disappear. "Believe me, Inga, there is a lot more to joining a political party than just a signature on a piece of paper. You are much too young to realize how much you can get involved in

175

something like this. I myself have been able to stay clear from political activities, but I can assure you that I know a lot of people who are not at all happy with the way things are. . . ." The battle was over.

I never joined.

———————

Now, while I am walking the last few steps back home, I think very much about Papa. If he were home we would not be so hungry. . . . Oh, that bakery smelled good! Maybe the prisoners of war will not be released until the Western Allies are in Berlin. . . . Sure! That's it. As soon as the Americans and the British are here, Papa will come home also. . . . Rotten war—I want my father!

But when are the Western Allies going to come to Berlin? What would we do if they don't ever come?

Simple . . . then I just won't stay in Berlin. There are other places. I try to picture myself leaving Berlin. . . . The rubble and the ruins and the ashes and the broken trees, the desolation and the murder and the rape and the hunger and the fear . . . all behind me. . . . The captain never leaves the sinking ship? . . . I am not the captain! . . . and who says Berlin is a sinking ship? . . . My Berlin, my beautiful Berlin. I know I can never leave you . . . never. Not until you are gracious and gorgeous and happy again. . . .

Du mein Berlin, Berlin, Du Perle an der Spree:
wer dich erst kennt, Berlin, der sagt dir nie ade. . . .

I am humming the familiar tune. It's silly to love a city so much. Why do I? Maybe it's like the mother who has five children, and one is always sick. At that moment she concentrates all her love on the sick child. . . . What does it say in the song . . . "the pearl of the river Spree" . . . Berlin will live again, some day. . . .

"Hello, Mama. I'm back."

"Yes, darling." She is sitting at the kitchen table, her forearms resting flat on the top, in between her fingers is a piece of paper, which she rolls up, then rolls out again, over and over. Her eyes are looking through the window, but it does not seem she sees anything in particular. If I did not know my mother better, I would say she has given herself time off from work and is just relaxing. Maybe it is the frown on her face, or the sadness in her eyes, or the hidden tension in her movement that alerts me to the fact that something is wrong.

"How was your day?" she says, without changing her position or looking at me.

"All right." This is not the time to tell her anything about Annie, or about the baker family.

"What's wrong, Mama?"

Her voice sounds tired. "A lot of things are wrong, Inga. A lot of things. . . ." Normally she talks very fast—today her speech is slow. A horrible thought comes to my mind.

"Papa. . .?" I must have said it out loud.

"No, thank God, that is something we can still hope for, that Papa is all right. . . ."

I breathe a sigh of relief. What else can there be that is horrible?

"What is it then?"

"We not only have to live with hunger, despair, and terror; now we will also have to live with shame and guilt. . . ."

"What do you mean 'shame and guilt,' Mama? The shame and guilt go to the account of the Russians!" I am rather annoyed at Mama. "They are the ones who have to live with it, not we."

"They are not the only ones who committed crimes, Inga." Mama has to pause a moment. She slowly rises and walks towards the window. She leans on the windowsill as if she needs support for the next words.

"My country, my people. . . . I don't think I will ever be able to believe it. . . ."

"Believe what?" I cannot conceal my impatience.

177

"When the British and American troops entered West Germany, they found concentration camps filled with thousands of dying, starving people. They found mass graves of men, women, and children who had been murdered. They found in these camps gas chambers where these people had been gassed en masse. . . ."

I feel myself get ice-cold with anger.

"That is a filthy, rotten lie. Mama, don't you see what they are trying to do? They are trying to whitewash what they did to us by making it look as if we were all criminals! I will never believe it, never!"

"I cannot believe it either, Inga, but I have to. . . . The evidence is there, the survivors are there to tell what happened. . . . And believe me, what they have to tell is more horrible than the wildest distorted imagining any murderer could possibly think up. . . ."

Now I am really angry at my mother.

"Mama, how can you possibly believe such a wild lie? How can you? I know our government was not the best in the world, but mass murder? There has to be another explanation. . . . Anyway, if it were true, would not someone outside the government have known? I find it hard to believe that something like this can in any way go unnoticed by people. Someone, somewhere, had to know—don't you see that?"

"That is what I have been telling myself all the time I was thinking about this whole affair. . . ." Mama puts her hands up to her forehead. "My head is beginning to hurt from thinking. The same questions coming up over and over and over: how? why? when? How is it possible to conceal something so horrible? I just can't think any more. . .I'm tired. . . ."

My anger has not subsided. These beasts! That lie must have been cooked up by the Russians, just so they could say to the world, "What we did in Berlin and Eastern Germany was just reprisal—look what the Germans did!" Well, anybody who did belive that was just a fool! I, for one, would never believe it.

"Come, Mama, sit down and let me get you some coffee."

"No, darling, thank you. Now that you are home I want to get some sleep before I go out of my mind from questions without answers. . . ."

"It's still rather early, but maybe we should try and go to sleep for the night, Mama," I suggest. "Tomorrow is another day. . . ."

"Yes," Mama says, and her voice is filled with bitterness, "tomorrow is another day—one more sad, empty, horrible, hungry day. . . ."

"You'll see that I am right, Mama. One day we will all find out that it was not true at all, that someone who hated us cooked up this lie for revenge or something. . . ." But somehow, deep inside me, I cannot quite believe myself any more. One answer is just as horrible as the other, and both seem impossible to believe. . . .

I have a lot of thinking to do. But I cannot do it today. There is just so much a human being can handle in one day, and this one has had its fill. Anyway, I am not going to believe it—so there!

11

THIS DAY, SAY GOOD-BYE AND FORGET!

We still do not know exactly what is going on in Germany. Apparently some kind of emergency government has been established, since we have been issued ration cards. The amount is just a little bit too much to let you die, but certainly not enough to live on. We can exist just a little longer, but for what reason? To kill us slowly? I must say, some mathematician must have spent uncounted hours figuring exactly how much food a human being needs not to die. . . .

Now we cannot even complain. When we think of our hunger, of the rape of our city and its people, we are also forced to think of the people in concentration camps, whose fate has been like ours or worse, depending upon the individual circumstances. . . . An eye for an eye, a tooth for a tooth. . . . It is not easy to accept reprisal for the guilt of others.

I have learned to accept, at least in my mind, the authenticity of the charges made against Germany; in my heart I have not been able to reconcile myself with the recognition of the horrible truth. If I am quite honest with myself, then I must admit that hidden in the depth of my feelings for my country is still the small hope that it was either a mistake or a lie—that is human nature.

But for the sake of the people who suffered and died in the concentration camps, we have to acknowledge the truth and accept our fate. The innocent paid, but the victims were innocent too. It is a weird kind of justice, and one that I cannot ever condone, but I am not God. Somehow He must know what He is doing. . . .

Among all the turmoil of emotions I have to find answers, and I find those that make at least some kind of sense. Maybe there is even an answer in the background of our ancestors. Thousands of years ago those that were sacrificed to the gods had to be virgins, the symbol of innocence.

I can, at this point, not say whether I will ever be able to fully accept such a philosophy, since the God I believed in was kind and just and the events proved to be most confusing. But for now it helps me find my way.

Something else has come into my mind, which never before even touched it. How must Paula feel? All the time she has been with us—kind, loyal, helpful, a friend in need. Yet, her origin is the country which has caused millions of tragedies, whose people murdered, raped, and looted. And we, who are supposed to be her enemy, are the ones she loves.

I am beginning to see that God does know what He is doing: it is to teach the ugliness, the senselessness, the complete destructiveness of hate. . . . How can I hate Russia when I do not want the world to hate Germany? "Do unto others as you would have them do unto you. . . ." Somewhere, sometime, man has to break the chain of hate, of the terror without end. The event, the act that has taken place, must be despised, but a person who hates is self-destructive. How are we to know that our hate is directed towards the guilty and does not just happen to hit an innocent person?

I cannot point at the Russian troops without also pointing at my own country. Man must be able to forgive in order to be forgiven. Annie was right when she said, "If you fall into a mudpool, it is unimportant whether someone threw you into it or whether you fell in by yourself. You fall into the mud, you get dirty. . . ." So then, maybe people, all people, have a tendency to get dirty at times, and some through no fault of their

181

own. But it also teaches another lesson—watch out that you don't get pushed into the mud. . . .

Thus, I am teaching myself not to hate, but to be alert . . . to forgive and hope to be forgiven, to accept things that cannot be changed without losing hope for some change. All in all, I am much poorer in some ways but much richer in other ways than I was a year ago. The most important thing I have learned is still compassion. If you have never had a tooth pulled without anesthesia, you just cannot know how much it hurts.

Paula and I never talk about these things. She is my friend, I am her friend. Beyond that there is no need for other communication. Lately, I have been worried about her though. She eats less than before, and from day to day she looks thinner. We are trying in every way we possibly can to make her eat more, even to the point where we pretend to have more than we do. We put two days' rations on the table, then say, "I have had enough," but it is not easy to fool Paula. The mathematics of the ration card is just too simple and too obvious.

Today, earlier in the morning, she had looked especially sad. I decide to have a talk with her. Maybe something other than hunger is bothering her. But where is she?

"Mama, do you know where Paula is?"

"I don't really know. I believe she may have gone to the canal for a bit of fresh air."

It does not take long for me to find her. She is at our favorite spot, where we have a marvelous view but cannot be seen too easily by others. She is lying down in the grass, hands folded under her head, looking up into the sky.

"Hello."

"Angel." She sits up as I approach her.

"Why didn't you ask me to come with you? You know I like to be here too."

"Me must be alone," she says, not looking at me.

"Why?"

She does not answer. But I seldom give up on an important question.

"Why?" I repeat.

182

"You must know," she says.

"Know what?"

"That me must go back to Russia."

Well, of all the things to say! She is just saying that, she does not mean it.

"Paula, you're crazy. Why should you have to go back to Russia? It is simply ridiculous—you said yourself that you were going to stay in Germany—so how come suddenly you want to go back? Have we hurt you? Has anyone hurt you?"

She quickly puts her hand on mine. "Oh no, no, no! Nix hurt! Nobody! Me no want to—me must!"

"But in heaven's name, why?"

"Yesterday, me go Kommandanturra. Kommandant says all Russians must go back in Russia or no ration card."

"Paula, we've gone through this before. We told you we will share what we have with you. It cannot stay like this forever. Sooner or later we will have to get more to eat, if we can just last through this a little bit longer." By now I am a little panicky; she sounds this time as if she means it!

"Me tell Kommandant," Paula says, "but Kommandant says, 'You Russian—you must go back. If not go back, you no goott Russian. Peng-peng!'" She makes a motion with her finger as if she is pulling the trigger of a pistol.

My God, what a country! You have to threaten to kill in order to get your people back into it! I shudder.

And Paula has to go there. Never—I won't let her.

My imagination does not give up too easily. "I know what we'll do. We'll hide you so they can't find you! Nobody knows where you are anyway, do they?"

I have not noticed that Paula has not answered. I am too engrossed in my mental search for a good hiding place.

"I know, Paula!" I am enthusiastic. "We can use one of the empty rooms and make it look as if there is no room at all, and if we board it up it will work!" I am thinking back to the time when we hid from the invading Russians that one horrible night.

"Paula?"

She is looking at me, not saying a word. I have never seen her

183

cry before; it's funny how you never know with some people that they can be unhappy too. . . . You never look for a crack in the walls of the fortress. . . . Seeing the tears slowly run down her cheeks, I finally realize the inevitable truth. I know I will never see her again.

Before I have a chance to give in to my despair, she says, "Kommandant also said, 'Your friends, they hide you, they dead too!' "

"Who cares?" I have to scream at someone; I don't really know whom I am screaming at. "Who the devil cares? They might as well finish the job now! They have done so much already—a little bit more or less does not make much difference!"

But my anger delays the coming grief only for moments. I pull my knees up to my chest to hide my face, but even Paula cannot stop my sobbing.

It has been a nasty night.

Almost all night long I have been lying awake, trying to think of some way to keep Paula here, knowing all the time it will be in vain. Apart from the fact that Paula's own life is involved, it is also the life of other people: my two little sisters, Mama, maybe Omi and Opa too. For myself I don't honestly care. But with all involved I do not even have the right to try and persuade Paula to stay. That the Russians mean what they say when they threaten with death we all know.

For Paula's sake I should try and make the best of it so that she does not suffer more by seeing me so unhappy. But I cannot do that. There are times when I am able to hide what bothers me, but not now.

The saying "Man does not live by bread alone" has never been made more clear. I am, under the circumstances, always hungry, but today again I cannot eat. Today is the day Paula is leaving, and it seems as if the sky at least shows some kind of empathy—it is gray and dreary.

We make the good-bye fast. Paula does not have many things to pack, one medium-sized suitcase, that's all.

And then there is the bicycle. My own bicycle had been stolen by the Russians. They were crazy about bikes, and any time they could lay their hands on one, they did so—without asking, of course.

Where Paula got her bicycle I never knew. I think she said a Russian gave it to her, and since the Russian army did not attack Berlin riding bicycles, it can be assumed that it, too, was stolen. But since everything else was stolen and never found its way back to the owners, this time at least there seemed to have been some kind of strange justice involved—it had found a deserving owner.

"Me take bike to station," she is saying now, "then you go back home on bike."

"Oh no, Paula, I don't want the bike. Can't you take it to Russia with you?"

"No, can take only little bit."

We have decided to walk to the station together. Mama does not go for the idea, I know. There are too many Russian soldiers around, especially in a station that harbors trains heading for Russia. . . . I myself do not feel too comfortable, but I cannot possibly bring myself to let Paula go alone. At least I will see that she is on the train to her home town.

Besides, as long as I am with Paula, nothing will happen to me. As soon as she is on the train, I will take off in a hurry on the bike and race back home. The "shooting-in-broad-daylight" game is over by now, so nothing could happen to me too easily.

We have left early enough to be able to walk slowly. The suitcase has been placed on the baggage plate on the back of the bicycle, and Paula is leading the bike.

Neither one of us talks much. We make believe we are just taking a sightseeing tour, with only a casual remark now and then. Before we know it we have reached the station.

It is crowded with Russians, both civilians and soldiers, all headed for home. I wish all Russians were headed that way, except for Paula, of course. . . .

185

Paula leaves me for a few minutes to find out exactly when her train leaves, but I make sure she stays within my sight, just in case!

When she returns she says, "Angel, you go home now. Train not leave till evening."

I am not sure whether I should believe her. Maybe she just wants to make it easy for me. . . . Still, there is nothing I can do. And perhaps it is best that way. Besides, the Russian uniforms still create fear in me. In a way I am almost relieved to get it over with, for more than one reason.

"Will you write me, Paula?" It is a silly question; there is hardly any possibility that mail from Russia will ever reach a German civilian. . . . I wonder if even the Russian soldiers have a chance to hear from home. But I must have something to take the horror of finality away from me. . . .

Paula is no dumbbell. "Yes, Angel," she says.

"Soon?"

Maybe she can find someone to bring a letter. Maybe somebody will come visit Germany and deliver the letter personally. . . .

"Yes."

By now I have steeled myself against my feelings. I hate to make a show. None of these people will see me cry!

One quick hug—and then it is over.

On my way home, out of the corner of my eye, I see that some of the Russian soldiers are making remarks at me, but they are not threatening. Who the devil cares? . . . I am pedaling my new-old precious bike as fast as I can. With each downward push, I am stamping on someone or something.

Funny, my cheeks are not even wet, the wind in my face blows the tears right out of my eyes before they have a chance to run down.

———————

The rumors about the Western Allies and their possible participation in the occupation of Berlin have increased. Thank God, maybe soon life will change. . . . The rumors say that they will divide Berlin in sectors: American, British, French, and Russian. People have now a chance to play a game—which sector will ours be? Frankly, no one cares whether it is American or British; everybody likes them. The opinion about the French is divided; some say "It's okay," but others say "horrible!" Obviously no one wants to be a part of the Russian sector.

We all feel a little like figures in a game of chess. For years now we have been moved up and down, back and forth, left to right, some toppled over, some pulled out of the game, some captured. . . .

But when will we know?

It is not easy to get used to Paula's absence. The first few days are horrible. Now I have adjusted—up to a point.

Each time I get especially hungry I think of Paula. . . . And today I am especially hungry. Mama wants me to go downtown to pick up the new issue of ration cards. I am not looking forward to it; the temptation to step into the little bakery to buy a whole week's supply of bread and eat it up all at once is almost too strong to be ignored. Well, what has to be done has to be done. I have learned to fight temptation as one learns to ward off pesky flies.

I make it a point to go past the bakery, with its taunting fragrance of freshly baked bread, on the other side of the road.

After I have picked up our ration cards and am on my way back home, I cannot help but think that here, in my pocket, I have the means to fill my stomach enough just once, not to be left hungry . . . three little pieces of paper. . . . All I have to do is take one of them out, go across the road, go into the store, and—voilá!—I am not hungry any more! . . .

I stop for a moment. Across the road from me is the bakery. Maybe just one loaf? I do not really have to buy all three. Then what? Instead of eating two slices I can only eat one for quite a number of days. And how would Mama feel, seeing me hungry? She would probably give me some of her ration, and that would just not be fair. . . . No, no, I just can't do it.

But it is my ration card, issued to me, Inga, to do with as I please. . . .

187

"Miss," someone is saying to me, "I don't want to alarm you, but in case you have not noticed, there is a Russian soldier standing behind you. He has been looking at you for quite a while. . . ." Then quickly the man speaking to me is gone again.

That's just what I need now. A Russian bothering me! Can't these horrible people ever leave us alone?

I have to make a fast decision: shall I run, or shall I pretend not to have noticed and just walk away at normal speed, or shall I just go right up to him and say, "Get away from me, you. . .?" In my present mood I am more angry than afraid.

Let him come! There is only one of him, and there are quite a few German civilians around. I'm sure they would help me.

He is standing in front of me.

Out of the corner of my eye I notice that some of the passersby have also stopped. Are they just curious, or would they really help me? You never know with people. . . .

By now it is too late to run, although suddenly I want to.

"You, mother? Father?" he says.

That's a switch! They don't usually ask questions like these. I wonder what he is up to?

All I can do is nod.

He has started to fumble around in a canvas bag he is carrying over his shoulder.

My God! Does he have a weapon in there? Is he going to pull a gun?

Suddenly he is holding in his hand—a loaf of bread!

He offers it to me.

"You home; mother, father," he says with a smile.

For a moment I am thinking that maybe he means he wants to come home with me and am just ready to turn and run. But he puts the bread in my hand, turns about quickly, and walks away.

I stand there, startled, clutching the loaf of bread. The passersby drift away with envious glances.

It is the best loaf of bread we have ever eaten!

As for me, I have learned another lesson. I will never again prejudge, and I will never again judge all; any decision must be made on an individual basis.

Maybe the lessons I am learning are worth the price I am paying. . . .

We have a visitor today, my father's sister, Aunt Emma. She is elderly, about seventeen years older than my father. Papa had been a little surprise package that arrived in his parents' middle age. Cousin Hilda, whom we had meant to stay with during our odyssey to Tegel, is her daughter.

She is bright, hard-working, outspoken, and still good-looking. I remember that she always had her home filled with fascinating things—a paradise for a child—and as a result I was always thrilled to visit her.

"Have you heard from Walter yet, Lisa?" she asks Mama.

Mama shakes her head sadly.

"No, Emma. We have hopes that he may be in Denmark as a prisoner of war. In that case he could be sent home when the Western Allies come here."

"Well, let's hope you are right. I am beginning to wonder if any one of us can really be lucky enough to be spared. . . ."

She takes a very small package out of her handbag and gives it to Mama. "Here, make us a cup of good coffee."

Good coffee—that means real coffee! We have not seen this in months! That is just like Aunt Emma, she always manages to have something that most people are not able to get. How does she do it?

While Mama is making the coffee, we just sit there making small talk. Somehow, though, I have the eerie feeling that Aunt Emma's visit is not casual, that there is something she wants to tell us, but I cannot sense whether it is good or bad. . . .

After we have enjoyed the coffee, Aunt Emma says, "Lisa, there is something I have to tell you. It is a very sad, shocking

189

thing, and you must brace yourself to take it as well as you can. . . ."

We know that it does not concern Papa—she would not have asked about him at the beginning.

"Yes?" Mama asks apprehensively.

"Our brother Fritz, his wife, and his daughter are dead."

"Oh, my God. . . ." Mama tries hard to fight back the tears.

Aunt Emma herself is shaken. "The saddest and most shocking thing, though, is the way they died. They committed suicide."

"I can't believe that!" Mama is so shocked it temporarily overcomes her grief. "My God, Emma, they had everything in the world to live for. They were always the happiest couple, they had the nicest house, they even owned their home. I just can't. . . ."

"You will understand when I tell you," Aunt Emma interrupts her.

Suicide? Uncle Fritz and all his family? It cannot be true. . . . The last time I saw them they were so happy. In fact, it had always amazed me that despite the personal tragedy in their life they managed to be as happy as they were. . . . Aunt Elli was paralyzed for life, she had an incurable disease. Their daughter, Hanni, was an extremely pretty girl, at the end of the war about nineteen years old. I never knew them to be anything but cheerful. Everyone did their own best to help make things better for Aunt Elli. Uncle Fritz worked ten to twelve hours a day to provide the best of care, the daughter cared for the whole household, starting at a very early age. They owned their home, a beautiful brick house; Uncle Fritz had built most of it himself. Since he was a stonemason it was not too hard, but it still took many man-hours of work. It was, considering the circumstances, their life's work.

When was the last time I had seen them? Remembering it brought back memories. The evacuation of some of our belongings during the end of the war, when it had taken me three times as long to get back home as it would have under normal circumstances . . . the attack on the train, the little girl standing next to me, our refuge under the train, the bullet holes in the shop window. . . .

Thank goodness I had been able to spend such a peaceful night with my relatives before I set out on my journey back home. And now, dead? Somehow I cannot absorb it. I still hear Cousin Hanni joking to me about the good-looking soldiers I might meet on the train and whom I should beware of. I still see Uncle Fritz working as hard as ever, and as cheerful as ever; Aunt Elli's friendly good-bye wave from her sickbed. . . . Dead? Killed themselves? Why? How?

Aunt Emma is telling us.

Uncle Fritz and his family were told by the Russian Kommandant to leave their house, since the Russians wanted it for their troops. Uncle Fritz argued, pointing out that his wife was paralyzed. Where could he take her? He could not possibly carry her more than a mile. It was to no avail; they did not even assign them at least a temporary home.

Earlier, Aunt Emma tells us, Hanni had been torn away by the Russians from the sickbed of her mother, who knew what was in store for her daughter and had to listen to her cries for help. Then Uncle Fritz had been taken to the Kommandantura for interrogation—at least that's what they called it. None of the family had ever been politically involved in any way.

Their nerves were still raw from the previous ordeals. When they were ordered out of the house with nowhere to go, with an invalid who was unable to walk, it was too much. They carried Aunt Elli for a mile or so to one of the fields they still owned. Then they sat down and decided that they were going to end their lives.

Uncle Fritz wrote a few lines to explain their decision. Then, during the night, he dug up a gun he had buried somewhere. He shot his wife, his daughter, and then himself.

For a long time we sit in silence. There are times when shock is so great that there is no room for tears.

"I don't think I can ever tell Walter. . . ." The lines in Mama's face are sharp today, her complexion is gray.

For myself, I can only say that I am struggling to keep up my

191

belief in the self-taught lessons of the previous days. But both Mama and I have another rough night. . . .

———————

We have received word that Helen is coming. Hurrah! I like her. She is Mama's friend, has been since I was a baby. . . . Her sense of humor is refreshing, and right now in these horrible times her company is something to look forward to. She is outwardly not at all pretty or good-looking; it is hard to describe her physical unattractiveness, but when she talks, when she smiles—warm, radiant, friendly—the world seems only half as gray as it is. She is also full of courage and determination. "Nobody would steal the butter off her bread!" Mama used to say.

Helen's sense of duty was unsurpassed. She had taken on the management of two large apartment houses in a nice section of Berlin. Her work included cleaning the stairs, hallways, windows, carpets, basements, and attics, of both four-story buildings. I could not even climb the stairs without getting out of breath! She had to collect rent, see to it that repairs were made when needed, and perform all the other tasks that go along with a job like that. Since her husband had an eight-hour-a-day job, he could not help her much. How she did it neither Mama nor I could ever understand.

But Helen never lost her sense of humor.

Mama had saved the coffee grounds from Aunt Emma's visit; they could be used once more. . . . We had also found a new recipe for a sandwich spread. Some cereal had been issued—not much, but a little extra, which helped a great deal. We would put a teaspoonful of our precious grease (whatever it was no one ever knew), officially called "Butterschmalz," into a cooking pot, then add the cereal, let it brown slightly, add some water, pepper, and salt, and after it was cooled it made a rather unusual but not bad-tasting sandwich spread. Even that, of course, was a rarity and delicacy. You could also switch the flavor by adding parsley, basil, marjoram, or other spices.

This we had made in celebration of Helen's visit and we were planning to have a little feast: a slice of bread with the sandwich spread and coffee from the doubly brewed coffee grounds.

"Boy, oh boy! Do I smell real coffee here somewhere?" Helen's face is poking through the door. "Dare one enter these sacred halls?"

"Come right in." Mama is as happy as I am. "Oh, Helen, it is so good to see you."

"Yes, it has been a long time. . . . Here, I brought you something—a piece of potato cake. Have you ever had that?"

Oh good, I knew what potato cake was. We used to make it; it had a nice yellow color, smelled good and tempting, and was moist as if it was loaded with butter. Potatoes were boiled, peeled, then put through the mincer; baking powder, sugar, some butter-flavoring was added, and after it was baked you had a delicious brown-crusted cake.

What a lovely day! A good meal, nice company—almost like old times. . . .

Helen is enjoying her sandwich spread. "What is it? It tastes good." Mama is just grinning.

"Ah yes," Helen nods understandingly, "Lohengrin brand: 'never shalt thou ask me . . . ' right?"

We all laugh; it feels good to laugh again.

"I have an idea," Helen says. "Why don't Inga and I go on a little trip."

"A trip? What do you mean?"

"Well, I have a bike, Inga has a bike—and fifty miles from here are farmers who would be willing to exchange some things we need, like food, for some things they need, like clothing, or towels, or watches, or other useful things. So tomorrow morning, before dawn, we are going to ride down to Werder and see if we can't coax some farmer into parting with some potatoes, or flour, or maybe even butter. How about it?"

The expression on Mama's face shows mixed emotions.

"It sounds all right, Helen," she hesitates slightly, "but what about the Russians? You would have to go through miles and miles of Russian occupied territory. . . ."

193

"Nonsense!" Helen is, as always, self-confident. "You just have to know how to deal with them. If you show them you are afraid, they will hurt you, naturally. But I found that if you show them your teeth, they pull in their tails and take off!"

"Well, Helen, I can't say that this is the impression I got after all that happened. Maybe you don't know them as well as we do."

"Don't be such a chicken, Lisa. The times of open looting, rape, killing, and so on are over now. They know the Americans and British are coming soon; they are going to try their best to behave. . . ."

"I never thought of that." Mama looks at me with a question: "Inga?"

At the moment I can just nod. My feelings are unimportant right now.

"But what are we going to exchange, Mama?"

"Oh dear. . . ." Mama's face shows disappointment. "You are right. We don't have anything. . . ."

"Oh, come on Lisa, you must have something. What about an old pair of pants, or some jewelry, or some old sweater or so. . . ."

I have Papa's gold watch which we had been able to save from the Russians. Darned if I am going to give that. I am not going to part with it after all the turmoil through which we had saved it! I'd rather starve to death.

Mama has been wearing her wedding band on a crude chain around her neck. Looking at it now, I am sure she is thinking about Monika, Chris, and me. Momentarily I feel a little ashamed; I should not let her part with it, I should offer my watch instead. I don't, but then I am not a mother. . . .

"Walter will give me a new one when he comes home," Mama murmurs.

Sure—that is what he will do. He will understand.

"Good. Anything else you can come up with?" Helen is taking another sip of her coffee.

"What about that old pair of pants we found outside half-

194

buried in the ground, Mama? They won't fit Papa or anyone else I know. . . ."

"Of course, that's it!" Mama is happy now. "I have washed them, all they need is a good ironing; they are still in pretty good shape."

"See if you can come up with anything else you can spare, Lisa," Helen says before departing. "Anyway, what you have will probably already get us something. . . ."

She kisses us good-bye. "Be at my place tomorrow morning at four o'clock."

That means I have to get up at three at the latest—good grief! I hate to get up early! Well, I have no choice. Helen knows what she is doing.

———————

It is a long, long ride. Helen is fast; she takes long powerful strokes and is always ahead of me. Once in a while she rides a little slower so that I can catch up with her; then we ride side by side for a stretch.

Soon I realize what she is doing; being ahead of me, she can explore the area for Russians. If there are any, we ride as fast as we can. That is usually the case in the neighborhood of small towns or villages. When we have left these, we can go slower, since we hardly see any Russians. Even so, it is nerve-racking.

I am still weak from the many months of hunger and emotionally exhausted from the turmoil. Right now I am also very tired from the long, fast bicycle ride. Anyway, how are we going to do it? Do you just go up to someone's door and say, "Hello, I want you to give me some food, I am hungry. Could you use an old pair of pants?" Or, "Hello, my mother is sacrificing her wedding band so that her children can eat. Do you have some food?"

Not me. I won't. I will not go to anybody's door and beg. But it isn't begging, I tell myself; you have something they may want. Want? What—somebody else's wedding band? An old pair

195

of pants? Want? Ha-ha, that's funny! Suppose they laugh at me?

I begin to shake inside, just thinking about it. Being seventeen, I still have my feelings on my sleeve. The adult sophistication for dealing with a situation like this has not yet reached me.

But I also have optimism. Helen will know how to deal with this, she will show me how to do it. . . .

Okay, on we go.

It is really a pretty day. The fields are displaying their last, almost painful, attempt at growth, the trees are trying to hold on to their leaves, but the season takes its toll. Fall is here, soon the world will go to sleep for a while, covered with the warming, protecting blanket of snow. . . . It's the ice that goes with it that I don't like. . . .

High up in the sky, a falcon circles around; his movements look desperate. Will he find something to eat? I don't want to see whether he does or not. . . . Why does everything that lives have to eat? Why did God make it that way? The trees and the flowers live, they don't have to eat. But they must have rain, and good soil, and even manure. . . .

Well, enough of that. We have gone out to do something. The thought of going back home with nothing is more than I can bear. Mama would never let me know if she is disappointed, I know that, but all this for nothing? We shall see. I can at least try.

"You see this one coming up? That farmhouse there on the left?" Helen is looking back at me. "It looks like we should make this our first 'victim.' " She is laughing. How can she be so casual? Well, it's just as well. She has stopped, leans her bike against the garden fence, and motions to me to do the same. I let her go first. I want to see how she does it.

She opens the garden gate and walks towards the house door. I am just about ready to follow her, when out from somewhere comes a black flash of lightning, barking like crazy, rushing at us.

"Ooops!" Helen cries, grinning. She backs out and closes the gate quickly.

Safely behind the fence she shouts, "Hello, there! Hello there! Is anybody home?"

The dog is still barking wildly, jumping up and down against the gate. A window opens, a woman looks out, but with the dog barking we cannot hear what she is saying.

The woman must have been calling the dog back—he leaves, tail wagging, and disappears inside the house.

"Yes?"

The question does not sound too friendly. My heart is pounding. "We would like to ask you if you have some potatoes, or eggs, or butter, or anything else to exchange. . . ." Helen has to shout it fairly loud. "We have some things here that. . . ." Helen does not have a chance to finish.

"You city people!" the woman screams. "You come here every day and bother us, knowing darn well we don't have any more than you. But we work a lot harder for it than you, do you hear me? A lot harder!"

One side of the window has already been slammed shut. She leans out once more to yell.

"First it's the Russians that take everything, then it's you city folks. I have just about had enough of all this!" Bam! goes the other half of the window.

It's hard to tell whether it bothers Helen. I know her well enough to know that she can put up a good front.

"Well, you can't win them all," she says nonchalantly. Whistling, she mounts her bike again and takes off. I have no choice but to follow her.

I want to get away from that horrible scene as fast as I can. After about five hundred yards Helen stops. We both sit down in the grass for a few moments.

"Apparently this is a route too many people have already taken," she says. "What we have to do is hit the side roads where there is less chance that others have already been. . . ."

"Helen, I don't think I can go through with this."

"Oh, come on, Inga, don't be such a pussyfoot! So we've been yelled at once! You can't really blame them, you know. They are probably being bothered every day by people. There

197

comes a time when it gets just too much. It would be asking too much to be successful at the first try. . . ." She takes her handkerchief and is drying my tears. "Hush, hush, sweetheart, don't take it so hard. You'll see, the next time it will be better, and you'll get used to it. . . ."

"I'll never get used to begging!"

"Honey, we are not begging. We are just trying to provide food for our families, in any way we can. That is a responsibility we have, you know."

She has hit the right spot. The secret word is responsibility—I can't let them down: Mama, Chris, Monika, even Papa. . . . If Papa were home, he would do all this. . . . As it is, he is not and I am the oldest, so I have to try and take his place.

"Okay, let's try again."

And once again I am learning. . . .

Soon we come to a place that is not enclosed with a fence.

"Let's try here," says Helen.

I expect much the same procedure as the first time, but I steel myself. An elderly woman opens the door.

Helen repeats her speech. This woman is at least friendly.

"We don't have much ourselves," she says, almost apologetically. "I don't really know what I can give you. . . ." She looks as if she is at least trying.

"Do you have children?" The woman looks at Helen.

"Two." Then Helen points to me. "And this girl has two little sisters at home. . . ."

"Wait here," the woman says.

She returns with a small basket full of food. "I told my husband that since the Russians took away my wedding band, here was a chance to get one back," she says, smiling. She takes Mama's wedding band.

"I'll be waiting at the bike, Helen," I say. From here on in I can afford to be out of the picture without feeling like a heel, letting Helen do it all alone. . . .

Helen had brought quite a few things along with her. I never asked her how much or what. She finishes her deal with the woman and comes back cheerful.

198

"Not too bad for a start," she says. And then she shares all she has received with me; each of us gets one-half pound of flour, six eggs, one-quarter pound of butter and half a loaf of bread.

A big load falls off my shoulders; at least I will not return home empty-handed! From here on in, I don't care much what happens, as long as I get home safe and sound with my precious merchandise. As we continue on our trip, we are riding side by side, singing, "Wem Gott will rechte Gunst erweisen, den schickt er in die weite Welt. . . ." (Whom God wishes to favor, he sends out to explore the world.)

We have no more success. Some people are nice about their refusals, some not so nice. It is now getting close to afternoon— we must hurry. To be on the road after dark is still risky. And it is getting dark earlier now in fall.

I have begun to feel a little discouraged again. I had hoped to get more—if I divide what I have into three, then there is not much for anyone. . . . Still, it will help a little.

"We will try one more time," Helen says. She is discouraged too.

A man opens the door.

The usual scene: Helen saying her speech, the man shaking his head. Slowly, Helen walks away. I have stayed with the bikes; someone has to watch our precious loot.

The man looks at Helen walking away, her feet are dragging.

"Wait a minute!" he shouts.

Helen runs back. She beckons to me; the man has disappeared for a moment.

"He asked me if some apples would do," Helen whispers. "I told him anything would do, anything at all. He says he has quite a few apples. He said he could use a pair of pants to work in."

The man has returned with a huge basket of apples; I estimate about sixty pounds. Hurrah! We thank him very much, and divide the apples between us. We stuff them into bags and hang them on each side of our bikes.

Now that it is over, I am glad we came. Are they going to

make eyes at home! They probably think we will come home empty-handed!

The next task is to get everything home.

When the Russian soldiers see German civilians carrying full bags, they stop and search them. If they find anything they like they do not hesitate to take it. If you argue, you may end up in some Kommandant's office, and if he likes what he sees, he may just want more than what you are carrying. . . . These things still happen every day. We have heard this from neighbors, friends, relatives, who have all tried it, and know from experience. So it's best to go home unnoticed, and that is not easy.

We know one touchy point where, upon entering the city limits of Berlin again, we have to pass a guard. I know I will not feel safe until we have passed him.

"Frau, komm!" says the Russian guard. I must go inside the guardhouse. How I hate that expression! It was the phrase the Russian soldiers used before they raped the women. It still terrifies me.

"My daughter!" Helen says, pointing to me "Nix komm! Here, you can see here!" She opens her bag. "You see; apples, just apples!"

He looks into my bags too. The six eggs are in my handbag, dangling from the front of the bike. The rest of the food is under the apples at the bottom of the bag.

He fumbles around in the bag for a few moments, but decides against making us empty it all out. He looks at me, at first suspiciously, then with a grin. I'd rather have him look at me with suspicion than the grin. . . . Helen is watching. "Daughter, you come!" she says harshly, and she gives me a rough nudge to mount my bike. She keeps on yelling at me, stupid things that do not make much sense. I get the message. I scowl and get on my bike. With much gesticulation and threatening hand-waving, Helen continues to yell at me.

The Russian is baffled at first. Then he grins from ear to ear, points at Helen in a gesture that says, "Oh boy, better keep away from her!" and motions us to go on.

I have an eerie feeling that it had been close to developing into a touchy situation; I had smelled vodka. By now, the Russians behaved fairly civilized when sober, but when they had something to drink they did not care about the consequences. They always figured they would get away with it, and most of the time they did. If you reported to the Russian Kommandant that you had been molested, he would say sarcastically that you should bring him the soldier and he would punish him. Can you imagine a woman bringing a Russian soldier with a gun to the Kommandant?

All this went through my mind as we rode away from that place as if the devil was chasing us. After a mile of frantic pedaling, we breathed a sigh of relief. Then Helen looked at me, I looked at her, and we both burst out laughing.

"How did we do that?" Helen is almost choking. "Boy, that Russian must have a mean mother-in-law or something, the way he got scared when I started yelling!"

I am laughing so hard I can hardly answer. There is a little bit of hysteria in that laughter, but who cares? We are on our way, and fairly safe.

"You better go right on home, Inga," Helen remarks as we say good-bye at her front door. "Better not come in—your mother will be worried."

I thank her for everything and take off. On my way home I evaluate the events; one hundred miles on a bicycle, twelve hours on the road, humiliation, fear, one golden wedding band, one pair of pants—all for six eggs, half a loaf of bread, one-quarter pound of butter, one-half pound of flour, and thirty pounds of apples. . . . But for a few days, we will be rich and live a little.

When I arrive home, I fall onto my bed, exhausted. I do not even fully enjoy the happiness our loot has created. I sleep and sleep and sleep.

When I wake next morning and look out of the window, I see two men in uniforms approaching the house. Russians? Have they somehow discovered that we smuggled some food through yesterday and have now come to take it away again?

Wait a minute—these are not Russian uniforms. There is

201

something red on their hats, and their uniforms are a kind of brown, not dirty green like the Russians. . . . Who are they? They are wearing some kind of an armband. As they come closer, I see that it says—*M.P.*

With one jump I am out of my bed.

"Mother!" My voice is hoarse with excitement. "Mother, the British are here! The British are here!"

I in my nightgown and Mama, who is already dressed, are dancing around the room, singing: "We have won in the lottery! We have won in the lottery! We are British sector! We are British sector!"

Now things will change. Now, life will begin again. Now, we will be people again. Now, we will have food again. Now—Papa will come home again. . . ?

The reign of terror is over.

Those that were sent away they
knew, but now they receive back
not the faces they longed to see,
only a heap of ashes.

Aeschylus

12

ARE DAYS CHANGING?

That I have expected life to change immediately can only be attributed to my youth. Still, some very important things are different from the way it was before the Western Allies came. We dare walk on our streets again, day or night, and gradually a certain amount of faith in law and order has been restored within us.

The best thing that has happened is, of course, that the Russian troops have left our area. I still can't quite figure when it happened—all of a sudden they were gone! There were no more dirty uniforms but very neat, clean uniforms of a different color; no more gutteral sounds, but Western sounds spoken with politeness and even a certain amount of kindness. Politeness and kindness are in the tone of a voice; you don't have to understand the language.

Now and then there would be a fight between either the British or the American Military Police and some Russian military visitors if the latter misbehaved! The British and American troops came to the defense of the German population at any time—no questions asked! Of course, the official rule forbade "fraternization," but that was hardly ever enforced.

It was the children who started the relationships. . . . Children do not conceal their feelings, and they were just not afraid of the Americans and the British! It was the children who, on various occasions, came running home, "Mommy, Mommy, look what I've got!" holding in their hands some chocolate or a can of food or some fruit or nuts. It was the children who once in a while would arrive home holding the hand of an American or British soldier, saying, "I brought my friend along. . . ."

Between the Berlin population and the American and British troops there was seldom any animosity. We understood each other. Had the British and American troops not come when they did, a population of approximately four million people would have slowly, gradually, and in different ways, been exterminated. . . .

Some buses are running again, even the railroad in some areas; electricity was reinstated some time ago, most waterlines are repaired, here and there is a store with empty windows but at least some rationed supplies. It is very little, too little not to be still very hungry, but the most important thing is really the removal of the constant threat to life, of harassment, of cruelty, of terror. The Berliners can breathe again. . . .

The Allies are trying hard to lift up the beaten enemy and restore pride and the desire to rebuild. But even the Allies cannot eliminate the tragedies that are still occurring as a result of the war.

Day after day, and more each time, the prisoners of war are coming home from Russia. Each time I see them in rags, dirty, unshaven, hollow eyes displaying hopelessness and defeat, thin as skeletons, walking slowly with their backs bent as if the burden of life is too much for them—each time I see one of them I see all of Germany, and my heart sinks.

No fanfares for them. No band to welcome them home. No one greeting them. No one saying, "Thank you for risking your life for us. . . ." For some, not even a family. There is no sadder sight than the leftovers from a beaten, defeated army.

204

Would Papa look like this? I don't think I could bear the sight. . . . And now they do not even have respect. How can a country be respected when there was an Auschwitz, a Belsen, a Buchenwald? How can Germany ever erase the memory of what took place in those cooking pots of hell?

In my mind the question still is how it was possible to keep the murdering hidden from the German population, from the world. How? Maybe only one who has lived under total dictatorship can answer that question and analyze. And maybe the only way to find an answer is to put it on a personal basis.

Let me assume that our Jewish family physician, Dr. Ehrhardt, had not left for Palestine when he did. What would have happened? If he had let us know that he was to be taken to a concentration camp, we would have tried to hide him or get him out of the country. If there had not been enough time, we would have tried to get him free and would have done everything in our power to help him. In doing so, we would very likely have come across some of the facts of what was going on in concentration camps. We might have tried to join the underground or leave the country ourselves.

Or perhaps one day we would have gone to his office and found him absent. Upon inquiring as to his whereabouts, we would have been told that he had been taken away to a camp to be shipped out of the country. In which case there would hardly have been any necessity to inquire further, especially since this could have been his own decision. And since no one suspects a murder unless there is a corpse, we would not have had any reason to investigate further.

Concentration camps? Yes, we had heard of those. Maybe everybody had a different idea as to what they were. Mine was that of an internment camp, the kind that exists in every country in time of war; a place where people lived until the war was over so that they could not commit sabotage or be involved in fighting against their own country.

In my opinion, the only people who really knew the truth

205

about these camps were those who ordered the atrocities and those who guarded the camps, and that was an extremely small minority of the German population. Every country has sick people, the difference is only in their position; if they come to power, the country is doomed.

It was Germany's crime that it had let a sick, violent, and loud minority come to power.

Those who knew what was going on had every reason in the world to keep quiet about it to save their own skins. Is it so hard to understand then that the rest of the German population did not know what was going on?

There may have been a few people who, despite some suspicions they may have had, still kept quiet when they should have investigated. To understand these, without excusing them, it has to be understood what a dictatorship really is—the only tool it has working for it is terror, or else it would not need to be a dictatorship! Nothing teaches men more quickly to mind their own business than terror. It takes either a disaster or numerous known tragedies for some people to be shaken out of their lethargy and revolt against tyranny and terror. But even those who had suspicions were small in number.

The killer, with murder in his heart, works smoothly and swiftly, and I do not believe that he announces his intentions beforehand or proclaims his deeds afterwards; if he did, he would be stopped, so he has to keep quiet. Germany has been accused of many things: arrogance, self-righteousness, contempt for other countries or minorities, and various other evils. Some of these faults may apply to some of the German people, but the whole country is not insane or afflicted with the killer instinct.

When later I finally yielded to accepting the truth about the concentration camps—that the crime did happen, that it was done by my countrymen, that it did take place on German soil—I found myself being ashamed of even having been born in that country. Then, seeing the destruction, the suffering of the people, and the fact that the price was paid mostly by those

206

who had neither knowledge about it nor anything to do with it, shame and horror were replaced by great sadness.

I imagined the concentration camps: thousands of people dead, mutilated in either body or soul, treated worse than animals, deprived of every human right and justice, starved and beaten because a country made the wrong choice in leadership. . . . No matter how much I tell myself that it did take place here, in my country, I don't think I can ever fully accept the whole horrible truth. . . . And all the while we were sitting in our homes, complaining about air raids, living our daily lives, not knowing! When, in my thoughts, I reach that point, I know it is best to stop thinking before I go crazy.

But I also cannot hate my country. Too many people in it are good, and have suffered bitterly through no fault of their own. Too many people are like me, wandering about in a daze, asking the same questions. How could it happen? Why did it happen? How could we live here without knowing? Were we too complacent? Should we have questioned more? Investigated more? But how can you fight crime and evil when you don't even suspect it exists?

My parents did not believe in our kind of government because they did not approve of what it represented and stood for. Yet even they never suspected the amount of insanity, cruelty, and terror connected with these people.

Now the most horrible fact is the finality. The people who died in the concentration camps can never be brought back to life again. Those who suffered can never be expected to forget, and Germany can never erase from the documents of history what happened on its soil.

Thus, when I look back at what happened to the German population, of which I am one, my heart aches. Regardless of whether what happened was deserved or undeserved, the price was paid mostly by the innocent. If their blood and their suffering could have brought back to life the countless dead and suffering people in the concentration camps, then at least it would have been worthwhile.

207

Must there be throughout the history of mankind a never-ending chain of sin and reprisal, sin and reprisal, of an eye for an eye, a tooth for a tooth, striking mostly only the innocent? Will mankind never learn how to live in peace? And those who want peace, are they the weak? Will the bully always have the upper hand? How does a person who loves peace avoid conflict? Does anyone know the answer? Wishful thinking is not enough, nor does turning the back on a problem provide a solution. . . .

What man needs on this earth that we all share is a common denominator. . . . Should that denominator not be God, the Almighty? But what do the believers do when they are confronted with the faithless, the godless, the nonbelievers? Teach them? How can you teach when you are talking to a pointed gun instead of a living soul?

Anyway, where was God when all this happened? Where? Had He gone on vacation when people died in concentration camps? Did He look the other way when my city was burned to the ground, the fields devastated and made barren, my people raped, humiliated, and murdered, deprived of self-respect and pride, thrown to the ground and then, helpless and half-dead, still beaten? Where was He, the Almighty, when the children, innocent and bewildered, looked for answers from their parents who had neither answers nor food? Where? Was He, too a mockery, a figment of someone's intoxicated imagination?

No.

God did see. God did let it happen, all of it. In one gracious, blessed moment in eternity He raised man from the ground, gave him power and knowledge, but with knowledge also came sin. . . . And through sin more knowledge, and through more knowledge more sin, until the never-ending vicious circle alarmed the Almighty, and He sent man, in addition to a soul, His only Son, Whose death and resurrection was to be salvation. And for a while man grieved. . . . But man forgets. Pain lingers only while the wound is healing; after that, the memory of pain is erased from man's mind. It had been meant as a kindness by God—now it had turned into a weapon against man. . . .

Yes, God saw.

And if He did nothing to stop the slaughter, the destruction, the despair, then He still knew what He was doing, because God, our Father, never loses hope. . . . Hope that man, through grief and pain, will eventually learn. . . .

God does not know geographical borders. Man is His creation—that's all He sees. Some of us are trying harder than others to be good, some of us are luckier than others in having more feeling, more compassion, more understanding, more of a touch of soul than others; some of us are more selfish than others, some are more demanding than others, some are too sick, body and soul, to contribute to progress—but all of us are here, on this world, as men, and as such are God's children, whether we know it or not, whether we believe it or not, whether we like it or not.

Yet, responsible parents can never let a child do all it wants. As a parent who says to the child, "Don't touch the fire, it hurts" and the child will touch to find out if it really hurts—so God lets us know that certain things are wrong, certain things will bring harm, but we, like children, still try to find out. . . . Then, when we are burned, we cry for God's help. Maybe that is where the difference between a boy and a man will show.

Among all children, there are also the bullies. Their desire is power, at any price. They will stomp on the weaker children, push their way to the front, take from others what does not belong to them, and in short, terrorize the others. Certainly we cannot encourage such behavior. We will try and stop the bully from exercising his terror over the others. By the same token, the bullies among the adults must be stopped, and that cannot be done by simply walking away from them—the bully will take that as a sign of weakness. Hence, we come up with this conclusion: the price for freedom, for independence, for a good and honorable life is high, and the highest price to be paid is always human life.

Among peace-loving, intelligent people a battle can be fought without bloodshed, a battle of the minds, but it takes two to meet on the same level. Intelligence and reasoning against brute force is bound to lose unless it is backed up by an equal display

209

of power and force; one can only reason with someone who is also capable and willing to do so. Unfortunately, the bullies among us will not accept intelligent reasoning if it interferes with their own goal, which is power and conquest. Bullies must therefore be met with an equal amount of power and strength.

The moment we submit to the power and brute force of the bully, the moment we are not willing to sacrifice our lives for what we believe in, for what we know is good and right and sane, at that moment we may as well be dead. The moment we stop putting up our lives as a security for the victory of our souls, we have lost the right to live, for then we are nothing, a dim shape, just a form without concreteness . . . a shadow in the night, fleeting, dissolving, alone, leaving no trace. . . .

What a tragedy that I, a seventeen-year-old girl, and thousands of others like me, had to learn these philosophies by the death of millions. . . .

I did not arrive at these conclusions overnight. Sleepless nights, days of bitterness in our hunger and despair; the struggle between hate and love of mankind and its expensive sins; the up and down between hope and desperation, trying to hold onto some kind of dignity and pride that would help us to survive the humiliations; the tearing apart of our souls to search for answers; and, last but certainly not least, the daily, exhausting, grinding fight for sheer physical survival—these all preceded my newly found peace of mind.

But I thank God that I was lucky enough to find it.

———————————

Others were not so lucky. I have just met my friend from school evacuation days—Ursel, my brown-haired, hazel-eyed, chubby roommate. She really has not changed much . . . the same little coquettish look from the side, still a little dimple in her cheek, still self-cut bangs, her soft, brown eyes with a twinkle. . . . Even her way of walking has not changed—she takes long, slow strides as if she is planning every step, so that she won't stumble. . . . Funny that I never paid attention to that before, although, tracing back my memory, I do recall her way of walking just like that.

"You haven't changed a bit," I say a little enviously.

"Oh, how can you say that, Inga." Her voice is soft, but she is scolding me a little, I can tell. "I think I look a little prettier now, don't you?"

I must say it takes me by surprise. Everybody in Berlin has only one thought—how to get enough to eat to stay alive, and here she is thinking about how pretty she looks!

At the moment, I can only nod.

"You have changed," she says, looking me over from the side.

"How?"

"You look older. But most of all you look even thinner than the last time I saw you."

This time, though, I am prepared.

"How come you don't?"

But she is on guard.

"Maybe it's not in my nature to lose weight over anything," she says with a smile that I do not quite know how to interpret.

"When everybody is starving?" I cannot conceal my annoyance.

"I am not starving," she says, again with that smile.

"Come on now! Everybody in Berlin is starving, and you say you are not? What secret warehouse do you know of that we other poor mortals don't know?"

"Never mind," she evades a direct answer. "If I tell you that I am not hungry, then you will just have to believe me."

Well, that's just like her. She really has not changed. She still never proves a point, yet she expects you to believe her, and if you don't she acts deeply hurt. She changes the subject.

"How did you get through all this? All right?"

"So, so." What else is there to say?

"Is your father home yet?"

"No. But we hope he will be home soon, now that the British are here."

"Did he write you that?"

"No. We have not heard from him since last December."

"Then how do you know that he is still alive?"

I am doing a secret slow burn. She can be as lovable as a week-old kitten, but she can also be extremely infuriating.

"We just know!" My voice cannot conceal my anger.

She realizes she has gone too far. Her hand is gentle on my arm; the soft kitten is coming out. . . .

"I'm sorry, Inga, I did not want to hurt you. . . ."

My first impulse is to say to her, "You are only mad because you have no mother, and I do. And you are also jealous because I love my father and you don't love yours. . . ." But I leave these words as thoughts and say instead, "Forget it. Let's talk about something else."

The "do you remember" game has started, and we end up laughing.

"Ah, well, we were children then. . . ." I cut myself short. Was it only a little over a year ago? Do people grow up in such a short time? Normally not, I believe. A lifetime in one year. . . .

"Listen, Ursel, I am in a bit of a hurry today. Let's meet again, shall we?"

I am on my way to visit Helen. The bicycle, Paula's legacy to me, has been coming in handy. Not too many Germans nowadays own one. During my conversation with Ursel, I have been pushing it. After we have set a date to meet again, she says, "Where did you get that bike? It doesn't look like yours, if I remember right. . . ."

"Some other time. It's a long story. . . . I've got to hurry, I'm already a little late as it is."

"Well, dear, that is nothing new with you. . . ." It's one last little good-natured dig before we part. I have to grin along with her. Just like her, here I am late again because I am talking with her, and she rubs my tardiness in my face!

"And you could take some lessons in tactfulness." I cannot resist the remark, and before she has a chance to digest it, I mount my bike and am on my way.

One of the reasons for my trip is the fact that I have no job.

It is time for me to begin looking around to help earn some money again—not that it will bring in much more food, but the ration cards for working people are slightly higher than for those who do not work. Up to now Mama would not let me go to work, since there were too many Russians around. She herself cannot leave Monika, who is still only a baby, and nine-year-old Chris. I want to work; the diversion from the horrible memories would do me good.

Since I am under eighteen, I have not been called upon to work on the ruins as "Trümmer-Frau." Millions of Berliners have to work on the streets of Berlin removing rubble and pipes, steel beams and charred wooden beams, bricks and stones. The usable bricks have to be cleaned by hand and stacked for reconstruction. It is done by men and women alike, millions of skeletons in rags, who see, at the end of the day, a slice of bread more at their table than they would without doing this kind of work. . . .

There is a painting, a famous painting called "Rider, Death, and Devil." Death had been painted as the figure of a skeleton with a hood over its head. Somehow these half-dead people with scarves around their faces remind me of that painting. . . .

Soon I will be eighteen. I will most likely be one of them; I don't think I will mind, though. Each stone is one step towards rebuilding, out of the rubble, out of the ruins . . . away from the eyewitness of destruction and death. . . . My Berlin, my lovely Berlin, will be beautiful again.

If I don't collapse from hunger I might even be able to enjoy an extra slice of bread. . . . The hunger-edema has gone away by now. I consider myself fairly normal. I lost twenty-five pounds altogether in the eight or ten weeks of our self-imposed exile, but at least I am not losing any more. Since I was never overweight, twenty-five pounds less shows, of course. . . .

Maybe Helen will have a little "refreshment." She is a resourceful lady, and since she lives in the city and knows a lot of people through her job, she is bound to come upon a little extra here and there. . . . Horrible to think that way. . . . I really thought I was going to visit her, not hoping I could pick up a scrap from her table. . . . My God, what has this war done to us? Where is my pride? I am going to see her because I'm hoping she can guide me to where I can find work. Work . . . I will concentrate on that. It will help me get the thought of food out of my mind.

What a horrible disappointment: Helen is not home. I stand in front of the door for several minutes, not wanting to believe it. Maybe someone will come in a minute. Perhaps she is just around the corner at a neighbor's home. . . .

Finally I have to give up. It would be foolish for me to stay around waiting for someone to come. A forty-five-minute ride on the bicycle . . . I dread the long way back home, carrying my disappointment with me. . . .

I wonder who that is behind me, also on a bike. Does he have to ride everywhere I ride? What does he want, anyway? A flirtation or dating is the furthest thing from my mind in these days. The display of male-female relations the Russians gave is enough to last me a lifetime. I want no part of romance or sex or anything connected with it.

If I am completely honest with myself, then I must admit that it frightens me. . . .

A glance back shows me that he is getting closer. From what I can see, he is rather good-looking. Young, in his early twenties, perhaps. A thick mop of dark-blond, wavy hair. . . . But what does he want from me?

Well, I am going to give him a good chance to prove how fast he can ride! And away we go!

I am pedaling as fast as I can. But I have forgotten that I get out of breath easily nowadays, an extra bonus from fate. . . . He has almost reached my side.

I may be frightened, but I am neither stupid nor a coward. Problems are best met head-on! That has always been my policy; it is now.

Abruptly I stop and dismount. When he also stops and approaches me it does not come as a surprise; I am facing him, the bike like a fence between us.

"Good afternoon," he says. His lips are parted in a friendly

214

smile. Nice, clean teeth ... slightly suntanned face and arms, blue eyes, which are also smiling. That wins me over—smiling eyes do not mean any harm.

"Why did you follow me?" I demand.

Now he laughs.

"Why does anyone follow a pretty girl?"

Pretty? Me? That's a laugh! I have not been an ugly girl, but I was never unusually pretty. Now, in my skin-and-bones condition? He must be crazy! I don't believe it.

Still, after months and months of isolation this is—apart from the enemy—my first contact with any human being other than my family and close friends. I am almost eighteen years old, and I feel as if life has passed me by. Other girls my age, in normal times, would have dated on and off, gone dancing, or to parties, or sleigh riding or horseback riding—all the fun that teenagers have. . . .

And I? My generation of girls? We made ourselves ugly so that the Russian hordes would find us unattractive enough to pass us by in their search for "Frau"! In time that was not necessary anymore; who finds skeletons pretty? We did not have to work at ugliness then—life took care of that. Still, maybe there are people who look with their hearts instead of with their eyes. . . . Is he one of those? Am I lucky enough to talk to someone who looks a little deeper than the surface?

Right now, I wish I was pretty. For a moment I smile at him, but when he takes my hand, I pull away quickly. He is a man, and the Russians were also men. Men ... they can do some horrible things. They are cruel, and they can kill. . . .

"Are you afraid?" He is sensitive, fortunately. "I only wanted to shake hands with you, like all people do in Holland."

So he is Dutch. . . . Well, the Dutch are pretty nice people. Anyway, he does not look primitive, like the Russians. He is polite too.

"Why don't we walk side by side for a little while?" he suggests. I nod. That sounds fine.

It is good to talk to someone again. To someone nice, that is. We walk for about half an hour along the road, pushing our bikes. It feels almost like old times, before the hordes came. . . . Almost normal, as if there had not been a war. Such a good feeling. . . I have told him why I had wanted to visit my aunt. When I refer to Helen I always call her my aunt—a leftover from childhood days.

"Work?" he says. "You are looking for work?"

"It would help."

"Were you a member of the Party?" He is serious now, the light touch of flirtation has left his voice.

"No, but I was in the Hitler Youth, like everybody my age. You know, at the age of ten. . . ."

"I know," he interrupts me. "You don't have to tell me. Everyone is quite familiar with the proceedings of the Nazi Party." He stops for a moment to light a cigarette. "Oh, I'm sorry. . . ." He holds the pack over to me.

"No, thank you."

"Don't you smoke?"

"Now and then at home but never on the street."

"Why not on the street?"

"I don't really know. . . . It just doesn't look nice. Sitting down with a cup of coffee, or a glass of wine smoking a cigarette looks pretty, I think, but walking along a road. . . . I don't know, there is just something about it I don't like."

He looks at me serious and quizzical, but also, I can sense, with approval.

"Are you serious about going to work?" he continues.

"Of course."

"Do you speak English?"

"English, French, and German."

"Excellent. What other talents do you have?"

"Well, I can type and I know shorthand, but I don't regard these as talents. I am not too good in either one of these. . . ."

"That's unimportant; the main thing is that you can speak English. . . ."

"Why?"

"Have you ever thought of working for the Occupation Forces?"

216

Momentarily, I am surprised. The Occupation Forces? Would they have any German civilians working for them?

I ask him.

"The Occupation Forces need Germans to work for them, but because of the language difficulties and because most Germans were associated with the Nazi Party they find it difficult to find any," he says. And with a little grin, "The de-Nazification takes time, and the Allied Forces cannot wait until all the Germans have been de-Nazified."

Again I am puzzled. "De-Nazified?"

I don't know whether I am finding it amusing or sad.

He is pointing to a group of people working on the ruins, cleaning bricks, removing beams and columns.

"You see there? Almost every one of these people was a member of the Party, and so, after they have worked on the rubble heaps for about six months more or less, they can officially apply for de-Nazification. That is, the 'little Party people' can; the big ones are in Nuremberg and will be put on trial."

That is something new to me.

"Are all these people ex-Party members?"

"No," he says, "some work just so that they can get higher ration cards. But a lot of them have to work there; it is one way of washing away Party membership."

"How do you know all this?"

By now he has begun to puzzle me again. Besides, it just dawned on me that he hardly has an accent. . . . Before he has a chance to answer, I ask him about his lack of accent.

"I worked in Germany during the war."

"Where?"

"That's immaterial." He changes the subject.

"Well, how about working for the Allied Forces?"

"I think I would like that. But how do I go about doing it?"

"There is an employment office nearby. Actually it is called the Labor Office. Do you know where the Lietzensee is?"

I nod.

He gives me the address.

217

"Do they speak German there?"

"Oh, no," he says. "Once you are there you are on your own. If you cannot communicate with them, there is hardly any sense for you to ask for employment, is there?"

Well, that does make sense.

"Don't look so worried. You will be all right, and I would not be at all surprised if the next day you are already working somewhere."

We say good-bye. This time his handshake does not frighten me. It is firm but gentle; his hands are strong and tender at the same time.

"I will not ask you for a date," he says. "These are trying times, and you will have your hands full trying to fill a new job with people from a different country. It won't be easy. . . ."

He looks at me fondly. "Not that I would not like to. . . ." Then, quickly, he is on his bike and has disappeared among the crowd. The last glimpse I catch of him is that mop of dark-blond hair.

My way back home seems like a dream. The things that happen to me! A slight feeling of regret accompanies me; he was a nice young man. . . .

The possibility of working for the Allied Forces has never entered my head. My English is only school-English, and although we had excellent teachers, I am not at all sure I will make out all right. . . .

There is another thing. . . . How do I feel about the English? They were our enemy . . . but, more important even, how will they feel about me? I was their enemy too! Questions, questions, questions. The answers can only come from going to the employment office and finding out. If I don't try, I will never know, will I? An intelligent person never prejudges. They all had mothers and fathers like the Germans, ate and slept, laughed and cried, played and worked, knew love and sadness just as we do. . . . So what is "enemy"? Just a word, unless you feel it, and I don't feel it. They had acted like human beings when they entered Berlin, not like animals as the Russians had done. . . .

218

They and the Americans had brought the first rays of hope to the dying city. . . .

And surely they will not employ German civilians if they hate them, will they? That seems to answer the most important questions. There is one more problem, though.

Papa is not home yet. . . . How will he be able to adjust to the changed situation? When he left, he left a family and a nice home. Now the country is run by four different countries and more different languages spoken. Papa never liked to be told what to do or how to think—it was one of his reasons for not liking the Nazi doctrines.

Papa will come back to a country that is mud in the eyes of the world and a people who are third-class citizens among the nations. . . . I never had to lift a weapon against an English or American or French soldier, but he was trained to be their enemy as a soldier. . . . Suppose he finds his daughter working for the people he was supposed to regard as enemies. . . .

I recall that on his last leave, already sensing the hopelessness of the situation in Germany, he made the remark, "The English are rather fair fighters. If I am ever taken prisoner of war, I would prefer it to be the British. . . ."

Did he get his wish? During the last phases of the war none of the families ever really knew where the soldiers were. The troops were moved around fast; the letters took a long time to arrive at home, and the postal stamp and addresses only stated the field postal number. By the time the mail arrived, the soldier could have been anywhere on either the Eastern or the Western Front, or anywhere else in the world where there was a German soldier fighting.

"You say you were not a member of the Nazi Party?"

The clean-cut, polite, blue-eyed British officer is looking at me with an expression I cannot quite analyze. His eyes do not betray any of his feelings.

"No, only the B.D.M."

"Hmmm." He is holding a file folder in his hands, looking at it. "But you said that you worked in the Military Supply Office in Berlin. Was it not almost impossible not to be a member of the Party?"

"I don't really know. Maybe under different circumstances, but I was only sixteen when I worked there, going on seventeen. . . ." I put emphasis on the "seventeen." I don't want him to think he is talking to a child!

"Hmmm." He is turning a few pages in the folder, but I cannot see what the folder contains.

"Cigarette?" He holds the pack out to me. For a moment I hesitate; I want to work, and suppose they don't like girls smoking? But the fact is I do smoke, even if only occasionally—they may as well know that now.

"Thank you."

While he gives me a light, he says, "Didn't you want to join?"

"If there had been a lot of pressure I might have joined, I really don't know, but I was too young for them to bother much. I told them my parents wanted me to wait a while yet, that they thought I was too young. Anyway, I only worked there for a few months, maybe nine months or so; then the war was coming to an end and we were all sent home."

"Where did you learn to speak English?" He is not looking at me, he is still studying the folder.

"At school, of course."

He must have sensed the little touch of amused puzzlement in my answer. Where else could anyone learn a foreign language?

He is looking at me now.

"Would you like a cup of tea?"

Would I? He deserves a friendly smile for that. I nod, "Yes, please."

"Cream and sugar?"

Oh, boy! Cream and sugar—that makes my day complete! These are still treasures one does not get easily. . . . This is not bad, not bad at all. They are friendly, polite, thoughtful, clean-

220

looking . . . yes, I think I am going to enjoy working for the British.

The interview continues for about two hours.

Actually, it is not just an interview; it is an interrogation. He himself has told me so, and he is almost apologetic. "Usually I don't say this to people," he says, "but you are an honest, nice girl and I don't want to upset you by asking all these questions. I want you to realize that I must interrogate you; that is my duty. You are also an intelligent girl, and as such, you will understand that some things must be done under certain circumstances. . . ."

"Oh, I realize that. Do you think I would not do the same thing if the situation were reversed?"

My answers are taken down by a clerk. It is tiring to dig back into the past—my memory is only good when things interest me! There were a lot of things that really did not interest me, for which I now have to search my brain for answers, since now they interest others. . . .

To a lot of questions I do not have answers, simply because I don't know any. Others come easy; and so the time passes, and before I know it, it is lunchtime.

"Okay, Miss, that does it," the officer says.

"That does it?" What does that mean? My English is not yet so good that I am familiar with such phrases. . . . Is it bad or good? For a moment I feel a little uncomfortable, I don't quite know what to make of this. . . . My conscience is clear. I have, to the best of my ability, answered everything truthfully, but you never know, sometimes there are misunderstandings, especially when one has to talk in a foreign language. . . .

"Can I go now?"

"Don't you want to know where you are going to work?" He is smiling.

Work! That is a magic word!

"Come with me, please," he says, and he rises.

We go into another office.

"Dick, I want you to meet Miss L, or better, Inga." He turns to me once more. "Most of the time we call each other by first names, contrary to the German tradition," he smiles.

The other man has risen, and we shake hands.

"Okay," says my interrogator, "I will leave you two alone to discuss the details. Good-bye, good luck." A friendly wave with his hand, and he has left.

"Can you start tomorrow?" says the other one.

Tomorrow? Goodness, they sure don't waste any time! But it suits me fine—the sooner, the better!

"Yes."

"We look after our boys, but also after their families—that is important," says the other one, while he is busy searching for forms and papers in his desk.

"And one of the most important things is to get mail to them and to get mail from them to their families. So we have just finished establishing an Army Post Office here in Berlin, but we need people to staff it. It is mostly run by our own boys, but we need more help. Some boys are being discharged and are leaving for home, others are posted somewhere else, and so on. We need people who stay here, so that we don't have to keep on training. It is an important job, but it is also not an easy job. You will learn a lot about the geography of England," he grins.

Oh dear—geography was never my best subject in school!

He can see the apprehension on my face.

"Don't worry," he grins good-naturedly. "You will have good teachers. . . . Once you know the little tricks, it is really not too difficult."

"I can try," I say, half-heartedly.

"Ahh—you'll be fine!"

I wish I had his confidence!

"By the way, you will get the highest ration card there is. Everybody working for the Allied Forces gets this. You are also entitled to one hot meal a day—no coupons from your card, and just a few cents in cost."

My heart jumps into the air in leaps! Hurray, a little more to eat! How lucky can you get?

After all my papers have been filled out, rules read and questionnaires signed, a few instructions given, I am dismissed. To-morrow morning at eight o'clock a new life begins!

"By the way," he says as I'm leaving, "just in case it may interest you, at the moment there are only about five hundred Germans working for the Allied Forces in Berlin. You are one of the first Germans to work for us."

On my way back home, I am walking on air. In my head is a silly phrase, repeating itself over and over in a tune, "A new life begins, a new life begins, a new life begins. . . ."

And I owe it all to my strange, helpful, friendly Dutch friend, whom I will never see again. I don't even know his name.

13

NIGHT IS OVER—DAWN IS HERE

"Brrr . . . is it cold out there!" I do not take time to hang up my coat. I throw it over the chair and rush towards the little potbelly stove, which glows with warmth and comfort on this icy winter day. The regular big tile stove cannot be used; it only takes coal briquettes and we have not seen such things in months.

My hands are numb with cold. It feels good to rub them, so close to the fire.

"Don't rub the skin off your hands," Ursel says. "How many degrees do you think it is out there?"

"Twenty degrees below zero."

"You are kidding?"

"All you have to do is listen to the news. They said it would go down to twenty-two below during the night."

"Well," Ursel says nonchalantly, "Maybe we'd better get our fur coats out for bed tonight?"

"Fur coats, that's a good one." I pick up my coat to hang it in the wardrobe. "I don't even have a decent regular one to wear. . . ." I look at it, half amused, half disgusted—an Army blanket, dyed dark brown. I had been lucky enough to buy it from one of my colleagues in the British Army Post Office. A little "irregularity," all of us—British and Germans—had learned a few "irregularities". . . . No human being with even a resemblance of a heart could stay neutral at the plight of the Berlin population.

Harry had needed money to take his German "Fraulein" out (as he had told me with a broad grin), and I needed a coat. Somehow, a British Army blanket had found its way to me and some German marks their way to Harry. Thank God for the Harrys in the world. . . !

"There's coffee, or whatever you may want to call it," says Ursel, pointing to the coffeepot on the stove.

"Oh, good!" Sometimes she is quite thoughtful.

It is not the best coffee in the world, but it is nice and hot. I am beginning to feel warmer and more comfortable now.

"The least you can do is offer me a cigarette," Ursel says.

"Sorry—of course."

Each evening when I come home from work, we sit for a few moments before supper and talk about the events of the day. Most of the time I do the talking, since Ursel is not working. Once I had asked her why she was not getting herself a job.

"Me? Work? Not on your life. . . . With that little bit of extra food I would be getting, I would use more energy working than I would get out of it. At least at home I can sleep and forget that there is not enough to eat. . . ."

"I am not doing too badly," I told her.

"That's a joke, Inga, you are still skin and bones—and you say you are not doing too badly. . . . Still, we all must live the way we feel is fitting, so don't take offense."

Of course, that had taken place after we had decided to rent the downstairs room my grandparents could spare. We share the expense, which is minimal, and it helps my grandparents along a little. Apart from the expense for the room, we live independently from each other. At times it is fun, at times the lack of privacy is inconvenient, but all in all, so far, we have not had any problems.

"I think I'll go upstairs and get my supper," I am now saying to her.

"Why don't you wait a little longer, otherwise you may get hungry again before you go to bed."

She has a point there.

While I put more coal and wood on the fire, she says, "By the way, first the mother hen was here, and then the security guard. . . ."

I have grown accustomed to her way of referring to my mother and my grandfather—she has teased me many times about them and their protectiveness over me. Hidden beneath the sarcasm though, I detect, or so I think, a slight jealousy. . . . Both my mother and my grandfather have never concealed the fact that they don't like Ursel, and it had been a tough struggle to convince them to agree to our arrangement of moving in together. It was only my constant argument that Ursel did not have any real parents, and that she was probably the way she was because she needed love and some people to care for her, that finally made them agree—reluctantly, but they did.

"What did they want?"

"Mother hen just wanted to know if you were home already, and security guard wanted to borrow a spoonful of butter. I swear, Inga, he irritates me even more than your mother does. I bet he did not want to borrow the butter—he just wanted to check on me. I could swear he thinks I'm taking your food when you are not home!"

"Oh nonsense, Ursel!" But I am not so sure that she is not right. Opa does not trust Ursel at all, which at times irritates me a little too. Still, it is nothing unusual; in these days no one trusts anyone as far as food is concerned. The rations are still so small that hunger has not yet been replaced by at least a humanly normal amount of food. I am the best off; I have the highest ration card there is, plus one extra meal a day. But I still have not regained any of the weight I had lost. . . .

"Well, I'll read a little, while you are upstairs. . . . Hurry, will you?"

Upstairs, Omi and Opa are sitting at the kitchen table playing cards.

"The kitchen is the warmest place," Omi says. "We did not heat the bedroom. When we are ready to go to bed, we will take

226

the coals out of the kitchen stove and put them in the bedroom stove. That'll warm it up enough just to go to bed."

"Did you hear how cold it is going to get?" Opa asks. "They said it would be down to twenty-two degrees below. I just hope our pipes are not going to burst from the cold. . . ."

"How much firewood and coal do we have left?" If I hate anything it is being cold. The aspect of having nothing at all to warm the house with really frightens me. In summertime, at least, we only had hunger to cope with—now there is another threat—the cold. Is it never going to end?

"Maybe a week," Opa says. Both look gloomy. "She, downstairs," Opa points downwards, and with "she" he means Ursel, "is she ever going to go get a job?"

His dislike of Ursel is expressed in not calling her by name; "she" is the only way he refers to her.

"What has Ursel's working or not working got to do with our firewood situation?" I am already on the defensive.

"Plenty," Omi replies, instead of Opa. "If she had a job, she would be gone during the day also; that would mean that you need not heat the place until evening."

"Oh, come on now, she sleeps late, which means that she does not make a fire very early anyway. Besides, it is nice to come home to a warm place instead of an icy cold one. . . ."

"We could heat it for you shortly before you come home," Opa contradicts.

Up to a point they are right. But I do not want to go into it any further, and I change the subject while I am eating my supper.

"Ursel said that Mama was looking for me. Do you happen to know what she wanted?"

Before they have a chance to answer, Mama comes in.

"Hello, dear."

I kiss her, and she sits down for a moment.

"Are you planning to go anywhere tomorrow night?" she asks.

I have to laugh a little. "Where would I be going, Mama?"

227

"Well, you may just have planned something. I wanted to be sure you would be home."

"Why?"

"Helen is coming for a visit, and you know how much she likes you. I thought we'd spend some time together."

"That's fine, Mama. I always enjoy her visits too."

A little change is nice to look forward to. Helen always manages to make us laugh.

"You know, they say it is close to Siberian cold outside," Mama says.

"You're telling me!" Just to think of it makes me shiver. "I think I am going to bed real early tonight, I want to be asleep before it gets too cold even in bed. . . ."

"Put your coat over your featherbed, Inga, that way you keep the warmth in."

"Okay, Mama. Good night everybody."

Ursel puts the book aside as I enter. "Well, what bad things about me did they have to tell you this time?" she asks, with a little sneer.

"We did not talk about you at all, Ursel," I lie. "All we discussed was the firewood situation."

"Well, let's get undressed and talk a little in bed, shall we?"

"Undressed?! That's a joke! You mean let's get dressed to go to bed, don't you?"

It really is a joke. To go to bed we change our day clothes to put on a long wool nightgown, a heavy sweater, a pair of old wool socks, and a wool shawl around our head. Once the fire in the potbelly stove is out, it gets so cold that in the morning when we wake up our toothpaste is frozen in the tube. A cup of leftover coffee on my bedside table turns into a piece of solid ice and my eyebrows are white from my breath, which turns to moisture and then to frost.

We are no sight to tempt any Peeping Tom, that's for sure! Each night when we go through this act, we end up giggling our stomachs sore, but it is a giggle mixed with slight hysteria. When I think of the coming weeks with nothing to heat the stove, I feel like anything else but giggling!

"Here." Ursel is throwing something over to my bed. A bonbon—what a nice surprise! "Anything new at work?"

"Kind of. . . ." I do not say any more on purpose—let her guess a little for a change. . . .

"Oh, come on, Inga, tell me." She knows that when she puts that tone into her voice, that soft little plea, I can hardly keep up my attempt at mystery!

"Well, all right . . . Arnold asked me out for a date."

"And?"

"And nothing. I said no."

"Inga, you are crazy! Why didn't you accept?"

"We have gone through this before, Ursel. Arnold is a nice person, I like to work with him, but that's all. He really holds no personal attraction for me, and I don't go out with anyone I do not care for at least a little bit."

I throw a cigarette over to her side.

"Thanks," she says, lighting it, "but I think you are a fool. Here you are working for the British, you have plenty of chances to go out with some nice dates, and you always say no. I don't understand you. If it were me, I would go whether I liked him or not. . . ."

"Ursel! How can you? I just don't believe you. You are saying these things because. . . ." I check myself. I do not want to remind her of some things that I know must hurt her.

"Do you want to know the truth, Inga?" She is sitting up in bed now. It is not often that she shows genuine signs of emotion one way or the other, but this time she lets the mask of indifference fall. "Do you really want to know how I feel about these things? It is very simple. When the Russians came into our basement, the first one who threw himself on me horrified me. The second one disgusted me. The third time it did not bother me at all. One learns fast. . . . I learned then to adjust myself to certain facts of life, and I swore then that I would make these facts work for me instead of against me. . . ."

She is inhaling the cigarette smoke with a deep breath. Her unusually slim fingers are beating a nervous rhythm on the feather bed. "I told myself this: 'So what! you are not a virgin

229

anymore, so who cares? The world is not going to come to an end because of that. . . .' Well? What was I supposed to do? Kill myself over it?" Her voice is now on the defensive. "Oh no, I love life too much! I did not ask to be put into that situation. I was thrown into it without any fault of my own. There was nothing I could do about it—nothing. The ones that could have helped, all the brave gentlemen down in the basement with us"—now she is full of contempt—"all these brave . . . you know what they did? Nothing! They were only too happy that it was not their wife or their daughter! No, sir . . . I am going to live my life trying to get what I can. It's everyone for himself, that's what I learned in those days. . . . I am for me. For me alone."

For a while I cannot say anything; I am shocked, and my heart hurts for her. So that's what happened to her. . . . I have to try somehow to make her forget. But can I? I can at least try. . . .

"I'm sorry, Ursel," I say gently.

"Don't be." She is now her good old carefree self, "Don't be, dear, I'll make out all right. . . ."

"I don't think you mean all you say. I know you better than that!"

"Do you now?" She is defiant. "Just give me a life philosophy that beats mine. Can you?"

"Of course. So something bad happened, but one can live through it without losing faith, you know. I agree to what you said about it not being the end of the world, but there is a lot ahead of us yet in life that we can look forward to. We don't have to resign to the negative viewpoint."

"Oh, Inga, you are an incorrigible optimist," she says, and her hazel eyes show just a trace of sadness, "but I guess that's why I like you so much."

"And I like you too much to just let you go ahead and be all negative," I say. "Anyway, maybe we better talk about something else. I'm not too eager to talk about those days yet. . . ."

"You have to admit one thing, though," Ursel continues. "Our generation has had a rotten deal from life. Pulled away from home several times, growing up with air raids, an enemy

230

invasion, hunger, cold, no future—what else is there to think about?"

"Well, don't you see anything nice coming up in the future?"

"Yep," she says dryly, "a long, cold winter!"

"Oh, you! Honestly—you always have to be negative! Can't you ever think about anything nice!"

"I'll do that when I see it."

"Some of the things that are nice cannot be seen. . . ."

"Oh, Inga, stop being such a philosopher. It does not suit you. . . ."

She turns over to the other side and puts out her light.

I don't know why I am so irritated with her. . . . Maybe it's because she always manages to get me into an argument and then she somehow leaves the argument unfinished and unsolved. I hate that!

Well, the only thing to do now is to go to sleep.

The potbelly stove is only dimly red now. The fire has burned down to almost nothing but ashes. A last piece of charred wood has fallen deeper, right into the ashes. There it tries with one last breath to rejuvenate itself on a small leftover piece of glow. Then that has to give up too. . . .

Outside, the storm is hitting the house in a frenzy, as if frustrated that it cannot reach its victims inside. Howling, demanding, moaning . . . sssshuuu . . . you in there . . . sssshhuuu . . . open up, let me in . . . ssshhhhuuuuu, ssssshhhhuuuuu. . . . Once in a while the trace of a draft makes the storm's demands very realistic. . . . It gets very cold in the room. Fire, please don't go out . . . burn! Burn forever, never go out. . . . I am afraid of the cold. I always have been. I used to have chilblains when I was a child. First they itch; then they hurt. Don't go out, fire. . . . Cold hurts too. Not just hunger . . . cold, too. I am afraid of it, almost more than of the hunger. People can get sick when they are too cold. I don't want to get sick. I can't afford to get sick. If I do, then good-bye extra ration card. . . . Good-bye-one-extra-meal-a-day. . . . Papa? Where are you? If you were home, we would not be cold. Or hungry. You would take care of us . . . I know.

Anyway, everybody is cold. We are not the only people in Germany who have nothing to put into their stoves. . . . Why isn't Papa home yet? Why does he have to be one of the last? Suppose. . . . suppose he never comes home again? He has to come home! He will! I know he will. . . . But if he doesn't? I have to face it, these things do happen. People do get killed in wars. I should know, I saw enough of them. . . . If he doesn't come home, I will have to support my family. I am the oldest. We have not heard from him for so long, almost a year. But he will come home! Yes-sir-he-will!

The storm is hitting at the flower boxes; click, click-clack-click . . . sssshhhuuuuhhhhh. . . . Walpurgis Night? Dante's Inferno? Nonsense . . . just a little old winter storm in Germany. Go to sleep, Inga. Just go to sleep. . . . For a few more days you will be warm, what are you worried about?

"Don't worry, little one," the doctor says. A mop of white hair, white gloves, white coat, white smile, white beard—he is all white! At first he frightens me a little, but his smile is kind. But why is he so white? All over? And there on my knee, which he examines, there is a huge white bandage. What's wrong with my knee? It is twice the size it should be. . . . I can't move it.

"Don't worry," the doctor says again. He looks a little bit like. . . . I know—like God. But, of course, I know he isn't! Now I know, my operation! I am in the hospital, I had a knee operation. I wish I could move my leg though.

"You must not walk on it!" the doctor says; his face is very serious now. Ha-ha, that's funny. I must not walk on it! I cannot walk on it! There's a funny howling outside—I wish that would stop. . . . The room is all white too. So is my bed . . . and the sheets. Everything is white. That howling outside bothers me. . . . Oh, I know what it is. It is an air raid. I think I will look out of the window to see what an air raid looks like. . . . My bed is right next to the window, I am on the top of the roofs. . . . Hey, that looks beautiful, all that red coming down from the sky . . . beautiful . . . nice and warm.

The bombs are all red, like fire, and warm. I can feel the warmth coming from them as they hit close by. Except I don't like to hear all these people screaming.... What are they screaming about, it's so nice and warm.... Ah yes, I am supposed to be in the air raid shelter. How can I be in the air raid shelter if I cannot walk? Ha-ha, that is funny. People are really comics. I am supposed to be in an air raid shelter—but how do I get there? Well, first I have to get out of bed. Oh, that leg of mine weighs a ton! Let's see; that chair there ... I have to get that chair. There we are! Okay, now to heave my leg onto it ... one, two, three, there! I am on roller skates— the chair is a roller skate! I whiz around the room like a witch on a broom ... zzzziiiing ... once around the corner! Zzzzziiiiiiinnnnnnnggggg ... once more ... hey, that is fun! Outside the noise is infernal. The ack-ack, the bombs falling, the people screaming, the explosions.... I don't like that roller skating anymore ... I am afraid.... I have to get out of here. Where is the door? Mama, get me out of here, please! I'm afraid! I have to get to the air raid shelter, I have to! Papa, why don't you come to get me out of here? You are supposed to take care of me! I can't move my leg.... Near the window, yes there, there is a bomb. It is blowing itself up like a balloon ready to pop ... and when it pops it will explode! I have to get away.... Papa, take me away from here ... there, that bomb is getting ready to pop! No! No! No! ...

My own screaming wakes me up. Ursel is standing next to me, holding my hand, shivering.

"My God, Inga. What's wrong? You have been screaming as if somebody was murdering you...."

She has lit a cigarette for me, holding it out to me.

"Here, take a puff."

"It was just a nightmare.... Remember when I was in the hospital for my knee operation? There was an air raid, and they didn't have time to take me down to the air raid shelter. I was so scared. I couldn't walk. My leg had water in it after the operation, you know, and finally I took a chair, somehow managed to get my leg on it, and shoved myself, leg and all, towards the elevator."

Ursel has started giggling.

233

"What's so funny?"

"I am sorry, darling," she is giggling even harder, "but you know I can't help picturing you with a stiff, bandaged leg on a chair, pushing it ahead of you like a giant-sized salami! . . . I just can't help it; but it must have looked hilarious!"

I have to join her, it must have looked funny! We are both sitting on the bed, and we are laughing as if we don't have a care in the world. . . .

———

Today the weather is no different from yesterday. It is still twenty-two degrees below freezing, but the storm has subsided. Now it is just a clear, icy cold, the kind that gets in your nostrils and makes them tingle, that makes the snow give a cracking sound under your feet without moving it an inch either way, the kind that makes your breath visible like a cloud of smoke. . . .

When I arrive home, Helen is already there. She has brought along some cookies and enough coffee for one cup for each of us—real coffee!

"Your mother has just told me about your firewood situation," she greets me. "With Christmas so close, that is certainly not a nice thing to look forward to. . . . But you know, Lisa, pardon me if I say so, but you are all a bunch of fools."

Helen has always been outspoken, and what she says usually makes good sense. We can hardly argue with her now.

"Why?"

"Because, my dear ladies, you do not see the wood for the trees. . . ."

"What do you mean, Helen?"

"For Pete's sake, Lisa, use your imagination! Look out of the window. What do you see?"

Mama and I both go to see what is so wonderful out there. "A street," we both say at the same time.

"Naturally!" Helen is a little impatient, "but on that street? On that street are, on each side of it, rows and rows of trees!

Good, marvelous trees. And trees make good firewood, you know." She is grinning now.

"Helen, you don't mean. . . ."

"Oh yes, I do mean!" she interrupts. "One nice dark night we are going to fell a tree!"

"You are absolutely crazy, Helen!" Mama does not quite know what else to say, neither do I. "First of all, it is illegal, secondly we do not know how to fell a tree! How do you suggest we do it? It is dangerous if you don't know what you are doing, Helen".

"Fiddlesticks!" Helen says. "In times like these nobody talks about what is legal and what is not! When you have frozen to death or starved to death—do you think anybody is going to come and say to your surviving relatives, 'Sorry, it was illegal so we let these people starve and freeze to death?' Anyway, whom are you hurting? That tree is not going to mind it one darn bit! Besides, it is right in front of your window and keeps all the sunlight out."

As always, Helen makes good sense. Excellent sense!

"But how do we do it?" I ask, with a slight shudder .

"Well, we have to have tools. Most of all we need a big, strong, sharp saw. Do you have one?'"

"Oh, yes," Mama says. "Walter always had one to take care of branches from our own trees. For some strange reason nobody bothered to steal it along with everything else. . . ."

"Fine. Make sure it's sharp, though. Now then, I will read up a little at home on how to fell a tree. What are books for? I have quite a few good ones at home. I will come loaded with knowledge about how to fell a tree!"

"It sounds good, Helen," I finally throw in my two cents worth. "Just one thing bothers me; those trees out there are about eighty years old and about two feet in diameter. . . ."

Helen scratches her head. "Tell you the truth, that has me a little worried, too. It won't be easy. But do we have a choice?"

"No."

"That settles it, then. The day after tomorrow it is supposed to go up to only fifteen degrees below, so it won't be too cold. I have a nasty suspicion, though, that we won't feel the cold at all," she adds, with a sly grin.

"Operation Wood-Felling" is supposed to take place two days from now, starting at about eleven o'clock at night. By that time most people will be asleep. We will have to work quietly so that we do not arouse unnecessary suspicion. I must say I am looking forward to it with very mixed emotions!

The two days have gone by fast. Much too fast for my liking! At this time, I'm not too sure which is the lesser of two evils: our desperate firewood situation—coal is completely unobtainable; we have not seen any in months—or the impending adventure of felling a tree two feet thick and seventy feet high! I must admit that when I think of it, I don't feel the cold any more! I am sure Mama feels the same way.

It is a bright moonlit night. Frankly, we would have preferred it to have been darker, but we could not wait. We have enough firewood to last only a few more days.

We have arranged it very well, there are four of us. We have asked Erna Peters if she wanted to come in on the deal, and she has happily agreed. That makes it perfect; we can take turns sawing, two at a time, while the other two are resting.

The street is deserted except for us. People are still suffering from the memories of the Russians and the curfew, and have developed a habit of being in their homes by at least nine o'clock in the evening. The only threat might be a patrolling police car. If it is the British Military Police we have nothing to worry about; they close their eyes to these things. Also I have a plus since I work for the British.

The German police patrol is a different matter. First of all, they have a strictly official interest in enforcing the law, and the law says you cannot go and cut down a tree that belongs to the city or state. But there is also the human factor; they are Germans too, and they too have no firewood in their homes. Enforcing the law, therefore, is made more pleasant by the

236

natural human trait of jealousy. Taking that into consideration, we have decided upon an action which is not that of a law-abiding citizen: bribery! We have no scruples about that at all. No one is going to be hurt by our action—as a matter of fact we save the state the expense of several death certificates. . . .

Without firewood, we cannot cook and therefore, not eat. Without firewood, we cannot survive twenty-two degrees below zero. It is a matter of survival.

The decision is that if a German police patrol car comes by, we will offer them a share of our loot. We are sure that it will work.

Felling the tree is teamwork.

Helen and Mama are working together, Erna and I are the other team. But first we have to use the ax to cut a dent into the bottom of the tree where we will be sawing. It is not easy. When it is my turn, I have the hardest time finding the same spot . . . besides, the ax is very heavy. My weight is still below one hundred pounds, when it should be around one hundred and twenty to be normal for my size and my age. But we manage.

We can now start the first incision with the saw.

"Helen, are you sure it is on the correct side? Remember, if you made a mistake, the tree will fall on the house!" Mama cannot quite conceal the anxiety in her voice.

Frankly I agree with her. I don't feel so good either. But there is not much time to think; we must hurry.

"Lisa, of course I have checked it over and over to make sure nothing can happen. . . ." Helen is just a little hurt.

"Okay then, here we go; back-forth, one-two, back-forth, one-two, back-forth, one-two. . . ."

Helen and Mama have started. We are taking turns by the clock; every team does seven minutes, which is about how long we can each saw without collapsing.

The task is not easy. The wood is green and moist. The saw gets stuck with almost every cut. By the time each one of us has taken three turns we are not feeling the cold (just as Helen had predicted!). Instead, we are bathed in sweat. Fortunately, the

237

warm woolen clothing underneath our coats and slacks soaks up the moisture, or else we would all get pneumonia. It takes several hours before we see the end.

To my horror I realize that felling the tree is not the only work that has to be done. How are we going to move it, once it is down?

As if Helen has read my thoughts, she says, "Come on, we are soon through, just a little longer. When it is felled, we are going to have to saw it into pieces of about three feet in length so that we can move it into the shed."

"How are we going to move it?"

"You'll see," Helen says.

"Hey, Mama, there is a car coming, I think."

"Oh, dear . . . no need to take chances," Helen says, grabbing the saw. "Everybody run! Into the house. And no lights on! Grab everything and move!"

Inside, panting, perspiring, tired out and weak, we watch to see what happens. Unless the headlights of the car hit the spot where we have been sawing, chances are that our misdeed won't be detected.

The German police patrol turns around again and moves away.

Thank God!

"Poohh, that was close," Mama says, relieved. "But I think we are going to be pretty safe from now on. They usually don't come more than once a night."

I wish I could stay inside. But I have to continue like everybody else—can't break up the team!

And away we go again. One-two, back-forth, one-two, back-forth. . . .

"All right now," Helen says. "Inga and Erna, get out of the way and prepare yourself for a big bang! The tree is just about ready to fall, and it will be a crash. The moment it hits the ground, grab everything and run into the house. No lights on, okay? If anybody comes, we are inside sleeping. Get the message?"

238

With a grin Helen has finished her speech, and we are now waiting for the big bang.

A slow, heavy crackling starts. A sound, like a moan from a wounded soul. . . . A tremble, a tremor now. . . .

Oh my God, what are we doing. . . . That beautiful tree. . . .

And it doesn't fall with a loud fast bang. It bends slowly, as if it hesitates. The branches on top get entangled in the branches of the two surrounding trees, as if they are trying to hold on to them to stop from falling. . . .

> Outside, where road and fence meet,
> there grows a linden tree. . . .
> It held within its branches so many dreams for me. . . .

No, no thoughts like that! That's life—we must live! Then why, why do I feel like crying?

Gently, as if it wants to save its branches from damage, it lays down its crown on the ground. One more last sigh from the branches, then everything is quite still again. It is over.

———

"Hey, Inga! What are you going to give me for Crishmesh?" At the Post Office Harry is teasing me, of course; he is grinning all over his face.

"I know what he wants for Christmas!" Arnold throws in, with a sly grin on his face. "What he wants for Christmas are his ten front teeth!" The other soldiers have all heard it and are roaring with laughter. Poor Harry, he just had to have almost all his front upper teeth pulled. Now he looks, despite his otherwise so handsome face, a little like a figure from a comic book.

"Aw—shuddup!" Harry is unperturbed. He has grown accustomed to the teasing by now.

"Seriously now, Inga, what would you like for Christmas. Any little thing we can get you?" Arnold is, as always, very nice.

"There are so many things I want for Christmas that I can't begin to tell you. . . ."

239

"Oh?" Arnold is surprised. "I never thought of you as being greedy, so you must be joking. But what is the joke?"

"The things I want you can't give me, Arnold." I want my father home; I would like to have a life ahead where I don't have to worry where the firewood is coming from, or the next meal; I would like to have the Russians all back in Russia, so that my beautiful city is not split any more; I would like to have the bakers' son back for them. . . . I could go on and on.

"What you need right now, Ingie, is a shot of good old Scotch whisky!" That remark has come from Billy.

Darling Bill, he senses what is going on inside me. He is fortyish, married, Scotch, dark-haired, wears dark, horn-rimmed glasses, and is about the most considerate, kindest man in the world. Whether he knows it or not, he replaces Papa for me. . . .

He can never say my name correctly; he always calls me "Ingie." Sometimes, quite secretly and hardly ever admitted even to myself, I wish Papa were a little more like Billy!

"We can't drink while we are on duty, Billy!"

"At Christmas we can. And today is Christmas! Merry Christmas everybody!" He is holding up a sparkling bottle of Scotch.

A big cheer from the crowd, "Hey, look at that! Scotch from the Scotch! The old rascal! Where did you hide that, hey?"

I can hardly admit that I never drank whisky before, can I? So as the bottle makes the round, with everybody taking a swig, I do too!

It goes down my throat like fire, Brrrr. . . ! The others are laughing—my face is, as always, an open book. After about five minutes or so I begin to feel very good, though! We sit around and chat.

"Are you well again, Ingie?" Bill's voice shows concern.

"I am feeling rather good, Billy, thank you. I even gained four pounds while I was in the hospital."

"Gee, I am glad to hear that, Ingie. You know, you really are a silly girl; you should have let us know that you were sick. Didn't you realize what you were doing to yourself when you kept on working?" He is scolding me a little, but would he understand if I told him why?

He has taken off his glasses now, holding them in his hand. He always does that when he is about to become very serious about something.

"I will never forget that horrible scream coming from you when I tried to help you out of your jacket, you foolish girl. It frightened us almost out of our wits. We didn't know what was wrong with you."

"I'm so sorry, Billy, I didn't mean to scream like that—it just came out of me, I couldn't help it. . . ."

"Don't apologize," he says, twirling the spectacles in his hand, "that's not the reason I brought up the subject. I just want to know why you kept yourself going for so long without saying anything. . . ."

"Billy, I can't tell you. Please don't insist. I just can't." He has been bothering me about that for a long time now.

"Listen, Ingie, I know that the first attack of pleurisy is extremely painful. No human being's sense of duty is so great that one could walk around with that pain without great difficulty. So, I-want-to-know!"

Now he sounds like Papa!

"All right. You want to know, do you! It is a very simple reason; while I am working, I am getting the highest ration card there is, and that is not enough to gain weight on. . . . What do you think would happen if I had to live on the lowest card? You tell me! And another thing, I am getting one meal a day extra here, don't I? Well, I need that meal . . . is that so hard to understand?"

My pride is hurt, my defense is anger. He made me say something I would rather not ever think about!

"Dear God!" His voice is really only a hoarse whisper. "Is it that bad still?"

"Yes!" I blurt out. He will hear no more from me!

I move back to my place. Billy is still sitting where I left him, spectacles in hand. He is looking down at them, but I doubt if he sees them. . . .

"Hey—doesh anybody have a mishletoe?" That is coming from Harry, of course.

"Whasshematter, Harry? You want to kisshh shomebody?" Arnold is imitating him. The others are holding their bellies with laughter. It is funny. Harry would be the last one to go around kissing girls!

"I jussh want to have one," Harry says stubbornly.

"Okay, here you are." Sammy has a mistletoe. He gives it to Harry, who comes walking right towards me. For heaven's sake, I can't believe he will. . . !

"Here, Inga," Harry is putting the mistletoe into the breast-pocket of my blouse, "now you have everybody coming to kissshhh you!"

What a nice bunch they are! I love them all so much. What a difference from the Russians, and how lucky we were to be British Sector; how lucky I am, working for them. . . .

As long as I live I will never forget my illness. For days on end I had been having terrible pains in my neck, my back, my shoulder. It was a matter of managing to go to work, just about making it, and then living through an agonizing day of pain. . . . Then returning home, just about managing that too, and going right to bed, where even sleep would not come because of the pain. A lot of work had fallen on Ursel's shoulders, and she was wonderful. Mama suspected I was not well, but somehow I managed to keep my condition from her, enough to let her think I was just a little under the weather.

After eight or ten days of this agony, I got to work as usual. I was so weak that I could not take off my heavy winter jacket (also made from a blanket) and I had to sit down first. Billy was nearby, working already, but he came to me, asking me if I did not feel well. I could not answer. The pain was so great that even the movement of my lips would have hurt. . . . He tried to take my jacket off, but when he moved my arm I started screaming, "Don't touch me!" My boss, a sergeant, came running. He tried to call an ambulance, but this was Germany, not England. No ambulance! He was disgusted. I heard him say, "Then for God's sake send a truck—anything!" No use. It's not that the hospital did not want to send it; they could not, because they did not have one.

242

By that time I was half unconscious with pain. I did not care what happened to me. My boss picked me up and carried me in his arms to the hospital, a ten-minute walk away from the A.P.O.

Sergeant Kent told the doctor that he wanted me to have the best of care, that he would pay all bills, that I was to get enough food, and so on. The doctor examined me, told the sergeant that I had had pleurisy for about eight to ten days, that today was the peak, and that from here on I would probably get better—that is, if no tuberculosis developed, due to my half-starved condition. With that, my benefactor was dismissed, but he promised to return next day.

I stayed in the hospital for about ten days, and each day Sergeant Kent came with a big bagful of delicious cakes. When he realized that I shared those with the other ten ladies in my room and also saved some for my family, he insisted on waiting in the room until I had eaten at least three myself. When I was dismissed from the hospital, I realized that my guardian angel had taken care again; no tuberculosis, no after effects. . . .

Now, here they all are, my darlings, all of them; Sergeant Kent, Billy, Harry, Arnold, Sammy . . . I am really feeling good right now—I guess the whisky is helping a little, too!

Merry Christmas, everybody! I love you all . . . all of you. I will try out this letter-sack holder. I wonder if it will hold me? Just for kicks. Sit-ting pret-ty, sit-ting pret-ty, daramdidam, sit-ting high now, daramdamdam. . . . Hey, look everybody, I am taller than you are. . . !

"That's enough whisky for Ingie," Billy says. Everybody is grinning a little.

Arnold comes toward me. What does he want? He is not going to push me into that letter-sack holder, is he? He quickly pulls me down to him, takes the misletoe out of my breast-pocket and holds it over my head. He is kissing me!

After the first second of shock, something funny is happening . . . a strange feeling. . . . His lips are firm but gentle at the

243

same time. . . . It's funny, I don't love Arnold, but I enjoy his kiss. . . . That's really strange, I don't understand it.

Everybody, of course, is watching, and I am blushing. But they laugh away my embarrassment and none of them are mean.

On my way home I am still puzzled, but another thought has entered my mind—I am not afraid of men. Maybe, some day, there will be love waiting for me, despite the Russians.

———————

Today is New Year's Eve. The last year, 1945, has certainly been one I would like to forget. . . .

1946 is on the doorstep—what will it bring?

The ground is covered with snow, but the biting cold has left Berlin. . . . Only a few more months, and springtime will be here. . . .

Right now, though, it still seems as if this winter will never end. I think it has been the longest winter of my life.

———————

After we had cut down the tree, the problem of getting it into the shed was considerable. Sawing it into three-foot pieces took much longer than we had anticipated. Cutting all the smaller branches off was an endlessly stretching task; at times it seemed as if we would never finish. . . . That first night we managed to cut off all the branches and saw two or three pieces off the thick trunk. Helen's inventiveness has been marvelous; she really thought of everything. We had four heavy-duty steel wheels, onto which her husband mounted four iron bars, so that it had been made into a convenient little wagon, about eight inches from the ground, with a handle in front to pull it. All we would have to do was to slide the logs onto it and pull it into the shed.

What no one took into consideration was the weight of the wood. The three-foot trunk pieces were heavier than any one of us would ever have suspected. No matter how hard we tried, the four of us could not budge them.

Finally, with two steel bars pushed underneath, we levered the log onto the little wagon. Moving the wagon was hardly easier. All four of us were pulling, pushing, heaving—it was a nightmare. We were afraid the wagon might not hold, but in that, at least, we were lucky. All the time we kept one eye out for approaching patrols—that was another nightmare.

In two nights we managed to get more than half of the tree into the house. We had to leave the rest out for a while in order to concentrate on sawing and hacking the pieces we had already brought in. Time was running out; we had to hurry. Another unpleasant surprise awaited us. When we happily put the first pieces of wood on the fire, we waited and waited and waited for the flame to catch, but nothing happened. The wood did not burn!

Of course we should have realized that freshly cut wood has so much moisture in it that it just will not burn! We had to dry it out first.

Now we had to hurry even more. In order to be able to use the fresh wood, we had to dry it out, for that we needed fire. In order to have fire we had to have something to make a fire with. . . . And our own firewood would last only three, at the most four more days. . . .

We worked like prisoners on a chain gang. Night after night, hardly getting any sleep, hungry, cold and exhausted—this was our life. Now, thinking back, I still shudder; I still feel the pain and weakness in my muscles, I still taste the salt of tears which I tried my hardest to suppress when I thought I could not go on and would collapse. . . .

But we did it. In about three weeks we had enough to last us through the winter, if spring should come fairly early. If spring would come early. . . .

———————

New Year's Eve. . . .

It has started to snow again. The snowflakes are dancing around outside, gay, lighthearted. . . . I wish I could be a snowflake. No, that's not true; their life is so short. But if it is a

245

happy life, is it not better to have a short but happy life instead of a long, agonizing one? Who says that my life will be long and agonizing? Isn't there a lot ahead of me yet? Who says it will be unhappy? Things change . . . Mama said that, and she was right. Things have already changed.

After I had told Billy the truth about why I concealed my illness, he must have realized why we were always disappearing when the Canteen came. . . . Why suddenly, come coffee break, all the Germans in the room would either disappear into the washroom or suddenly develop a mad and frantic desire for work. . . . Germans were not allowed to buy from the Canteen. Anyway, a few days after our conversation Sergeant Kent ordered a regular daily supply of tea with cream and sugar plus one bun for each German employee. How it was paid for we never knew, but I am sure the British Army did not pay for it. . . . Our supply must have come from the private pockets of our British soldiers and their sergeant. . . .

Thank you, Billy. Thank you, Sergeant Kent. Thank you, my beloved, kind, wonderful colleagues and friends. . . . As long as there are people like you in this world, it will be a good one.

I am alone in my room. Ursel is spending the holidays with her family. Mama is busy trying to fix something for us to eat so that we know a new year is here, in at least some small way. . . .

Money? Oh, we have money. But we can't buy anything with it. I bring my salary home, pay the rent for my room to Omi and Opa, give Mama the rest to do the shopping with. When we have bought all we are entitled to there is quite a chunk of money left. I keep a little for myself, but there is not much sense in doing even that. What could I buy with it? The only place one can buy anything extra is on the black market. We do not have anything anybody would want on the black market. . . . Everything of value we had is all now somewhere in Russia.

Save? What for? Rumors say that the German mark will be

devalued soon, anyway—so what is the sense in saving? What money we have left after shopping is not an intentional saving, it is just left over, that's all. We would gladly spend it on food! Or even clothing. Or shoes. Or bedding. Or towels. Or. . . .

Sometimes we hear a rumor about "Care Packages." We have not received a single one. Once in a while there is an extra ration of the "Butterschmalz," the undefinable kind of lard—but it helps a great deal. If it is true about the "Care Packages," who gets them?

On the black market are great amounts of goodies: coffee, sugar, butter, ham, canned goods, bread, cigarettes, cookies. But who can afford five hundred marks (one month's salary) for a pound of coffee? Or eight hundred marks for a pound of butter? Or five hundred marks for a loaf of bread? What we have left over from salaries or other income (pensions, child support, widow's pension, or other sources) is not enough to take to the black market. . . .

I have a suspicion that somebody, somewhere, is getting richer by the minute. . . . Still, things could be worse.

Tomorrow is the beginning of a new year. Life will get better. Maybe even my father will be home one of these days.

The firewood is crackling in the stove. The coffeepot is, as always, on top. It contains only "ersatz coffee" (some kind of chicory and toasted wheat) but it is hot, and when I add the luxury of cream and sugar it does not taste too bad. I fix myself a cup, it tastes sweet and somehow, in its warmth, comforting. . . . I light a cigarette, put my chair close to the window, and look outside.

Snow is still falling—clean and cold, but not frightening any more. As a matter of fact, the world outside is quite beautiful. . . . If it weren't for my memories, I could even imagine that there had never been a war; the snow has covered almost all traces. Even the ruins look pretty now; only the outline suggests destruction.

Was Christmas just a week ago? Christmas . . . I would like to forget about that, for a while. Ever since our experience last spring, sitting on the roadside not knowing where to turn, the

247

religious meaning of Christmas has to be put aside temporarily. If anybody had recited the Christmas story this year, with the phrase "for there was no room at the inn," I would have started yelling so loud even the dead would have heard me. . . .

No, this year Christmas was strictly a matter of: it came, and it went. Some things are best forgotten.

The other aspects of the "merry season" were hardly merry: still no word from Papa, still not enough to eat, still no sign of great things to come, one way or another.

Once again, as so often this past year, my thoughts wander into a painful direction, looking for answers. . . . Have I found them all yet?

All I know is that I do not want war, ever. I want peace, and so do many others like me. But what is the price for peace—how does one achieve it?

The answer would be very simple if all people in this world wanted the same thing. Neville Chamberlain wanted peace when he made a pact with Adolf Hitler. . . . Did he know that he was selling his soul to the devil for the sake of peace? Is it enough just to want peace?

No. To make a pact with the devil will cost lives, not save lives. . . . There has to be something else.

As long as different people live together in this world, with different philosophies, different aims, different personalities, different desires, but most important, different morals, to have peace requires something else. What?

The picture of the little sparrow comes to my mind; it had happened on a lovely, sunshiny day. I was looking out of the window, enjoying the tranquility of the day, when I noticed two sparrows. The bigger, stronger one was on top of the other, pecking away at the little one's head so viciously, so without mercy, so brutally, that in a fit of fury I raced outside, hoping to separate the two. As I approached them the big one let go, giving the little sparrow a chance to get away. The little one, exhausted and in panic, tried to get away—but lo and behold, that big vicious sparrow, a few yards away and with the threat

248

of my presence gone, went right after him again and started the same brutal attack! Well, if that didn't take the cake!

I had watched fights taking place in nature, and most of them looked more vicious than they really were. Most of the time when the rival, or enemy, or whatever it may be called, showed signs of defeat, the stronger one would let go, satisfied with his victory. . . . Seldom had I seen an already defeated enemy being chased again—nature usually does not show malicious cruelty. The fight for survival exists, but it seldom is a fight to the death, unless sheer existence is involved, in accordance with the theory that the big fish eat the little fish, and so on. Now this big nasty sparrow proved that there can be an exception to the rule. . . .

I felt myself get cold with anger. Again I went right after the two sparrows, with the intention of catching the big one. At that moment I was not sure what I would have done had I caught him. . . .

Naturally they flew away again, into some thornbushes. As fast as I could, I followed right into the bushes. I did not even feel that it hurt—anger was greater than a little pain. Then, finally, I saw the little one escape and the big one disappeared soon after.

Thinking about this incident now, I remember the feeling of reward for having helped the helpless and possibly saved the little sparrow from a very senseless death. In this particular case, sheer survival was not involved, since sparrows do not eat sparrows! But it does raise another question—are we, as human beings, subject to the same rule of "survival of the fittest" as everything else in nature?

Maybe at one time we were, but since man began to think about himself, values had been established that should overcome the primitiveness of some of the more cruel aspects and events in nature. Man called it "civilization."

Unfortunately the degree of civilization is a completely individual thing.

In my country, just recently, civilization was replaced by

249

viciousness, hunger for power, brutality and sadism; logic and reasoning by fanaticism, in the ranks of my own countrymen at first; then it was displayed a second time by the people who conquered the city. But this time they were not just a sick percentage. This time they were the majority—a majority of beings devoid of feelings, morals, or any concepts of humanity.

The disciples of hell had been let loose a second time. . . . This time they spoke a different language, that was the only difference. So then, how does the peace-loving person defend himself against brutal assault, or the ideological conquest, which can do just as much damage? Do we go to the bully, the assaulter, and say, "Look here, fellow, I want peace. I want to be your friend, I have no ill intentions towards you, I want to help you live a good life, but please leave my life alone too. I like the way I live. . . ." If he is out for conquest, if he is hungry for power, and he wants you to live the kind of way he believes in, and if in addition to this he has no morals, no feeling, no compassion—then you are in trouble, friend! Because no matter how much you want peace, if he does not, then he will come and clobber you!

Which leads me to the only answer available, that those who want peace cannot afford to be weak. Moral as well as physical courage, firm beliefs, a feeling for justice and what is right, a certain amount of unselfishness and compassion—all these are strengths. But another strength is needed, too, when you deal with brute force: the strength of a good and adequate defense.

My little friend, the sparrow, had no defense of his own, he was weak. Somehow fate had thrown me into his path as his defense; I was stronger than his enemy, the big cruel sparrow. . . . But what would have happened had I not been there?

Life has been teaching me a lot of things. And though I learned a lot, the memories of the past year are still raw. God only knows if I will ever forget them. . . .

Paula? I have never heard from her again. Maybe I never will. One chapter that has to be closed . . . one that hurts. . . .

Annie? She has finally recovered; a basic desire to be healthy and happy came through strong finally. The last I have heard of her, since her place of residence also became British Sector, was that she, too, was working for the British.

Mrs. Stromberg has moved to a new place of residence. Strangely enough it is the little house the Russian guard used to occupy farther up the road, the place that always represented fear to Erna Peters and me when we had to go for water. Otherwise she is unchanged—for better or worse, as always with her!

Omi and Opa are keeping the shed clean as a whistle. Who knows, some day they may have some chickens again to lay eggs. . . . Maybe even a goat. . . . The flowerboxes are not yet repainted due to lack of paint, but they are repaired and are just waiting for some seeds. . . . Maybe in the spring there will be flowers again. Who knows?

The baker and his wife, the Gaertners, had asked me as soon as we were assigned to be British Sector to go to the Allied Kommandantura to see if they could find out anything about their son. Of course, I agreed. Mr. Gaertner and I went; Mrs. Gaertner stayed at home to tend the bakery shop. I always knew it was wise to find the right people, and since I could speak English I was lucky enough to get through to a rather high-ranking British officer. He was polite and very sympathetic, and promised to check with the Russians about the boy. It was then (already then) that I first noted that all was not well. With my supersensitivity I could detect, already then, a note of "we are not getting along too well with the Russians". . . . I could sense he had not much hope the Gaertners would ever see their son again, but who would have had the heart to tell them that? I told Mr. Gaertner that the British would do everything in their power to find out where the son was, and that I was sure there was hope that they would soon hear from him. They never did.

Uncle Carl had visited us once. He was working at a fairly good job, and he looked well. We did not once discuss the events in the basement. When he came it dawned on us, with a very guilty conscience, that in our flight from home we never wondered where he had disappeared to! His presence was proof

251

that he had not done too badly, which relieved us a great deal.

Uncle Fritz, Aunt Evi and their children have a new home. I believe the old home had too many memories. . . . I am happy for them. I would have done the same thing. Who can live staring at a spot that holds the memory of the exchange of one human life for another, even if unplanned?

Mr. and Mrs. Schulmann? . . . No, I cannot face the dead. Not yet. That also goes for Uncle Fritz, Aunt Elli, and Hanni. I cannot permit myself to think about them yet. They must stay out of my mind, maybe forever. Perhaps the day will come when I can face the kind of death they died. . . . For now, I must keep them somewhere where my heart cannot reach them.

Let's turn the radio on. It's too quiet in here. . . . In an hour or so I will go over to Mama's room to toast in the New Year with some kind of liquid. I don't know what it is, but I think she has some little surprise. Mama always does.

> *The Heavens praise Him, His power, His splendor,*
> *Resounding God's name over oceans and earth.*
> *His might is eternal; By His grace and His glory*
> *His word divine by man is heard. . . .*

I have always loved that piece of music. Beethoven Opus #48. . . .

I think maybe I better not stay here alone. Perhaps I should go over to see Mama and my two sisters now. Omi and Opa will be there, too.

It is a relief to enter into an atmosphere of togetherness. Chris is holding Monika by the hand and is helping her walk. How fast they grow . . . Chris looks so adorable, trying to be very grown-up. Her blonde hair is neat—Mama had set it in curlers previously—now it falls down in blonde, shiny curls, with a red ribbon in the back.

"Look at my ribbon!" She is very proud of it.

Monika pulls away at her hand, she wants to keep going! It isn't every day that she has so much exercise. It is past her bedtime. But she still wants to walk.

Omi and Opa are sitting quietly, watching the little ones. Mama is busy laying out the glasses.

"Punch!" she says proudly. "Helen gave me some red wine when she was last here for a visit, and I saved it. We are going to have hot punch."

"Oh, Mama, that is marvelous."

"We also have some doughnuts. They are not too good but better than nothing . . . and that's about all they are made from—nothing!"

We all laugh. We are alive together here, why shouldn't we laugh?

Before we know it, it is midnight—time to toast in the New Year. We are standing close to each other. The radio is announcing that the New Year is almost here.

Mama has filled the glasses. I like the red color of the punch. . . .

From somewhere, from amongst the ashes, the ruins, saved from destruction, someone must have been able to find a lonely church bell and restored it to where it belongs. As the gong on the radio announces that the New Year is here, the year 1946, we hear, vague and a little forlorn, almost shy and restrained, the sound of the church bell, while from the radio comes the powerful voice of Beethoven's music again, "The heavens praise Him, His power, His splendor. . . ." But even the great composer's divine creation cannot overpower the mellow voice coming from the one, lonely, single church bell on that New Year's Eve in Berlin.

———————

Two days later the mailman brings a letter from Denmark.

Papa is alive!

In springtime he will be home. . . .

What was it Mama had said? "Life changes, there is never a standstill. . . ."

I have learned by now that in life things rarely change fast.

But they do change.

I have learned that nothing good comes easy.

253

But if you work at it hard enough, it will come.

I have learned that sometimes it is wise to close one's eyes to the inequities in life.

But with enough goodwill, most of them can be overcome.

I have learned that before one can take, one must give.

But giving is made easy if we have faith.

I have learned that few really want to fight and destroy.

But those who do must be fought against to preserve what we believe in, so long as we are sure that what we believe in is right.

My country, infested with an evil, was conquered by people of two different world philosophies. Shouldn't the value and validity of a philosophy be judged by the actions of the people who represent it?

Perhaps the most important thing I have learned is the acknowledgment of good and evil. We, as human beings, are as much a part of the counter-balance of nature as everything else around us. We cannot accept the existence of good without acknowledging also the existence of evil. We all know what God is, but few of us, at the age of seventeen, have come face to face with the devil. To the young among us, evil, in the shape and form of the devil, is hard to recognize.

The devil is hunger, destruction, terror; the devil is hypocrisy, dishonesty, deceit; the devil is false values, selfishness, cowardice, and lack of faith; the devil, in his lack of compassion or human feeling, stamps on those who lie defeated on the ground, and he has no scruples. The devil exploits the weak and the ignorant and uses their emotions for his own selfish means, conquest.

If you sell your soul to the devil for the sake of peace, you sell it to the cause of war!

I have learned so many things I cannot recite them all. Soon we will be a complete family again. Things will not become better by miracle, we will have to work for them. As one problem is solved, another will replace it.

When Papa has come back home, life will be better, I know

that. Even then, there will be problems—other problems, those that I don't know of yet. . . . Still, I think I will 'cross that bridge when I come to it.

After all, I have crossed quite a few bridges before, haven't I?

A time to die, or to be born,
A time of rape: a time to mourn . . .
What price, oh Lord, to pay for birth?
"Look for me in the stars above:
I sent you peace, you men of earth . . .
You made the scars—I gave you love."